CYCLING
in and around
Cape Town

36 Cycle rides in the
Cape Peninsula and the Boland

TIM ANDERSON
COLIN DUTKIEWICZ

Published by Struik Timmins
(a member of the Struik Group (Pty) Ltd)
Struik House
Oswald Pirow Street
Foreshore
Cape Town
8001

Reg. No. 54/00965/07
First published in 1990

Designer: Tracey Carstens
Maps: Lellyn Creamer
Typesetting: BellSet, Cape Town
Reproduction: BellSet, Cape Town
Printed and bound by National Book Printers, Goodwood

ISBN 0 86978 366 1

CONTENTS

Northern suburbs/Cape Flats

Country rides

Appendix

AUTHORS' INTRODUCTION
AND EXPLANATION OF ROUTE DESCRIPTIONS

This book is for everyone and anyone who enjoys being outdoors on a bicycle and needs ideas for interesting places to pedal to Cape Town and its immediate hinterland. It is for absolute beginners as well as for fairly experienced cyclists.

It is especially for those who like to ride in a group, maybe as a family, while exploring this beautiful area and discovering a little more about the interesting sights and wonderful views along the way.

Some of the cyclists we have in mind may be fit, competitive athletes with costly hi-tech bikes. Others may be content to ride faithful old bangers left over from schooldays, and not feel bad about walking up the hills.

No matter who they are, we see all of them as lovers of the outdoors, enjoying the exhilarating sense of freedom in cycling, and revelling in the rare magnificence of the area's scenery.

Our book describes 36 bicycle outings in this wondrous region, each with route instructions that we have checked out personally, and some notes about what you might see or do along the way. Also mentioned are some appropriate eating establishments which were acceptable at the time of writing; however, restaurants tend to change hands or staff so often that it is risky to guarantee their quality.

All our recommended rides are graded according to length and the level of physical effort they demand. A few are relatively arduous while others are gentle outings suitable for the very young, the very old, the weak and the timid. We think there's something for everyone but we hope to coax cautious beginners into progressing gradually through every ride in the book. Some of the nicest and most spectacular destinations are up or over the hills and require a fair measure of effort to reach, but most riders will agree that it's usually worth it.

In some instances people will need to drive or catch public transport to the starting points of the rides. Because they might be living anywhere within, or beyond, Cape Town we've simplified our instructions by writing as if everyone would start from the city centre. Most people will be able to work out their own short cuts or alternative routes for getting to the starting points of the rides.

Our book is NOT intended as a comprehensive guide to cycling. However, for the benefit of beginners and those with little technical knowledge of bicycles, our opening chapters offer some abbreviated information about choosing bicycles, equipping them, taking care of them, and avoiding the embarrassment of inadvertently becoming separated from them.

Inevitably, some people may find our information too elementary; others may find it too technical. Certain points we mention are matters of opinion (and we say so).

Our purpose, however, has been mainly to give enough advice for the new cyclist to maximize his enjoyment of sightseeing while minimizing the effort of pedalling. As in all other pastimes and sports, some basic general knowledge can be amazingly rewarding in terms of added pleasure and satisfaction – not to speak of spending one's money more effectively.

Foreign or out-of-town visitors who want to cycle in the Cape should try to borrow bikes, because hire shops are rather rare.

Explanation of route descriptions

The rides are grouped according to geographical area, and graded according to physical demand on the rider. The gradings are very conservative and are as follows:

A = Short – up to 15 km
B = Medium – 15-30 km
C = Long – more than 30 km

1 = Easy and level
2 = Undulating; small hills
3 = Strenuous; big hills

Every ride description gives the following information:
Features – a summary of what the ride offers. Suitability or otherwise for beginners or family outings. Safety considerations of route – e.g. whether it runs through lonely or poorly-policed areas.
Grade and distance – just that, plus actual riding time.
Best times – of day and year, according to traffic, sun, wind, etc.
Special information – anything relating to the ride which doesn't fall easily into the route description, e.g. historical background details.
Sustenance – where you can buy food or meals during the outing. Where we haven't personally tried the establishments we say so. There may be other good places on the routes which are not mentioned – simply because we haven't tried them or are not aware of them.
Getting there – abbreviated directions for getting to the starting point by car or by public transport, if any.
Doing the ride – route directions, with landmarks and oddments of interesting information.

Request to readers

If you find any of our route descriptions or maps misleading, inadequate or ambiguous, please let us know by sending a letter, with the corrected information, to Struik Timmins, PO Box 1144 Cape Town 8000.

Here's to meeting you on the road.

Colin Dutkiewicz
Tim Anderson
1990

CHOOSING A BIKE

Types of bikes

The most common bicycles today are known as ***racing bikes.*** The majority of people reading this book will probably have one of these, or be thinking of buying one. If you don't already have one, don't be put off by this 'racing' description. You don't have to be a hot-shot cyclist to ride an ordinary racing bike; in fact they're much easier and safer to ride than the heavy 'sit-up-and-beg' bikes generally used in the past.

The quality and sophistication of the parts and materials used for racing bikes varies widely; their prices reflect this. Most racing bikes are wholly mass produced, and from the riding point of view even the cheapest among them are quite adequate for many people. However, depending on how much they're used, the moving parts of cheap ones will wear out more rapidly than those of expensive ones.

At the other end of the scale, the expensive mass-produced bikes are adequate for quite competitive cyclists. These pricier machines may also feature subtle technology which adds greatly to the ease and pleasure of recreational riding. In addition, the more expensively engineered bike will justify its cost because it lasts longer – provided it's properly taken care of.

'Hand-built' bikes naturally cost a good deal more, but they still use selected mass-produced components for all their moving parts. Hand-builts may incorporate super-lightweight alloy tubing, special jointing techniques, and the builder's particular ideas on frame and fork 'geometry' (dimensions and angles). Hand-built bikes can be amazingly light; the most sophisticated examples may be specially tailored for the shape and capabilities of a particular champion rider.

Knowledgeable cyclists favour certain types and makes of components and may order a semi-hand-built bike just to get these. Other cyclists have physiques which are not comfortable on standard frames designed for 'average' riders. These cyclists will require hand-built frames, possibly with quite ordinary components, which will naturally cost more. (Rigidity, by the way, is an important factor in a bicycle frame, because a surprisingly large amount of the rider's effort can be spent on literally flexing the frame rather than propelling the bike forward.)

Mountain bikes (more correctly referred to as all-terrain bikes or 'ATBs') are, in the best examples, strongly made yet surprisingly light. They usually have three ranges of gears, wide-section block-tread tyres, and a geometry which ensures that the bike is manageable at slow speeds or on rough ground. However, some ATBs on the market are needlessly heavy and of relatively crude construction.

Mountain bikes have a high 'rolling resistance', which means that quite a lot of the rider's effort is absorbed in overcoming friction between the ground and the large 'footprint' of the tyres. This is compensated for by the effectiveness of the gears – at the expense of lost speed on flat sections. They can be fitted with slimmer tyres, which, with the rather upright riding position and huge range of gears, makes them attractive touring bikes. However, slim tyres will 'de-mountainize' a mountain bike.

Tandems (two-seaters), have to be specially ordered and therefore are expensive. They are exhilaratingly fast on level roads, but only experienced and fairly strong riders can get them up hills without enormous effort.

Because they have to seat two people, tandems need extended frames which flex longitudinally and waste some of the riders' effort. This factor, and the heaviness of the machines, means that these two-man bikes have a disappointing mixed-terrain performance compared with the conventional one-man bike.

Unorthodox bikes, whether they're unicycles, tricycles, BMXs, strange imports or 'recumbents', are not likely to interest most of the people who need this book. However, many of the short rides featured are quite suitable for family outings with children on BMXs – just make sure they are in good order and that the brakes work!

Recumbents are wonderful for sightseeing because the rider lies back in comfort. This position does not strain the rider's back and posterior, allows for very efficient pedalling and minimizes forward wind resistance. Also, the recumbent rider's low position lowers the centre of gravity of the rider and bike, which permits good speed on bends. For these reasons recumbents can move pretty fast.

Unfortunately these machines have to be specially built, which makes them expensive. They also require a somewhat different riding technique which takes time and practice to master and makes for difficult handling in slow traffic. Nevertheless, a practised rider on a recumbent will go faster than if he rides a conventional bike.

There are minor bicycle adaptations which may interest the experimentally-inclined cyclist. For instance, more and more people are experimenting with 'disc' or 'faired' wheels. These use detachable material to fill in the gaps between the spokes. The effect is to reduce air turbulence caused by the spokes as the wheel rotates. Turbulence sabotages streamlining and therefore slows the rider down. The new plastic moulded wheels are particularly suitable for fairing.

Another way of reducing friction is by using fairings over the whole bicycle. Normally, a cyclist rides in a sort of 'scoop' position which produces a great deal of wind resistance. By enclosing the whole bicycle in a lightweight nacelle or fairing, the wind resistance is reduced enormously. Apart from the saving of effort, maximum speed can increase phenomenally.

Without going to these lengths, a noticeable speed increase can be obtained by attaching a relatively small air deflector to the handlebar. You may have noticed that quite a lot of trucks have a large plastic bulge attached to the front of the load box to give a similar effect. This gives a really meaningful saving in fuel consumption, so you can understand what effect streamlining can have on your endurance.

In cycling it's important to keep in mind that the human body is very weak in relation to its mass. When it applies its strength to a machine such as a bicycle, little bits of the small amount of power the body does develop can easily be wasted.

You may think that speed is of no consequence to you, but energy wasted while cruising along without much effort is still being wasted. This will become evident when you turn round to come home against the wind! Not to mention the fatigue you will feel when you do get home.

The right bike for you

If you're very new to cycling you'll need suggestions about bicycle type, size, make and accessories. We'd like to offer advice about what you should expect to pay, but bicycle prices are rising so fast that any figures mentioned will be out of date before long. However, keep in mind that bicycles are cheap compared with the cost of their constituent parts bought separately. In other words it works out cheaper to buy a fairly high specification bicycle at the outset than to replace worn components with more durable versions later on.

Find a well-established cycle shop, speak to an experienced assistant, tell your adviser what you want the bike for, and if possible give him an idea of how fit you think you might get. You're unlikely to get knowledgeable advice in a chain store, and in any case such a shop does not generally provide after-sales adjustments and service.

Common sense recommends a standard mass-produced racing bike of reputable make and with minimal equipment. An expertly checked second-hand bike might be entirely satisfactory, and if you take reasonable care of it you may be able to get a useful trade-in or pass it down to a younger member of your family one day.

If you can afford it, your bicycle should have a superior quality frame. This will make it worthwhile to convert the bike to a higher overall specification at a later date, if you wish to do so.

Apart from the frame, don't buy any expensive accessories that you will not need for your envisaged cycling activities. Wait until you've gained enough knowledge and experience to know exactly what you want in relation to the kind of cycling you really intend doing – and are able to do!

There are three basic factors that influence your selection: purpose, price and pride. New cyclists may *think* they'll never do more than potter round the suburbs, but the unforeseen delights of cycling may spur them on to greater things, or they may find a hidden physical talent which inspires them to try more challenging rides and even competitive cycling.

Sometimes a reluctant cyclist may have to do far more riding than he intends in order to encourage or accompany other cycling members of the family. On the other hand, a hopeful new cyclist may discover chronic backache, latent physical idleness, accident proneness, or traffic phobia – leaving him with a redundant bicycle.

Ego can be a problem in choosing a bike. Many people get a thrill from owning, riding, and caring for a beautiful hand-made competition bicycle – and why not? But be warned: they are very costly. Their spares and repairs are correspondingly expensive. Before you decide to spend a small fortune on a high-specification bike, consider the fact that a fit and experienced cyclist on a modest bike will always completely outstrip an unfit or overweight cyclist on an exotic racer. Out on the road you may feel distinctly put down and financially cheated when fit people riding far lesser bikes easily overtake you and your fancy machine. Also bear in mind that high-specification lightweight components only last as long as they should when cared for correctly.

So, unless and until you discover a latent athletic talent, take the bicycle shop's advice, and buy a bike which matches your cycling intentions, your physical characteristics and your fitness level. By the same reasoning, don't over-flatter a relatively modest bike with needlessly exotic optional components.

Incidentally, ladies should not buy ladies' bikes – i.e., those without a crossbar. Unless you are determined to wear a skirt, a gent's bike with crossbar is preferable, being stronger and far stiffer (energy-conserving), especially if you ride hard.

Our suggestion is that you go for the best locally mass-produced bike you can afford. Mid-price-range production bikes are good enough for a fairly fit rider, even in competitive events. Stick to a well known, long-established make.

For youngsters who need serviceable bikes to get to school and sports events, durability is the prime consideration. Such bikes need mudguards to keep wet road dirt off uniforms. They are best fitted with hub gears rather than derailing gears, which frequently get damaged in typical school environments. They need strong rims and fairly heavy tyres which can endure chronic under-inflation.

There are three sensible reasons for buying a mountain bike. One reason is that you intend to use it for mountain trail-riding – a thoroughly pleasurable and companionable pastime. The number of organized outings and competitions is increasing, but at present there are not many suitable tracks where mountain bikes are permitted – officialdom still tends to classify them with motorized trail bikes and their often irresponsible and intrusive riders.

A second reason is that you intend to do a good deal of touring, maybe carrying camping equipment, rain-gear, food and so on; mountain bikes fitted with slim tyres and proper carriers are very good for this purpose. A third reason is that people who suffer backache on racing bikes often find mountain bikes don't give this problem.

If you buy a mountain bike, it's a good idea to get two sets of wheels and tyres for it – fat ones for mountain tracks, and lighter lower-friction tyres for road riding.

If you're thinking of a tandem because you want to ride as a couple, first try to borrow one and see how you really like it. Tandems allow continuous conversation

The main parts of a bicycle.

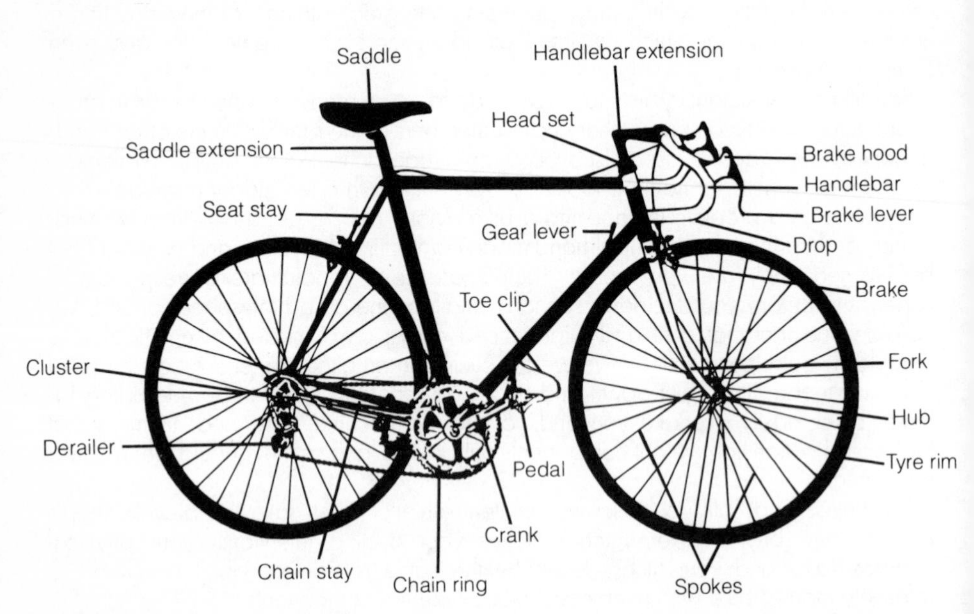

between their riders, something which is almost impossible for cyclists under typical single-file-in-traffic conditions. They are also excitingly rapid on level or gently hilly country. However, it's hard work to drive them up hills, especially when the crew is a physically mismatched pair, such as a tough young man and a dainty woman or child. Of course, the pedalling burden of this muscular disparity is the price of togetherness, and maybe also a measure of love! Because of their long wheelbases, tandems are relatively difficult to steer. Without a good deal of practice in the riding technique, they can be scary for the front rider when hurtling down a winding descent – not to speak of nerve-wracking for the stoker (rear rider) who has no direct control over the steering. In addition, their length and awkwardness can make tandems difficult to transport.

Tailoring your bike

In a good cycle shop you're not obliged to buy a machine wholly 'off-the-shelf'. Some of the components are optional and choosing the right ones can make a world of difference to your pedalling enjoyment. If you let a salesman hustle you, or you get carried away in your eagerness to get on your new bike as soon as possible, then you may end up very disappointed and blame all the wrong things.

Frames: There's much more to frame design than the obvious purpose of connecting the moving parts to each other and providing a perch for the saddle. The lengths of the various frame parts and the angles between them have a considerable influence on the ridability of a bike and the comfort and efficiency of the rider. Small differences in the geometry of a frame can make an enormous difference to the 'feel' of a bike, its stability and cornering potential.

Mass-produced bikes are usually available in several standard frame sizes. Do not compromise with the correct size for your body shape just because, say, the colour you like is available only in the wrong-sized frame. Both undersized and oversized frames can be uncomfortable and may reduce the efficiency of the rider's energy usage, no matter what compensatory adjustments he makes.

Many South Africans are much taller than the average European – and most locally-available bikes are designed and proportioned according to European criteria. Thus, many tall South Africans ride bikes with undersized frames. A marginally undersized frame has certain advantages, but beyond that margin the compensatory saddle and handlebar adjustments that you have to make detrimentally affect the overall geometry of the bike, resulting in under-performance and rider discomfort.

DO NOT buy an oversized frame for a growing child, reasoning that he'll grow up to fit it. A youngster on a bike too big for him cannot have the degree of balance and control necessary for his safety. Even an adult on an oversized frame is at a disadvantage.

Most frames are made of thin alloy-steel seamless tubing. In all but very cheap frames the ends of the constituent tubes are assembled into pre-formed sockets known as 'lugs', and then fixed by welding or (better) by surface alloying ('brazing'). The lighter the frame the thinner the walls of the tubing (its 'gauge')have to be; the lighter (thinner) the gauge the more exotic (and costly) the alloy must be in order to maintain the necessary strength.

To minimize flexing, good frames have tube ends with thicker walls in the vicinity of the lugs. These are known as 'double butted' tubes. In the best frames, all the tube pieces should be double butted.

Traditionally, frame tubing has been circular and of uniform diameter, but the quest for higher cycling performance has prompted new stress research. The outcome has been frames with elements of differing diameters, and not necessarily circular. The overall effect has been an improvement in the unavoidable compromise between strength, rigidity and lightness.

You may hear the cognoscenti referring to frame tubing as 'Reynolds', and then a three-digit suffix. Reynolds is a major manufacturer of seamless tubing and assigns numbers such as '531' to its various product lines. Such a number fully denotes the composition and physical properties of the tubing. These numbers have become an industry standard world-wide and are a convenient shorthand for quality and characteristics of bike frame material. In the higher price range you will come across Columbus and Cannondale tubings.

Saddles: The normal seating position for conventional racing bicycles is an ergonomic catastrophe. The most distressing focus of this is the saddle – a device which, if unsuitable or not carefully positioned and angled, can make life very uncomfortable for the rider.

Insist that the shop allows you to test several saddles, each for a distance of at least 30 km, if there's any chance that you will ever ride that far. Alternatively, you may be able to borrow a bike to try out its saddle. Of course if you don't expect to ride further than 10 or 20 km, the saddle isn't so important.

The price of saddles is not necessarily an indication of how comfortable they will be. What one rider may find quite tolerable can be unacceptable to another rider. Foam and sheepskin covers will not help much in relieving a shape that simply does not suit your crotch.

Generally a slim saddle is better and minimizes chafing. However, female pelvic bone geometry differs from that of males and women often find it more comfortable to have a wider saddle.

Gears: Gearing is another element which you may need to have changed on an off-the-shelf bike. Regardless of their fitness, people vary enormously in strength and endurance, so the gear ratios chosen for a bike should match the user's riding capability.

There are two types of gear system. One is the old but tried-and-tested epicyclic two- or three-speed hub gear. It is a fine device that is difficult to damage, can run more-or-less without adjustment for a lifetime, and imposes minimal wear on the chain. However there are only three ratios and they are necessarily very widely spaced; even then the low isn't low enough for some hills and the high isn't high enough for maximum speed under favourable conditions. A secondary drawback is that the width of the three-speed hub is too great for narrow racing wheels.

The other gear system is the derailing type gear system, now highly refined and quite reliable provided you know how to change gears correctly and learn how to adjust the mechanism – which is quite often necessary.

The original system was devised in France and called 'Derailleur' – a derivative of the French-adopted English word 'derail'. It is sometimes spelt as De Railleur, as for a surname, but this is misleading. We've chosen to revert to the English spelling. Thus the system is a 'derailer' because it changes gears by *derailing* the chain onto various other gears. Note that the derailer *component* is the particular gadget which actually leans against the chain to move it.

Derailing gear systems and their chains should be of better engineering quality than the rest of the bike in order to minimize cog wear and chain stretch, which result in the chain 'jumping' and 'skidding' after a fair amount of use. Quality, however does not compensate for bad changing technique, rough usage, or lack of maintenance.

For children and beginner cyclists a five-speed derailer is easy to get used to and quite satisfactory. The 10- or 12-speed derailers require an additional shift lever and may confuse newcomers.

To be able to change derailer gears correctly you must listen to the sound of the chain and finely adjust the gear lever position to eliminate the clattering and rubbing sounds which indicate maladjustment. Failure to do this will result in rapid wear and the inconvenience of gears jumping to the next ratio while you're pedalling.

If you're hard of hearing or mechanically very insensitive you may not be able to make this adjustment and therefore you should consider 'click-stop' gear selectors.

These are ideal so long as they're kept in near-perfect adjustment. However, because cogs wear and chain and control cables gradually stretch, the 'click' settings get progressively displaced until the rider may not be able to engage the appropriate gear – this will mean a trip to the serviceman.

You will have to trust your dealer to determine the actual ratios of the gears. However, by the time your initial gear set is worn enough to need replacement, you'll know better what you prefer.

A typical twelve-speed gear set suitable for an averagely strong and fairly fit man might have a front gear pair comprising a 42-tooth gear alongside a 53-tooth gear. The rear set or 'cluster' might increase incrementally from 13 teeth on the smallest up to 24 on the biggest.

On the road this means that for getting up steep hills he would set his chain to run on the smaller front gear (also known as a 'blade' or 'chain wheel') and the largest cluster gear. Thus for every revolution of his legs his rear road wheel would rotate 42 ÷ 24 = 1,75 times.

Downhill or on the level with the wind behind him he'd shift the chain so that it ran on the larger (front) gear and the smallest cluster gear so that his wheel would then turn 53 ÷ 13 = 4,1 times for every revolution of his legs.

In other words, other things being equal, he could apply approximately 4,1 ÷ 1,75 = 2,3 times more power to his wheel when going uphill than he would be able to on the level. Alternatively, when trying to speed along the level, he would only have 1 ÷ 2,3 (about 43%) of the power theoretically available to him. According to the road gradient and the wind and how he was feeling he would select various other combinations of gears from the 12 available. These may not sound like big differences but they have a profound effect on how tired one becomes when riding, and how quickly one starts getting tired.

According to the sex, age, strength and fitness of the rider, gear combinations should differ from the ones just discussed. For instance, usually a female rider will need a 48-tooth larger front blade and perhaps a 14 to 26 cluster.

An important factor in choosing gear ratios is to know how well your legs 'spin'. People with long heavy legs, (especially if they're not cycling fit), usually find it difficult to move their legs round as rapidly as people with comparatively short or lighter legs. This means that for successful fast cycling the slow spinner will need different gearing from the fast spinner.

Highly competitive cyclists have a choice of blades and clusters. In an event such as the famous Rapport Tour they may have the combinations changed from day to day to give optimum performance whatever the terrain.

Tyres and wheels: There's much to be said for narrow ('one-inch') wheels which, with correctly inflated tyres, help give minimum rolling resistance. These narrow wheels come in two different types, one shaped to suit conventional beaded 'clincher' tyres and the other to suit unbeaded 'tubular' tyres. (Note that despite metrication the nominal width of tyres is customarily stated in imperial units.)

Wider wheels have wider tyres with a larger footprint. In dry weather the theoretically greater adhesion that they provide is unnoticeable, but in wet weather the wider tyre is more suitable for inexperienced riders. However, the widest of tyre footprints is little help against the commonest causes of skids – oil and oily residues on the road, and wet (painted) road markings. By the way, treadless ('slick') tyres are sometimes used in dry-weather speed events.

Tyres wider than $1\frac{1}{8}$ inch have comparatively thick treads which in theory confer greater protection against punctures. However, beaded racing tyre inner tubes are so easily and quickly changed at the roadside that a puncture is more of an irritation than a menace, unless you're actually racing.

On the other hand, tyres wider than $1\frac{1}{8}$ inch are almost invariably fitted with locally-made inner tubes, and these have always been maddeningly porous compared with imported tubes. If your bike has the commonplace $1\frac{1}{4}$ or $1\frac{3}{8}$ inch tyres you will need to pump the tyres daily to keep them properly inflated.

Leisure cyclists try to avoid rainy days, and if they do get caught out they're prepared to ride unhurriedly on slippery wet roads. They can thus afford to disregard the matter of adhesion, and pay attention to the greater mass and higher rolling friction of wider-section tyres. Overall, we strongly recommend the 1-inch wheels – or, at the most, $1\frac{1}{8}$ inch.

Cycle tyres, like car tyres, have different 'profiles', which means that the differences between inner and outer diameters vary. Low profile cycle tyres are usefully lighter but give a discernibly bumpier ride and are more susceptible to puncture by stones – especially if under-inflated. They are also less tolerant to over-inflation, which may cause a blow-out.

When a tyre is described as 700 x 23, it means the nominal diameter is 700 mm and the distance from rim to outer edge of tyre is 23 mm (*not* the width of the tyre, although width and profile are related). Thus the second number in a tyre description describes the profile. For general use, 700 x 23 is fine.

Tubular tyres ('tubbies') completely enclose their inner tubes, the circumferential joint edges of the tyre being finely stitched together. The tyre slips over the shallow-grooved rim like an elastic band, with the joint against the rim, and is prevented from working itself off by a removable cement.

Because they do not have wire beads moulded into them, the sides of tubulars can be very thin and hence the tyre will be very light. In addition, the simple grooved profile of the wheel rim gives a much lighter wheel/tyre combination than can be achieved with beaded tyres. Tubulars are standard for serious road and track racing, especially because top riders have support vehicles carrying spare wheels which the crew change in a flash, *BUT,* if you're not in this league they are a lot more expensive than beaded tyres, mainly because of their stitched construction. Not only that, but a cyclist using them must carry with him at least two spare tyres (complete with inner tubes) because of the tubbies' susceptibility to punctures. A punctured tubbie has to be partially unstitched for repair, a job that is almost impossible to do at the roadside.

Cyclists whose enthusiasm is matched by the size of their wallets may have two sets of wheels and tyres, one with beaded tyres for cruising around and training, the other reserved for competitions. For first-time cyclists, even those buying expensive bikes, we firmly recommend beaded tyres, especially if your main foreseeable interest will be weekend sightseeing trips. Even in competitions, the advantages of tubulars are likely to be insignificant compared with the factors of your athletic ability and fitness.

Notice that racing tyre valves have a knurled sleeve which has to be loosened to let the air in before you attach the pump connector. Don't forget to re-tighten it after pumping up.

Mountain bike tyres are built more like car tyres, with a similar type of valve (and pump), and a massive block-pattern tread.

With regard to wheels, high-quality steel rims are somewhat heavier but certainly cheaper than aluminium alloy wheels. Aluminium wheels can only be straightened if the buckle or wobble is minimal. More serious buckling can often be repaired in the case of steel wheels, which are also less easily damaged during tyre-changing.

Most wheels have 32 or (preferably) 36 spokes. Top-range bikes use double-butted spokes (thicker towards their ends) and even elliptical-section spokes to minimize forward air friction. Well galvanized or high-quality chromed spokes look better for longer, but most spokes are electro-galvanized or plated poorly and rust very quickly. Thus, for cosmetic reasons it's best to buy top-quality spokes, but they're expensive. Stainless steel spokes look better for longer but develop rust-like staining which requires continual polishing away for good appearance. Stainless steel is very hard and spokes made of it are inclined to snap in use. *Never* try to tension or replace spokes yourself.

Always choose wheels equipped with quick-release axles rather than the kind which have to be loosened with a spanner. Not only does this make for faster and less messy wheel removal, but it means you don't have to carry heavy wheel spanners.

Brakes: In the low-to-medium price range, centre-pull calliper brakes give the best and most dependable action. Their mechanical principle is superior to that of side-pull brakes but the latter are more popular because they are easier to adjust. Your dealer will show you the difference between centre- and side-pull.

Unless side-pull brakes are expensively engineered and carefully maintained their mechanism is inclined to exert an unequal force on the arms carrying the brake blocks. This reduces the active retarding effect so that the potential advantage is lost. Not only does the uneven pull unnecessarily stress the wheel rim, but it tends to leave one of the brake blocks in contact with the rim after releasing the brake.

Mountain bikes should always have centre-pull brakes because the gripping power on the blocks is greater and because they cope better with being dirtied.

Be sure your brakes are 'hooded' by nacelles over the 'works'. These are not for decoration and streamlining; they are important hand-holds for certain riding positions.

Also be sure that 'all-weather' brake blocks are fitted, otherwise you will not be able to stop if the blocks get wet. Remember, however, that even these blocks do not work immediately. The road wheels have to turn a couple of times while the blocks wipe off the free water before actually biting the dried rims. Do not be tempted to fit over-hard blocks; these last longer, but the harder the block the longer it takes to stop the wheel. Some bikes have two sets of brake levers to cater for alternative hand positions while riding. These are positively dangerous despite being marketed as 'safety brakes'. They lack leverage, especially once the cables stretch or the block adjustment backs off. They also needlessly add mass and air resistance.

Pedals and cranks: For children and beginners the rubber block pedal has advantages, especially if the rider wears tackies or slip-slops. Metal ('rat-trap') pedals are slippery for leather shoes and will soon damage soft-bottomed shoes like tackies.

Ordinary metal pedals are supposed to be used with toe clips, which are fine as long as one's feet remain on the pedals. However, some experience is necessary before a foot can be slipped in and out of toe clips easily and safely in stop-start traffic conditions. Toe clips are not a good idea for young children who may panic if they feel they can't get a foot out.

Modern racing pedals are also metal but do not require toe clips. Instead, they use a system first developed for ski boots, resembling press-studs, with little sockets on the pedals and corresponding spigots (cleats) on the cycling shoes. This is a very safe system in traffic and gives an important mechanical advantage.

With traditional pedals the rider's power can only be transferred while his legs press down on the pedals; if he tries to extend the duration of his power stroke by also pulling backwards on the pedals his feet will just slide out of the toe clips. With 'clipless' pedals the rider's foot stays attached to the pedal regardless of the direction in which he is pulling.

Although there is no engineering reason why the clipless system shouldn't be applied to slightly modified rat-trap pedals, it is only available with high-quality and very costly racing pedals, which must be used with expensive cycling shoes.

It is possible to fit the shoe cleats to certain kinds of running shoe, which will cut down somewhat on the total cost. Ensure that the shoe does not have a thick cushion sole and take great care to align the cleats properly.

Note that it will turn out cheaper in the end to buy a bike already fitted with clipless pedals than to buy them separately later. This applies to most of the bicycle accessories discussed here.

As far as cranks are concerned, the 'cotterless' pedal cranks are preferable, although more expensive. In these, the cranks have tapered square holes which are forced up firmly on the correspondingly shaped ends of the shaft connecting the cranks.

Cranks attached with traditional loose cotters are inclined to work loose, mainly because the cotters that are generally available are too soft. If the looseness is not corrected immediately, the cotters will distort, and invariably the user will over-tighten them with a hammer so that they are difficult to remove. A strong or heavy rider may well shear a loose or distorted cotter, and this can cause an accident, not to speak of pain!

Handlebars: Apart from the material used, these vary principally in width (span) and depth of drop. In theory, the greater the drop the further the rider can get his head down, and the more streamlined he will be. However, most people find the best theoretical position far too extreme, causing cricked necks, backaches, and sore eyes – and it makes it difficult to appreciate the scenery. A modest drop is preferable.

Wide handlebars obviously give the rider greater leverage when turning. This is necessary for mountain bikes, and bikes fitted with large footprint tyres that need more effort to swivel them on the road surface.

For racing and touring bikes the exact width is not very critical so long as it corresponds roughly with the rider's shoulder width. Remember that some of the rider's weight is 'propped up' by his arms, so if they are splayed or constricted because the handlebar width is wrong, the arms and shoulders will tire easily.

Riding comfort is greatly affected by the proportions and height setting of the handlebar bracket. This bracket, together with the top end of the 'fork stem' into which it clamps, the swivel bearings and other associated bits and pieces, constitute the 'head set'. Some brackets 'reach forward' more than others, and this type is usually more comfortable for tall people. Comfort and fatigue are closely associated with the relationship between handlebar and saddle adjustment.

Handlebars should be fitted with sponge rubber tubing rather than 'handlebar tape'. Although it offers slightly more wind resistance, the rubber is very comfortable in all weathers, especially if your hands 'tingle' on rough roads or in cold weather.

Avoid the so-called 'triathlon handlebars'. These allow a restful position on an uncrowded open road, but are unsuitable where nimble steering and/or continual braking is necessary. Most fun-ride and race organizers do not allow them.

There have been occasional instances of handlebars breaking inside the head set

– an extremely dangerous occurrence. These fractures are caused by metal fatigue. A good cycle dealer knows which makes of handlebar were involved and will not sell them – but check with him in any case. The heavier or stronger you are the more important it is to have a reliable handlebar.

Setting up your new bike

There's a close interrelationship between the shape, dimensions and adjustments of a bike. By taking a bit of trouble to get the combination right for your particular anatomy you'll enjoy sustained comfortable riding and not waste energy.

In addition to the adjustments you make for the sake of comfort, you can make some 'hardware' adjustments to improve the bike's mechanical efficiency and increase the longevity of its moving parts, as well as ensure your personal safety.

It was mentioned earlier that the fixed parameters of a bike are referred to as the 'geometry' of the design, the merits and demerits of which lead to unending debates among the experts. Fortunately, as far as the geometry goes, all you need be concerned about at this stage is that a knowledgeable and experienced cyclist, probably someone at your dealer's, should supply you with a bike of the correct frame size and then make the main adjustments to suit your build.

The anatomical adjustments are saddle height, saddle fore-and-aft position, handlebar height, handlebar fore-and-aft position, and handlebar tilt. It's unlikely that even the expert will get it exactly right for you first time, so don't be afraid to go back for fine-tuning after a few weeks. Take special note of backache, wrist ache, neck-crick, and whether your legs get sore above or below the knees. These are clues your adviser will need.

The saddle: If you don't have access to an expert, you'll have to start with rule-of-thumb positions which you can improve on later by trial and error. Remember that your most vulnerable points are your knees – any odd feeling in the knee should be treated by adjusting your saddle immediately. Start by setting the saddle height. First move the saddle so that it's horizontal when looked at from the side. Now sit on the saddle with one hand squeezing a brake lever and the other hand supporting you against a wall so that you and the bike are vertical.

The *minimum* saddle height should be such that you can put your *heel* on the pedal when it's at its lowest position, with your leg straight at the knee. The other foot should not be on the ground when you do this, but on the opposite pedal. Repeat with the other leg on the other pedal in case your legs are of unequal length (not uncommon); adjust for your shorter leg. Wear the shoes you expect to cycle in when you make this setting.

From this lowest adjustment you can expect to raise the saddle 2 to 3 cm by trial and error, moving it about 5 mm at a time and trying it for an extended period. You can also test it by going on a hard enough ride to make your leg muscles ache. If, apart from any other aches, your legs are sore mostly above the knees, then probably your saddle is too low. If they're sore mostly below the knees, it could be too high.

To find the best fore-and-aft position for the saddle, lean the bike slightly to one side and let a weighted string hang from the nose (front) of the saddle almost to the ground, like a plumb bob. The saddle will be within the best range if the string hangs between 6 and 8 cm behind the shaft which passes through the bottom of the frame (known as the 'bottom bracket') to connect the left and right pedal cranks. (Shaft, bearings, and associated parts are collectively referred to as a 'hanger set'.)

This is another adjustment you can check out by a road trial. Provided you have reasonably good balance, find a quiet road and see if you can ride 'no hands' while sitting upright. If you find you can't easily hold the position or can't get upright at all, then most likely your saddle is too far forward. If you can only do it by bending alarmingly far backwards at the waist then the saddle is probably too far back.

Another check can be done by going on a long ride. If your wrists, and perhaps also your shoulders, are sore, then most likely too much of your body mass is being supported on your arms because your saddle is too far back. You can also experiment with saddle tilt, but only after adjusting the handlebar as follows:

The handlebar: For mainly sightseeing rides, the top of the handlebar should not be above the level of the saddle, provided the handlebar drop is moderate. For competitive riding the handlebar can be up to 3 cm lower; it's worth lowering it especially for the occasional competitive event. The lower position allows better leg action (especially with clipless pedals) and somewhat reduced wind resistance – but very likely at the cost of a sore back and cricked neck if you're not used to it. The handlebar should be swivelled so that the handle ends are horizontal, or *slightly* tilted downwards at their rear ends.

The handlebar height is set by moving the handlebar bracket up or down in the stem tube of the front fork. You will first need to loosen the bracket locking bolt, the head of which projects above the stem of the bracket. Instead of a *projecting* bolt-head it may be a *recessed* bolt-head with a hexagon-shaped socket hole. If so, you will need to buy an Allen key which fits this socket and functions as a spanner. After loosening the bolt half-a-dozen turns you will probably have to knock it free by giving it a sharp whack with a lump of wood. Don't over-tighten the bolt; check tightness by gripping the front wheel between your knees and trying to force the handlebar to swivel inside the fork stem. It should swivel, but only under considerable force.

If you raise the bracket, be very sure to leave enough of it inside the stem tube for safety; not less than 5 cm. If this doesn't give you enough height it may mean the frame is too small for you. Longer brackets are available, but if you get one make sure it's a very reputable make and of forged material. A lot of pressure is exerted on the bracket because it supports your upper body mass, and it also endures heavy alternated flexing as you pull on the handlebar going uphill; the two stresses can eventually cause a fatigue fracture of the part, especially if you are strong and heavy.

As mentioned earlier, handlebar brackets come with different forward reaches. With the handlebar at saddle height, any sense of an over-curled back or of pain in the backbone suggests that a longer-reaching bracket is required. Here again, the longer the reach the more severe the stress on the headset. Contemplate what would happen if your handlebar and brake levers suddenly disappeared because your bracket broke on a downhill ride; it is certainly a good investment to have a top-quality bracket.

The headset bearings: After you've retightened the handlebar bracket in the fork stem, check that the headset bearings are correctly adjusted. If the handlebar feels as if it's binding or dragging when it's 'steered' with the front wheel off the ground, then the headset bearings have been set up too tightly.

To check if the bearings are too loose, rest the front wheel on the ground, squeeze the front brake, and firmly try to jiggle the handlebar/stem tube assembly backwards and forwards inside the frame. If you see an actual free movement or feel a sort of 'knocking' inside the frame at this point then the bearings are too loose.

If you have faith in your mechanical abilities, you can tighten or loosen the headset bearings yourself by turning the large adjustable nut just above the upper bearings.

This nut has a locking ring or locknut above it to prevent it working away from the set position. If you're not careful the essential act of tightening the locknut will disturb the adjustment. The trick is to make the adjusting nut slightly loose so that when you tighten the locknut it will squeeze the adjusting nut just the right amount tighter.

Once you've set its height, the handlebar should be rotated in its bracket so that the centrelines, or axes, of the ends you grip are parallel with the natural position of your hands as you ride.

The brakes: If necessary you can now move the brake lever positions so that when you're riding you can hook up the levers with your first two fingers without having to shift your hands from their normal riding grip. There should always be some free movement in the brake system so that, with your palms on the handlebar, your first two fingers can pull up the levers far enough for your remaining fingers to curl round them before the brake blocks actually begin to rub on the wheel rims.

If your brakes have adjusters at the lever ends as well as at the calliper ends, first set the callipers so that the brake blocks normally rest about 2 mm clear of the rims. Check that when the brakes are applied the blocks land squarely on the rims. If the blocks are too high they may rub the tyre; if too low you may lose friction in the area where the block fails to meet the rim. With new blocks, ensure they are fitted parallel with the rim by tightening their clamp bolts while the brakes are being lightly applied.

Even on a new bike, check that the brake block holders are facing the right way! One end of each holder is open so that the replaceable block can be inserted. The other end is closed so that the block cannot be shot out by the drag of the wheel rim as the brakes are applied. All the closed ends must be towards the *front* of the bike.

The final brake adjustment is at the lever end, the idea being that in a hard competitive event with the blocks wearing all the time the cyclist can tighten his brakes while he rides. Remember that on a new bike the brake cables will stretch quite a lot before stabilizing. Also remember that brake cables remain slightly elastic, causing a degree of sponginess when the levers are squeezed, especially for the (longer-cabled) back brake.

With brakes and handlebar now set up, you can return to the saddle and try out different tilts. A slight upward tilt at the front is often the most comfortable for touring. However, for sustained head-down hard riding this tilt is likely to cause pins and needles, or worse, in the region of the crutch.

The gears: Your dealer should adjust the gear-shift system for you, but in this case too the control cables will stretch quite soon and throw out some of the settings. By all means try re-setting it yourself, which will be a useful experience for when you want to make adjustments as the whole system gradually wears.

If you haven't used derailing gears before, first get your dealer or someone knowledgeable to show you how to work them, and if you don't catch on at once, don't be afraid to persist with questions until you really do understand. It is particularly important to appreciate that after the gear you want is engaged, the selector lever needs a little more jiggling until the chain runs freely and quietly. One so often sees (or rather *hears*) cyclists blithely riding along oblivious of the needless friction and wear occurring as their gear parts scrape and chatter because of incorrect positioning of the gear levers. Note that *unlike* the three-speed hub gear, the derailer requires that you keep the pedals turning while you change. However, take pressure off the pedals every time you do this to minimize the chain-stretching and gear-wearing jerk as the chain slips across.

In practice, changing is very easy provided you can *hear* what the chain's doing. Don't avoid using the gears because you're feeling strong enough to do without them; use them frequently so that the turning rate of your legs (their 'spin' or 'cadence') remains as constant as possible, regardless of gradient.

With derailers it is not necessary to select a specific gear, other than the highest for downhill speed and the lowest for steep hills. According to how your legs are taking the strain, just settle for whichever intermediate gear takes the strain off or maintains your rate of spin. There's no need to check which actual sprockets are engaged.

As a matter of interest, power pedalling utilizes mostly the so-called long-fibre muscles. These tire sooner than the short-fibre muscles that you use when pedalling rapidly. So if you concentrate on pedalling you may find you soon run out of steam.

The gears will need readjusting quite soon after you've bought the bike. You may also find the chain sometimes jumps off the front blades. These happenings are normal in a new bike, and a reputable dealer will expect to have to attend to them, along with the obligatory first service.

Here's how to make minor gear adjustments. We'll assume you have a standard 10 or 12-speed set, i.e. with two front gears/blades/wheels and a cluster of five or six sprockets (gears) at the back.

Prop your bike up vertically with the rear wheel off the ground; for this it's worth buying a simple stand made of bent rod which fits over and around the bottom bracket. Don't adjust gears while the bike is upside down – the slack part of the chain droops differently and usually leads to a false adjustment.

First check that the factory assembly was right! From a metre or so behind the bike, look carefully *between* the front blades to make sure that the gap between them is exactly in line with the middle sprocket of a five-speed cluster or, in the case of a six-speed cluster, the gap between third and fourth sprockets. If the alignment seems wrong, get back to your dealer before trying any adjustments.

Assuming all's well, turn the pedal crank forward and engage your highest gear combination – larger front blade with smallest cluster sprocket. Fiddle exact lever position for quietest running. From behind, keep an eye on that small sprocket and imagine a line running vertically through it; this imaginary line must pass symmetrically through the 'jockeys' (also called 'idlers' or 'pulleys'). If it doesn't, turn the *upper* adjusting screw ('stop') one way or the other to move the jockey over. (The jockey is the assembly of parts carrying the two small plastic cogs which the chain runs around under the cluster.) Now engage your lowest gear combination – smaller front blade with largest cluster. Check the alignment of the jockey with the large sprocket. If necessary move the *lower* adjusting screw to make it right.

If you have difficulty in making the chain ride far enough across onto the smallest or largest cluster, it may be because the cable from the shift lever is either too tight or too slack to give sufficient range of movement. It is easily adjusted by the knurled nut or barrel on the short piece of cable just above the jockey. You may also find that the shift levers don't stay in position, in which case tighten up the friction-nut/wing-nut on the shift lever.

Now check out the front derailer. First make sure the chain guide is clamped to the frame so that the underside of it is about 3 mm above the chain on the larger blade. There are two 'limit screws' on the mechanism. Their main purpose is to prevent the chain running right off the blades when you shift between high and low ranges, so you can easily set them by trial and error while cranking the pedals around by hand.

However, if you screw them in too far in an effort to make doubly sure the chain won't ride off, you will find they inhibit the chain movement so that you won't be able to engage the highest or lowest rear sprockets.

You may need to loosen the chain guide clamps to make a final twisting adjustment to prevent the chain from scraping on the guide cheeks – where it would soon wear a groove right through the guide if not attended to. If you have trouble getting enough range of movement on the front derailer shift lever, try turning the adjusting nut at the mechanism end of the cable.

Now take your screwdriver and make a road test. You may find that under riding conditions the chain occasionally rides off the blades or the outer sprocket gears. Correct such tendencies with *slight* adjustments of the appropriate screws – the settings may be quite sensitive.

Here's a useful tip: if the chain does unexpectedly ride off the larger blade and end up hanging on the pedal crank, it is not necessary to stop and get oily hands re-threading it. Just move the shift lever a little in the direction it goes when you change to the smaller blade, and keep pedalling. You'll find the chain wheel will pick up and replace the chain by itself.

Whenever possible, use the larger blade only with the three smallest cluster sprockets, and the smaller blade only with the three largest sprockets. If you make a habit of this it will minimize chain stretch and sprocket tooth wear as well as reducing friction and improving pedalling efficiency. It will also reduce the frequency of readjustments.

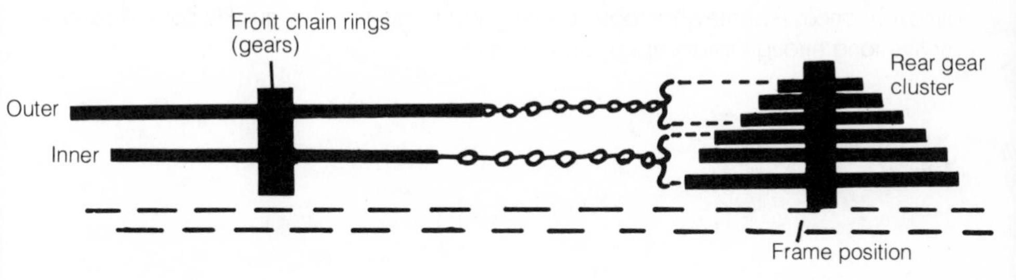

As far as possible try to use the outer front chain ring with the outer three cluster gears, and the inner front chain ring with the inner three cluster gears, as illustrated.

Wheel and hanger bearings: Check these for tightness. Start with the front wheel, which, when off the ground and with the bike vertical, should roll round by itself under the weight of the tube valve until it comes to rest with the valve at the bottom. If it doesn't, either one of the brake blocks is not quite clear of the rim, or the bearings are too tight. Now check for looseness by trying to move the wheel rim from side to side between the forks. If you see a movement or sense a knocking feeling then the bearings are too loose.

If you understand how to move the axle cones in and out then adjust the bearings, but if you're not sure, go to your dealer rather than inadvertently damage something. As with adjustment of the headset bearings, bear in mind that the locknut for the cones can disturb the bearing adjustment when you tighten it. Be sure to hold the cone with a cone spanner when you tighten the locknut.

After you have learnt how a correctly adjusted front wheel should feel, check the back wheel. Unless it's removed from the bike this wheel will not roll round under the valve weight because of the friction in the free-wheel mechanism. But you can still try rocking the rim in the fork to check for looseness. It's actually better to adjust the rear wheel bearings after taking the wheel out.

The hanger bearings are easily checked for looseness by holding a crank and trying to rock the shaft up and down in the bearings (slip the chain off first). If you feel a knocking, make sure it's not loose pedal bearings. Check for hanger bearing tightness by laying the bike on its side, pedals off the ground, and ensuring the whole chain wheel and crank assembly turns freely under the lightest touch. If it turns with a bumping or corrugated feeling then the bearings are already damaged, probably from over-tightening, and must be replaced.

Hanger bearings are set by screwing the adjusting cup in or out and locking it with the locking ring. The usual precautions must be taken against squeezing the bearings when the locking ring is tightened. Special spanners are needed to turn cup and ring, and the job is not as easy as for the wheel bearings.

Pedal bearings are less critical than the other bearings, but should still be checked for binding or undue wobble. Most of them can be adjusted in much the same way as wheel bearings, although some bikes have cheap pedals which have sleeve bearings and no provision for adjustment.

Generally all bike bearings should be set up *slightly* too loose rather than too tight. Under riding conditions bearings heat up a little, which tends to tighten them, especially the hanger bearings. A somewhat over-tightened bearing causes actual damage almost at once. A somewhat loose bearing will begin to wear quickly but will usually survive long enough to accept a readjustment.

BICYCLE EQUIPMENT AND MAINTENANCE

Equipping your bike

Avoid festooning your bike with nonessential accessories which defeat the object of buying a lightweight machine in the first place. The following should prove most useful:

Distance-recorders and computers which can be read easily while riding are necessary for following most of the route suggestions in this book, or for recording your own trailblazing. There is the old-fashioned hub-positioned 'cyclometer', which may be difficult to read while you ride, or the modern 'computer' which fits on the handlebar and has many additional functions. They tend to get stolen if left on the bike, so try to get the type that you can remove when necessary.

Lights: A white headlight is useful as a warning to errant pedestrians, but almost completely useless for showing the cyclist anything on the road surface unless it's pitch dark and he's moving very slowly.

A cyclist's greatest danger comes from being run down from behind, day or night. If you expect to be out at dusk or dark (which is most unwise), fit a bright red rear light, preferably a headlight with a red globe. It is possible to get halogen globes which last well and give a brilliant light. The globe should be rated to cope with the high voltage which can develop in a dynamo on a speeding bike.

Lightweight dynamos driven off the crown of the tyre (as distinct from the sidewall) are kindest to your tyres. However, dynamos cause noticeable drag and lights driven by them go out when you stop and dim when you toil up hills – which are the occasions when you are at your most vulnerable. Therefore you should also have a *strong* battery-powered rear light which you can switch on and off under such conditions. The ones which fix to your leg give you a better chance of being seen by following traffic because the light waves up and down conspicuously.

Be sure your bike is fitted with a large red rear reflector (a legal requirement), positioned so that it doesn't get obscured by your tool kit or clothing.

A bell or a hooter is a legal requirement. A hooter is more reliable. Fit it pointing downwards so it doesn't act as an airbrake.

A rear-view mirror is useful in theory. In practice, however, cycling mirrors give an inadequate rear view. If you do fit one, make quite sure it doesn't project outside the width of your handlebar. Any side-projection such as a mirror is a hazard, especially if fitted to the handlebar; vehicles occasionally pass terrifyingly close (or you wobble), and it needs only the slightest knock on the item that is projecting to throw you off balance. The so-called 'safety flags' also project but are more yielding; however, few of them are made well enough to withstand daily use for very long.

Tyre pumps are essential and should be of good quality, fitted with the kind of washer which can be readily replaced. Some pumps have an internal gadget which takes the guessing out of inflating to the correct pressure. Such pumps are much more expensive and somewhat heavier. Pumps sometimes get jolted out of their clips on bumpy roads; use a short length of Velcro tape to bind the pump to the frame. It's sensible to buy a little pressure gauge, especially if you use low profile tyres. Never pump your tyres from the inflator at a service station – there's a high risk of bursting the tyre.

Water bottles: Taking continual sips of fluid on a hot or hard ride is easier on your digestion than drinking whole cups of liquid. Fit one or even two bottle clips to your bike. Get stainless rather than chromed clips, and wrap rings of masking tape round your frame tube under the clip clamps, to prevent the paint coming off and rust starting.

It's not essential to have a proper cyclist's water bottle, although the streamlined types are very smart. Some of the better frames have screw holes for water bottle holders. Many cyclists use an empty plastic fruit juice bottle, partly because bottles tend to be jolted right out of their clips, and in a competitive event where you don't want to stop there's no regret in losing a disposable bottle.

Carry bags: Carrying a jersey, rain cape, camera, flask, *padkos*, etc. in a backpack is inconvenient, uncomfortable, and aggravates any incipient backache. Much better is a small waterproof zip bag which fits neatly to the handlebar and can be quickly slipped off its bracket if you need to leave the bike. Most dealers have an extensive selection of cycling and touring bags.

Tools: Carry only what you know how to use. If you have beaded tyres, three good quality tyre-levers are mandatory, along with two spare inner tubes. Keep the traditional puncture-repair outfit at home, or take it along only on very long trips. Rather check your bike regularly than have to carry heavy tools on long rides just in case something goes wrong.

Cheap multi-purpose spanners are almost useless – they never seem to fit anything properly and they snap very easily. On a longish trip rather take a small 'shifting spanner' (4-inch), a pair of small pliers, a smallish screwdriver and appropriate Allen keys if your bike needs them. If you do not have quick-release wheels, buy a good ring spanner to fit the axle nuts.

It is important to carry a supply of rags to clean your hands, which are likely to get oily while fixing a rear puncture or replacing a jumped off chain. Also take a couple of coins to make an emergency phone call. Keep the tools in a well-made waterproof bag securely strapped under the saddle.

Locking chain: A nuisance, but often necessary if you want to leave your bike for a while for calls of nature, taking photos, going into a shop and for travelling by train. Get a piece of *substantial* galvanized chain (not stranded cable), long enough to wrap around a big lamppost. A comparatively solid padlock, preferably all brass, is better than a combination lock – which you may not be able to undo if it's dark. Always take the chain through your front wheel as well as your frame when you secure the bike; there's a substantial trade in stolen front wheels.

Torch: If you don't have a removable battery-powered lamp you'll need a small bright torch for cycling at night in a deserted area. It's maddening to have mechanical trouble in the pitch dark and not be able to see what you're doing.

Maps: These are not really equipment and they're seldom essential. Nevertheless, good large-scale maps add very greatly to the interest of planning, doing, and reminiscing about a ride.

Map Studio's *Cape Town and Environs Street Guide* is almost essential for following many of the rides in this book, and is a useful thing to have in the home anyway. It includes the principal surrounding country towns.

The '1:50 000' (meaning that 1 m measured on the map with a ruler would represent 50 km to cycle) official 'topographical' (showing the hills and valleys) survey maps are excellent and cheap. You can buy them at the Government Surveys and Mapping office in Rhodes Avenue, Mowbray, or order them by phoning (021) 689-9721. Some outdoor-sports and book shops have specialized maps for hiking trails running in the vicinity of rides which interest you (not necessarily rides in this book). Such maps often include information of specific interest to hikers and cyclists.

Equipping yourself

Some dealers do better business out of cycling clothes than out of cycles, especially since it became fashionable to go around in expensive Lycra clothing whether or not one actually does any cycling. This is not to deny the merits of well-designed gear. If you're a keen cyclist, the best cycling gear (i.e., that designed primarily for utility rather than style) can add to your cycling comfort and reduce your air friction.

The bright colours of the clothing are attractive, but also conspicuous. Depending on your self-image you may feel such gear is inappropriate for a weak rider or a beginner, especially if the clothes are emblazoned with the names of famous cyclists or mighty sponsors.

Helmets are likely to become a legal requirement and more and more event organizers are already insisting on them. The actual risk of severe head injury is very low, but just the possibility of brain damage makes it worthwhile to wear a helmet.

At present there are no formally-approved local standards for cycling helmets. The vast majority of helmets available are imported, and only some of them are marked as complying with recognized American or European safety standards. These are the ANSI, SNELL and BSI standards.

Our advice is to look for the lightest and most airy rigid helmet you can find, and don't be prejudiced by a comparatively low price.

On *any* helmet, the straps, their adjustment and anchoring methods are extremely important. The straps must prevent the helmet from tipping forward or backward on your head under impact. A helmet which jerks off or gets knocked out of position before or as you hit something is obviously useless.

Before buying a helmet, check this point by tightening the chin strap to a *comfortably bearable* tension and getting someone to try pushing the helmet off your head forwards, backwards, and sideways. If it moves out of position under anything less than a hard neck-jarring shove then don't buy it. Have a look at how the strap ends are fixed into the dome. Pull on both sides of the chin strap to see if there's a tendency for it to work loose.

In choosing the right size, you may need to allow for a sweatband under the helmet, but don't be tempted to get one that is too large for comfort – it will shift out of position on your head. Most helmets have an absorbent lining, but in many examples this is a plastic foam which will make you sweat even more, and it is not amenable to regular cleaning. If there's any choice, then a bright yellow or a white helmet is most conspicuous in traffic.

Cycling shorts: These have a substantial cushion of chamois leather ('shammy') sewn into the crutch region, which is a great alleviator of discomfort on long or hot rides. Make sure it really is chamois and not a plastic substitute which is worse than nothing.

White shorts are best for summer use, black is worst – it transfers heat through to your legs. The opposite applies in winter. For maximum comfort, cycling shorts should be worn without underwear.

Cycling 'longs': It is not a good idea to ride in tracksuit trousers unless the weather is extremely cold or your knee joints are unusually susceptible to ordinary levels of cold. In these cases, rather buy the proper long-legged cycling pants – which are very expensive. If you have knee problems, keep your knees warm with sections of old *wool* socks pulled over them.

Glasses: Wrap-around plastic (never glass) 'shades' are very useful in protecting your eyes from ultraviolet light, glare and wind, as well as grit and insects. They also protect prescription spectacles if you happen to wear them. In fact, eye protection relaxes your whole head and neck, thereby increasing riding comfort. When you buy your shades make sure they are guaranteed to filter out a given percentage of ultraviolet light; many makes of sunglasses, irrespective of price or brand, do not. If they don't, and are merely darkened for the sake of appearance, your pupils will open to compensate for the darkening, thereby letting in even more ultraviolet than if you were shadeless. In this way your eyes could be severely damaged.

Opticians usually stock or can order clear or tinted optically correct plastic 'safety' specs with side-pieces. These are surprisingly cheap and effective.

You will probably need to rig elastic to the side-pieces of the shades to stop them flying off in the wind. Smart-looking elasticized spec-retainers for securing skiing goggles are available in Europe; you might be able to get one. Also, a tiny patch of foam rubber stuck under the bridge of the glasses protects your nose during a longish ride. Certain fluids, available in car-accessory shops, can be applied to shades and spectacless to give you quite good vision even when it's raining.

Shoes: Proper cycling shoes incorporate gadgets which keep your feet attached to the pedals for a longer period than it takes to complete the press-down power stroke of your legs. The technique for extending the press-down into a 'pull-around' has to be practised, but once he has learnt it the cyclist enjoys a decided power-transfer advantage. Still better (and easier to use) is the clipless system described earlier. However, cycling shoes are expensive, and the clipless system is especially so.

Old tackies will do for the sort of riding described in this book, but their soft soles will get damaged fairly quickly. Worn running shoes are a good compromise – their soles are hard enough to stand up to metal pedals, they're comfortable, lightweight, and unaffected by rain.

Wear simple *cotton* running socks when cycling, especially if you have sweaty feet.

Shirts/jerseys: A quality cycling jersey has pockets and is a sensible but costly garment for cool weather cycling. In warmer weather some people find them hot and clingy like T-shirts. It's difficult to get a proper cycling jersey which isn't plastered with advertising, but they *are* available if you insist.

Any casual shirt you fancy is entirely adequate; in cooler weather you can wear a T-shirt underneath. In cold weather it is quite important that whatever you're wearing does not work up and leave a band of unprotected flesh, especially around the kidneys.

During a sunny bike ride you can get very burnt without feeling hot. Some people need to wear sleeves and collars for solar protection, but in hot weather where this might be uncomfortable, rather resort to a good sun filter cream.

Cycling gloves: These are rarely necessary unless you suffer from bad circulation or want to prevent your hands from getting weatherbeaten. In extremely cold weather leather cycling gloves prevent chilblains but don't really keep your hands warm.

Cold hands may not trouble you but they can desensitize and weaken your hand muscles for steering, braking, and gear-shifting. Cycling gloves with thick woolly sleeves/socks pulled over the top are fine provided you can still stick your fingers out.

Rain gear: If you have to ride to work or school in all weathers, then proper two-piece rain gear made of material which 'breathes' is essential. However, it is rather heavy, very expensive, and awkward to cycle in. We don't recommend cycling capes – they tend to get hooked on the handlebar or blown up over your face by a gust of wind, both of which occurrences are highly dangerous.

People who ride for relaxation should stay at home on wet days. Apart from the discomfort of getting wet, slippery roads, reduced visibility and stinging spray in the eyes greatly increase the accident risk. If the weather looks merely showery, then take a light windcheater and a good quality neat-fitting woollen jersey to wear. Real wool garments continue to feel bearably comfortable when wet, although wind makes the entrapped water cold. If you don't want to carry a windcheater, don't laugh at the idea of carrying a plastic garden refuse bag. Cut slits in the two bottom corners, and in the middle of the bottom seam, so that you can put your arms and head through – this is amazingly effective at keeping out much of the wind and the rain.

Compass: This may sound like an unnecessary item, but you'll find a cheap pocket compass useful for following the route descriptions in this book. A compass enables you to act on an instruction such as 'ride eastwards' without having to digest the mass of written instructions which might follow.

Maintaining your bike

Once a bicycle is 'run-in' and properly set up by someone competent it needs very little adjustment and maintenance unless you damage something. The most vulnerable component is the derailer gear system. If you are ham-fisted at mechanical tasks (as distinct from merely lacking knowledge), then you'll have to rely on your favourite cycle shop for upkeep – don't try anything more ambitious than fixing a puncture.

If you do depend on a shop, you must expect to pay a fair amount. Cycling nowadays is a fast-growing and prosperous trade; good mechanics are scarce and have to be well paid, and there are high mark-ups on spares and accessories.

When you go to a professional cycle workshop and ask for your bike to be 'checked', you are almost certain to get landed with a fixed-price standard 'service' of one kind or another, and the ultimate bill is likely to include some parts which you'll be told it's in your best interest (and well it may be) to have replaced. Get quotes before having any work done – the size of the quote may persuade you to do the job yourself, which will eventually help you get more out of the sport.

Obviously it's more economical to do your own adjustments and some of your own repairs if you can. Nevertheless, we recommend leaving the following jobs to the professionals:

- Straightening wheels
- Straightening anything that's bent (sometimes bending makes the metal crack, which you may not notice until the part collapses at some awkward moment).
- Replacing bearings
- Replacing gear parts

As explained in the section on adjusting your new bike, various parts will bed-in, stretch, or generally settle down, the overall effect being to upset the original settings. Thus, after two or three hundred kilometres, your new bike should be ready for readjustment, after which it should be satisfactory for another 1 000 to 2 000 km unless you ride fast and hard. Remember that the better the quality of moving parts the longer they will last and the longer they should maintain adjustment, provided they were set up correctly in the first place. One of the best simple checks on your bike is to lift it a few centimetres off the ground and let it bounce on its tyres. Any rattle or thud should be investigated as it might indicate that something is broken or loose.

Here are a few practical tips about key aspects of running maintenance:

Wheels: Looking at the bike end-on, the wheels must run centrally between their respective forks, with equal gaps between each wheel rim and the adjacent arm of its fork. If a wheel keeps shifting to one side, it's usually because the quick-release lever on the axle spindle isn't tight enough.

Wheels get dented and buckled when you hit stones and bad road bumps, which is bound to happen sooner or later. Sometimes a spoke breaks. Youngsters often ride off a kerb or 'jump' their bikes up a kerb – both practices are bad for wheels and tyres, especially genuine racing wheels. Any of these occurrences may cause a wheel to develop a wobble, sideways and/or up and down.

Both kinds of wobble can be dangerous at speed. They reduce braking efficiency, make the brakes screech, accelerate tyre wear, cause (more) spokes to break, and may lead to cracks in the wheel rim. However, a wheel 2 or 3 mm out of true is tolerable for pottering around on scenic excursions.

Inspect rims for damage and cracks. Rim damage can cause tyre blowouts.

Unless you have an instruction book, and plenty of time on your hands to practise, don't try to straighten a wheel – the job is something of an art.

Tyres: The golden rule is to keep them correctly inflated. Soft tyres lead to wheel damage, tyre damage and unnecessary friction with the road. But don't over-inflate, or the tube may burst. Every time you pump your tyres up, check for sharp objects embedded in the rubber; don't *dig* these out but pull them out carefully with small-nosed pliers.

Other than punctures, the commonest damage to tyres is to the sidewalls, which are comparatively thin compared with the tread. Sidewalls easily get cut by loose gravel and bits of junk in the road. Impact damage may not cut the tyre but can weaken it, causing it to bulge and eventually burst at the bulge. With beaded tyres, small cuts and minor bulges can be dealt with by a suitably cut 'gaiter' (rubberized canvas) stuck inside with rubber cement.

Tyre beads (and wheel rims too) are frequently damaged by tyre levers wielded by insensitive hands. Take it easy when attending to punctures, and use well designed tyre levers. Actually, very little force is needed to remove or replace a beaded tyre, especially one that's been on the wheel for some time.

If you don't mind the ever-increasing incidence of punctures you can use a tyre for pottering about the suburbs until it literally wears right through. But if you intend to enter competitive fun-rides or go on long scenic trips, keep a pair of fairly new tyres and put them on for these occasions. Take them off again afterwards. With practice you can easily swop both tyres within 15 minutes. Don't throw out worn tyres just because you're going to make a major excursion.

The back tyre is the 'driving' tyre and it also carries the major part of the load; therefore it will wear faster than the front tyre. When you notice that its tread is nearly gone, transfer it to the front and put a new one on the back.

Don't worry too much if the protective, semi-decorative rubber coating on a sidewall begins to peel off. This is often the result of perishing by sunlight and doesn't necessarily weaken the tyre.

For fixing punctures make sure you have a stock of *small* patent patches. For some odd reason these sizes are often hard to get, and the patch you're obliged to use for a narrow-section racing tube may be far too big for the job and need to be 'folded' around the tube. In this case, use two coins larger than the patch; stick the patch in position and use the coins as a press to keep the patch squeezed against the tube. Put pressure on the coins with a weight or a strong bulldog clip.

You can also cut the patch down to size, but if you use the patent type with silver paper backing this is not ideal. If the transparent plastic film doesn't peel off easily after attaching the patch, leave it on; it won't do any harm inside the tyre.

Frames and forks: Check your frame by carefully centring the wheels in their forks, then stand back and view the bike end-on: the wheels should be in exactly the same vertical plane. If they're not, the frame and/or the front fork is twisted. Go to your bicycle expert and get an opinion on how bad the twist is – a small amount of twist is tolerable, but there are several other factors to take into consideration.

Frame twist can be caused by a combination of a weak (poor quality) frame and a strong rider, but the commonest cause is a collision of some kind. Collisions are also the main cause of front fork damage; children often bump up a kerb or overestimate the power of their brakes and barge into the garage door. Such impacts may bend the front fork backwards.

Sometimes it's better to leave a minor front fork bend than to straighten it. Never try to straighten a front fork yourself; the job needs know-how and skill and may even be too risky to be worth doing at all.

Gears and chains: Gear adjustment was covered in an earlier section (see p.12 – 13). If you find that no amount of adjustment will give you consistent gear changes it is probably because the jockey assembly is worn or the tension spring in it fatigued or broken. We don't recommend you undertake this repair yourself.

You may find that, after a lot of use, the chain occasionally skips teeth while you are using the smallest sprocket and pedalling hard – you'll feel a hard, disconcerting jerk. This indicates the need for a new chain – soon, because the jerking will accelerate the rate of chain stretch and will damage or even break the sprocket teeth.

Technically it is undesirable to fit a new chain to a worn cluster; if you can afford it, both should be replaced. Second best is to replace only the small sprocket on the cluster, provided it is the type which allows individual sprockets to be replaced – and even so you may well find dealers don't carry separate sprockets as spares.

However, unless you're a highly competitive rider, it is satisfactory to use a new chain with a moderately worn cluster. A good quality cluster should last you through two or even three chains. After that, it's best to replace the front chain wheels as well (being much bigger, these wear comparatively slowly).

The key to long chain and sprocket life lies in regular cleaning and oiling. Buy a 'link-pin extractor' from your dealer and ask him to demonstrate how to push out one of the pins on a chain so that it can be removed from the bike.

Once you have done that, wipe off the worst of the oily muck then coil up the chain, lay it flat in a tin, and cover it with engine cleaning fluid bought from a car accessory shop. Swish it around with an old brush. Take it out and squirt it hard with water (preferably hot water). Dry it as quickly as you can (with a hair dryer). Hang it up by one end and pour plenty of thin clean oil onto the top end of the chain. Let the oil run down by itself and drain off into a tin under the chain. Coil up the chain a few times, then hang it up by the other end and oil it again. Allow time for all the surplus oil to drip off – more than enough will stay behind. The surplus oil will be slightly gritty; pour it through a coffee filter before re-using it.

Cleaning the cluster and chain wheels is much more tedious. It is unwise to use engine cleaner or other solvent in case it gets into the bearings where it will not only attack the lubricant but will also carry in loose dirt. Rather set aside time to work over all the gears with old rags. Take care not to leave bits of thread behind. Do the cleaning every month or so rather than wait for it to get unpleasantly mucky.

The jockey parts should be wiped thoroughly clean too. You can oil the jockey joints and wheels but there's no need to put more oil on the gears – there will be enough on the chain. When you replace the chain and reconnect its ends, be sure to press back the chain pin so that it projects an equal distance each side.

Provided you get the special tools to remove and replace it, you can service the cluster yourself by first removing all loose dirt with rags, then dunking it in engine cleaner. Several dunks (change the fluid each time) and a great deal of swirling around will be needed. Wash it very thoroughly with hot water, inside and out. Dry it quickly and completely. Then squirt copious quantities of oil into the guts, spin the mechanism around to distribute the oil, then let the surplus drain out.

Don't forget to clean and oil the shift mechanisms.

Remember that excess oil on exposed parts increases the buildup of dirt, so refrain from over-enthusiastic oiling.

Cables: We've already dealt with adjustments to the gadgets which are operated by the cables, so now for the cables themselves. Their weakest points are their extreme ends ('terminals') and where they bend quite sharply.

Inspect the ends frequently; replace the cables as soon as you see individual strands broken. Wipe grease or Vaseline onto the cable ends regularly to delay the onset of rust. Periodically, and with new cables, pull them out of their sheaths, wipe off loose dirt, and soak them in thin oil. Drain off all surplus. (Old or thickened oil inside a cable sheath may make the cable action sluggish.) The point of the oiling is not so much lubrication as rust prevention.

When you up-end your bike, to repair a puncture for example, take great care not to kink the brake cables where they join the levers on the handlebar. When you replace brake cables be sure to buy them at least as long as the old ones.

Water and rust: If you've been out in the rain it is essential to wipe down your bike as soon as you get home. Use an absorbent cloth or old chamois, then finish with a hair dryer. Pay special attention to the wheel rims, the cables, and the chromed parts, including spokes.

Chrome is supposed to offer protection, but nowadays it is rarely of sufficient quality to be much more than decorative. Once the underlying metal begins to corrode there's no stopping it, and before long the chrome will start lifting and peeling.

If you do a lot of riding in rain, or somehow get your bike thoroughly wet, water will get into the bearings and gradually emulsify with the oil or grease. This will diminish the lubrication effect. Also, the bearing surfaces will begin to pit from rusting. The only remedy is regular cleaning and overhaul of all bearings. In any case, this should be done annually if you ride a fair amount.

Use grease rather than oil for the wheel, hanger, and headset bearings. Grease keeps water out better than oil does, and also makes it easier to fit the bearing balls. Do not pack the bearings solid with grease; if you do, the grease will congeal in the same way milk turns into butter when it is churned.

Cycling Safety

Whether you're driving a truck, riding a bike or walking, any form of traffic encounter is potentially risky. However, most mishaps are preventable or avoidable if you're alert, humble and defensive.

Everyone hears chilling stories about cycling accidents, but courteous behaviour and consistent safe riding rarely make news. There are thousands of active cyclists who've never had any kind of traffic accident.

The following points have a bearing on cycling safety:

- Large numbers of road users are not, and never will be, good 'natural' drivers, even though they may try to be. It's futile to shout at them or remonstrate with them or expect them not to do outrageous things. Many thoroughly bad or hopelessly incompetent drivers are very nice people who consider themselves responsible citizens and careful road users. You may be one of them!
- A considerable number of people (including cyclists) have partially defective vision. Inadequate 'binocular vision' is common, which means that although the affected drivers/riders do their best to be careful, they cannot accurately judge their distances, forward or sideways, from other objects in the road. Drivers may also have poor 'peripheral vision', which means that when looking ahead they may be physically *unable* to see objects alongside or just in front of them.
- On certain days and at certain times of the day motorists are more irritable, tired, reckless, or full of beer than at other times. Apply your common sense to work out when to avoid cycling.
- Timing is also a factor in anticipating other hazards. For example, drivers towing twin-hulled boats (the widths of which they usually underestimate) are very likely to be on the roads early on weekend mornings and late weekend evenings. In addition, it is always harder to see at dusk than at night.
- Most drivers (and pedestrians) completely underestimate the speed of cyclists, and do not appreciate that a fast-moving cyclist cannot stop quickly.
- After making all allowances and excuses for dreadful driving, you must accept that there will always be some drivers around who are nothing less than public menaces to all other road users. The cyclist's only safeguards against these people are prayer and avoidance.

The cyclist's response to these and other possible threats to his safety is always to ride defensively, no matter how he is provoked. Here are some tips:

- Ride at least a metre away from the kerb or road-edge. You need this margin so that when overtaking vehicles pass too close you will have some escape latitude and not get forced against the kerb and so fall off your bike. It is *not* more safe to ride very close to the kerb.
- Buy a brilliantly coloured safety vest to wear (always) over your jersey/shirt. It greatly increases your visibility.
- Ride straight. Never swerve. Look well ahead for manhole-covers, stones and potholes in the road; *gradually* adjust your riding line to avoid them. This is especially important when riding in a group. Standard group cycling procedure is to avoid the obstacle and point down at the obstacle as you pass, alerting those behind.
- Never think that if a green traffic light is in your favour you have an unchallengeable right to pedal on regardless.

•Similarly, if a traffic officer or event-marshal beckons you on, don't assume nearby motorists will respect your right of way. They may not even have seen the officer!
•*Expect* every vehicle to turn without warning or without waiting, right across your line, left or right. If you always expect it then it won't surprise and annoy you.
•Don't blindly trust painted cycle paths. Early-morning motorists often back out of drives across them without proper care. Note that the new Traffic Ordinance ***requires*** you to use such paths if they are there.
•Be humble! If a bus passes you and seems to be pulling in too soon, then STOP so that it can get ahead before wiping you out. Also, never be afraid to get off your bike in an emergency.
•Continuously try to 'read' and anticipate the traffic situation around you so that you don't get caught up in someone else's accident.
•Don't ride two abreast unless you're on a really quiet road and very alert to possible traffic sounds behind you.
•For the same reason, *never* ride with a 'walkman'.
•If you get caught in bad light and don't have a good lamp, then either ride on the pavement or ride on the opposite side of the road so that you can see what's coming at you. (Of course that's illegal, but your life is more important in this case than staying on the right side of the law.)
•Avoid cycling straight into a low sun – drivers of cars with dirty windscreens may not see you against the strong glare.
•Never follow another cyclist too closely except in organized competitions, where 'slipstreaming','sucking' or 'drafting' is a calculated risk for the experienced rider.
•Habitually check for the presence of a driver in every stationary car ahead of you. *Expect* the driver to fling open his door just as you ride past.
•***Expect*** every stationary car ahead of you to pull into the traffic without warning.
•On a narrow or winding road, if you see or sense a truck and trailer rig overtaking you, *stop* as it passes, because the trailer may cut in on you even though the driver thinks he's well past you.
•If a driver deliberately stops or waits for you to cross or turn, don't stare with open-mouthed disbelief – courteously thank him and take the opportunity (but look out for impatient motorists who are wondering what the fellow's waiting for).
•Don't underestimate the risk of colliding with a pedestrian. A pedestrian is conditioned to sense an approaching *vehicle* – he may appear to look straight at you, yet not see you, and then step in your path.
•*Never* swear at, yell at, or graphically insult inconsiderate drivers. Their action was probably unintentional, and your outburst will only make them aggressive towards cyclists in general (and may thus indirectly cause injury to another cyclist).

Even with no other road-user in sight, carelessness and laziness can be your downfalls. Observing a few golden rules will successfully prevent this. These are:

•Keep your bike in good order – no loose wheels, no loose handlebar, no broken spokes, no 'whiskery' brake and gear cables (broken strands), bearings properly adjusted and oiled or greased, tyres correctly pumped up.
•In traffic and when going fast downhill, keep two fingers of each hand on the brake levers at the first position, so that you can stop quickly.
•Never apply brakes by 'grabbing' them. 'Squeeze' them on.

- Your front brake does most of the stopping work, but never apply it by itself otherwise your back wheel may slide out sideways and you'll come off the bike! Worse, you may get somersaulted over the handlebar. Use both brakes simultaneously.
- Don't wave to friends. Keep both hands on the bike and shout out your greetings.
- Don't attempt hand signals unless you're absolutely confident in one-handed control of your bike. In any case, most motorists will ignore your signals. If you're really struggling to change lanes or cross a stream of traffic, rather get off, wait for a gap, and run across the road wheeling your bike.
- Don't show off with 'no-hands' tricks.
- Don't let oil from your chain and gears drip onto your wheel rims and then possibly soak into the brake blocks.
- Wear shades. An insect hitting you in the eye at speed can cause a fall – and injure your eye.
- Experiment (with great care!) to see how far you can lean your bike on bends without catching the pedal or your toe on the ground and falling over. Don't pedal round sharp bends at speed; rather coast with your inside pedal/foot UP.
- Avoid fast cornering where a thin layer of gritty sand has been blown across a smooth tar road. Also avoid drifts of softer sand deposited by the southeaster. (Apart from the safety angle, sand picked up by the tyres will fall onto your chain and gears and act like grinding paste.)
- Remember that all painted road markings are extremely slippery when wet or slightly oily. When it rains after a long dry period, there will be both oil and water on the paint and the danger is even greater.
- Never tie a discarded jersey or jacket around your waist, in case a sleeve drops down and catches in your back wheel.
- Never carry shopping on the handlebar unless it's in a receptacle designed to fit there.
- Keep well behind other vehicles, even if they're going very slowly or giving useful wind and rain protection. A car or small truck can stop far quicker than a bicycle, and so there's a danger that you will run into the back of it.
- Never hold onto another vehicle to get a free ride uphill.
- If you do fall off in dense traffic (including other cyclists) try to have the presence of mind to lie still where you fall, so that following drivers/riders can avoid you. Move only when you've collected your wits and the traffic has passed.

1 Getting to know the Mother City

Features: You may think you know the city well enough, but walking around it with a guidebook when there's not much traffic about can be an eye-opener. On a summer's day, riding round town is distinctly cooler than walking, and if you're new to pedal-pushing, this is a suitable outing to familiarize yourself with your bike. Not recommended for unaccompanied women or children.
Grade and distance: A1; 7 km; 30 to 60 minutes total.
Best times: Saturday afternoons, summer mornings (finish by 07h00 on weekdays), summer evenings after 18h30. Avoid times when there is a lot of traffic, when the wind is high, and Friday evenings when too many vehicles are being mismanaged by inebriates. Sundays or public holidays are suitable except that most eateries will be closed.
Special information: Personal security is at risk when the city is quiet, especially downtown. Groups of felons are mostly into car theft or after foreign tourists and sailors, but anyone going through this area alone outside business hours is taking a chance. Riders should be quite safe if in groups of three or more. Note that muggers don't like working early mornings. Be sure to carry a substantial lock and chain in case you leave your bike unattended, and keep alert if you pause to take pictures. Take a guidebook with you.
Sustenance: Hardly worth it, but your best bet is the railway station where the restaurant and 'pie cart' have very long opening hours – but neither the fare nor the ambience is inspiring. The tearoom in the Gardens (access from Queen Victoria Street; outside tables) is very pleasant on a still day, but not very good value and doesn't open early. During weekdays, several small establishments in the street-level and underground shopping/business areas offer good-value breakfasts from 07h00 or even earlier.
Getting there: Leave your car somewhere not too isolated and where you can get to and from it unmolested. Avoid the station roof parking lot. We suggest the area between the station and the Civic Centre (Pay 'n Display).
Doing the ride: Follow the one-way signs towards Cape Town's great unconfessed practical joke – the assembly of crooked red pipes on the plaza between the Civic Centre and Standard Bank Centre, formerly the Cape Town Centre. Turn left and make your first unexpected discovery: you are in Longmarket Street – not THE Longmarket Street, but another, less famous one. Arrive in Adderley Street at the statues of Jan van Riebeeck and his wife Marie de la Queillerie.

Turn left, skirting the fountain, and continue up Adderley through the Riebeeck Street traffic lights. If you want to pick up information from Captour, it has an office at the entrance to the underground part of the Golden Acre (Strand Concourse) which you can reach by detouring onto the pavement at this point and going down the ramp parallel with Adderley Street.

Take note of the attractive mosaics on this side of the station. Cross the next set of lights, Strand Street, through the pedestrian lights outside the Golden Acre, and stop to see the 'War Stone' on the centre island near Hout Street. This marks the spot where the end of World War I was announced in the city. Ride right up Adderley Street past the Groote Kerk (1704), cross Bureau Street intersection and note the Cultural History

Museum on the left (formerly the Supreme Court, and before that the slave quarters, built in 1680), and ahead Government Avenue passing through the Gardens – vehicles, including ridden cycles, are not permitted.

Turn right with Adderley Street into Wale Street, ride past St George's Cathedral (1901) then right again at the second traffic light, into bumpy Burg Street. The Old Town House (1755 or 1761) is on the Burg/Longmarket south corner. Ride down the two blocks of Burg Street and cross historic Greenmarket Square (bumps to be expected on the cobbles), then turn left up Shortmarket Street (a one-way street).

Now turn left into Long Street, also one-way. Attempts are being made to preserve the Victorian character of Long Street by restoring some of the better designed old buildings; notice one of the recent restorations, The Blue Lodge. There are some absorbing second-hand bookshops along here, along with Morris the Butcher of sausage fame, a glass craftsman, and both pawnbrokers and pornbrokers.

Half a kilometre up, pass the refurbished Long Street Baths (heated swimming pool), and turn left at the traffic lights into Annandale Road. The warm old buildings on your left were built for the South African College, forerunner of UCT, and now house the Michaelis Art School, and in the grounds, the Little Theatre. The Labia cinema is diagonally opposite on the Rheede Street corner. Veer left, pass the Mount Nelson hotel entrance on the right, the top of Government Avenue almost opposite, and then the high wall of Cape Town High School. After the wall turn down left into Hatfield Street, passing the Hatfield Pizza and Pasta Factory.

About 400 m down on the left are the Great Synagogue and the Jewish Museum – this was formerly the Gardens Synagogue and contains exceptionally interesting artefacts and information about old Cape Town. The road changes name to St Johns but presents St Mary's (cathedral, 1891) on the corner of Roeland Street, after which it changes name again to Plein Street. Notice Stalplein with its military memorials and reputedly undying flame, and behind it Tuynhuys, the state president's residence adjoining the Houses of Parliament.

The next building houses the Receiver of Revenue. After this you come to short Spin Street which was significant for its 'slave tree', under which slave auctions were once held. On the centre island you can see the commemorative plaque set in the ground marking where the old tree used to stand. Carry on down Plein Street and then turn right into Darling Street (formerly Kaisersgracht) diagonally across from the main post office. The PO has very interesting exhibits in its Parliament Street foyer, including a 1629 postal stone.

Pass the Grand Parade (pretty dull and dirty on a Sunday) opposite the old City Hall, used mostly now as a library and concert hall. Built in 1905 in the Italian Renaissance style, it is seen to best advantage from the other side of the square, especially at night. Next to the City Hall is the far older and more historic, but dull-looking Drill Hall; opposite is the Boer War Memorial. Now cross Buitenkant Street and stop at the old Castle on your left. Surprisingly many Capetonians only visit it as schoolchildren (if at all). Restoration has been proceeding for nearly two decades and a visit is extremely worthwhile (good conducted tours are held regularly).

After the Castle turn left into Oswald Pirow Street and ride over the bridge next to the Good Hope Centre. From the highest point of the bridge a leftwards view, seldom photographed, gives a good impression of the changed skyline of the old city, now with its controversial ugly modern high-rises. Cross at the traffic lights for Hertzog Boulevard and pass the Culemborg railway goods depot on your right. Turn left onto the road running beneath Table Bay Boulevard, with the docks to your right.

When you arrive at the Heerengracht, turn left and take a look at the Bartolomeu Dias statue standing in the lawned traffic circle. Cross the circle and head up towards your starting point. Did you know that the whole of Adderley Street was once called Heerengracht? Part of it was renamed in 1850 to honour C.B. Adderley, a pro-South Africa British MP who played a major part in thwarting the British Government's plan to dump shiploads of convicts at the Cape.

Take good note of the intersection of Adderley Street with Hertzog Boulevard; this is the starting place of the Argus Cycle Tour – one of Cape Town's most exciting annual sporting events.

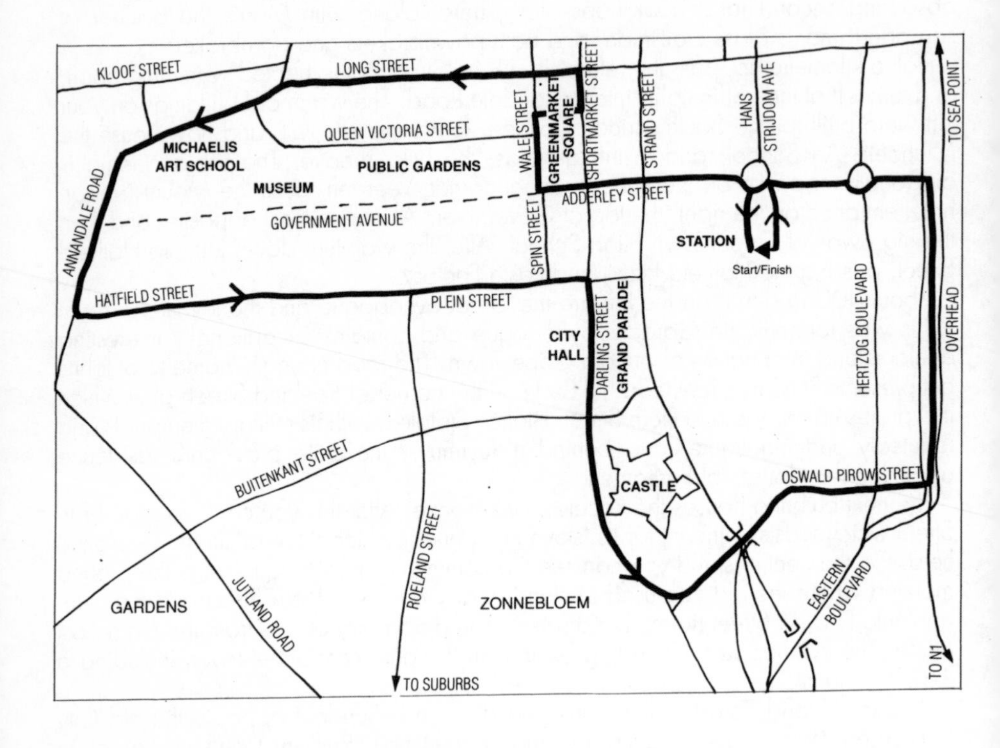

2 A harbour patrol

Features: Harbours fascinate most people, and Cape Town's partially historic harbour is no exception. A ride with no hills that is suitable for a family, but not for youngsters or women on their own. Policemen and other security personnel are present and there is a fair amount of traffic even over weekends.
Grade and distance: A1; 14 km; one to two hours, depending on the distractions.
Best times: For watching yachts sailing in and out, weekends and Wednesday evenings are the best. Sunsets are great but you should leave the harbour and downtown areas smartly after that. Any strong wind is unpleasant because there are no protective buildings and a lot of grit blowing around. Autumn tends to bring fog.
Special information: Private traffic is minimal in the harbour area but Spoornet/Portnet trucks and forklifts travel at breakneck speed. The greatest harbour danger, such as it is, is failing to see rail tracks and catching a wheel in the groove. Security control at the harbour entrance is minimal, but very occasionally and without prior warning officials get the jitters, so it's advisable to carry an identification document.
Sustenance: Best choices are Ferryman's in the Victoria Basin, or Seagulls next to Green Point Stadium. If you can afford the crayfish and mussels on offer (nothing else), Panama Jacks is open every day from noon to 20h00. At the time of writing, various eateries were being planned as part of the redeveloped Victoria Basin.
Getting there: Start in town; we suggest street or off-street parking in Oswald Pirow Street adjoining Struik House – opposite Spoornet's Culemborg goods depot.
Doing the ride: Ride northwards for 200 m, passing under the Table Bay Boulevard which becomes Eastern Boulevard somewhere above your head. You will have crossed two traffic lights by now. Swing left after the second set of lights and ride another 200 m to the customs and security gate – no hassle about entering. Swing right at the stop street, cross the railway, turn right and ride about 1 km to the Royal Cape Yacht Club on your left.

The road surface is wide and smooth but look out for ironmongery that has dropped off trucks – huge nails, baling wire, broken glass, lumps of wood. The 'scenery' usually consists of piles of imported hardwood and loads of scrap metal. Sometimes the monotony is relieved by vast stacks of cement or extended scatterings of grain attended by uncountable hosts of pigeons. The yacht club is for members only, but excellent views of the boats and associated activity can be had by detouring left to M berth, just before the building labelled SAS *Unite*, and wandering along the northeast-pointing arm of Duncan Dock. See if you can spot some of the foreign yachts – a giveaway is the washing hanging out to dry!

From the club, another 800 m brings you to Eastern Mole Road, just beyond the yacht lay-up basin. Panama Jacks is down this road, and there are usually all sorts of interesting harbour activities going on. You can also find your way to the Sturrock Dry Dock and, alongside Jackson Wharf, take a look at the extraordinarily grubby and vulnerable-looking foreign fishing boats.

Bearing northwards, the road doubles and brings you to the Ben Schoeman Dock, which is mostly used for coastal container traffic. About half a kilometre further on the road rises onto a bridge and presents a stop street. The left turn leads to the deep-sea container area, best not visited because of large trucks and machines shifting containers around. Turn right, ride to the security gate, about-turn, and go back the same way, but pass the point where you entered the harbour and carry on down parallel with Duncan Dock. If you see any loading or unloading that looks interesting, stop and take a closer look, but stay alert for railway shunting and for forklifts.

At the end of the straight, turn right into South Arm Road which takes you parallel to berths D to A, with Irvin and Johnson on the left. South Arm makes a T at the end, forming Elbow berth to the left and A berth to the right. Victoria Basin is the whole area enclosed to your left. The large building ahead houses the Portnet harbour control offices. This is a good spot to watch the comings and goings of ships.

Reverse down South Arm Road and carry on straight to the traffic circle; take the *first* of the several right-hand exits from the circle (don't go straight) which is East Pier Road. Continue past some steep cliffs and note the historic time-ball tower on the left (the ball used to be dropped at exactly noon daily so that ships could re-set their navigation clocks), then pass the Granger Bay customs exit turn-off, the Waterfront Brewery and the Sealink heliport area. Along this very bumpy section spot the live fish vendor and restaurant on your right before arriving at the end. The right turn goes to East Pier, opposite Elbow berth. You can go part of the way along the breakwater, but heavy construction work is usually in progress.

Return the same way, but detour onto all the quays where even on Sundays there is usually something interesting going on – pilot boats, tugs and service craft coming and going. Notice No. 4 Quay where the deservedly famous and much-lamented Harbour Café used to be, as well as the internationally-known Penny Ferry, a nostalgic low-cost attraction that has also fallen victim to progress.

You can leave the harbour and return to your car the way you came in, or leave through either the Granger Bay or Dock Road exit.

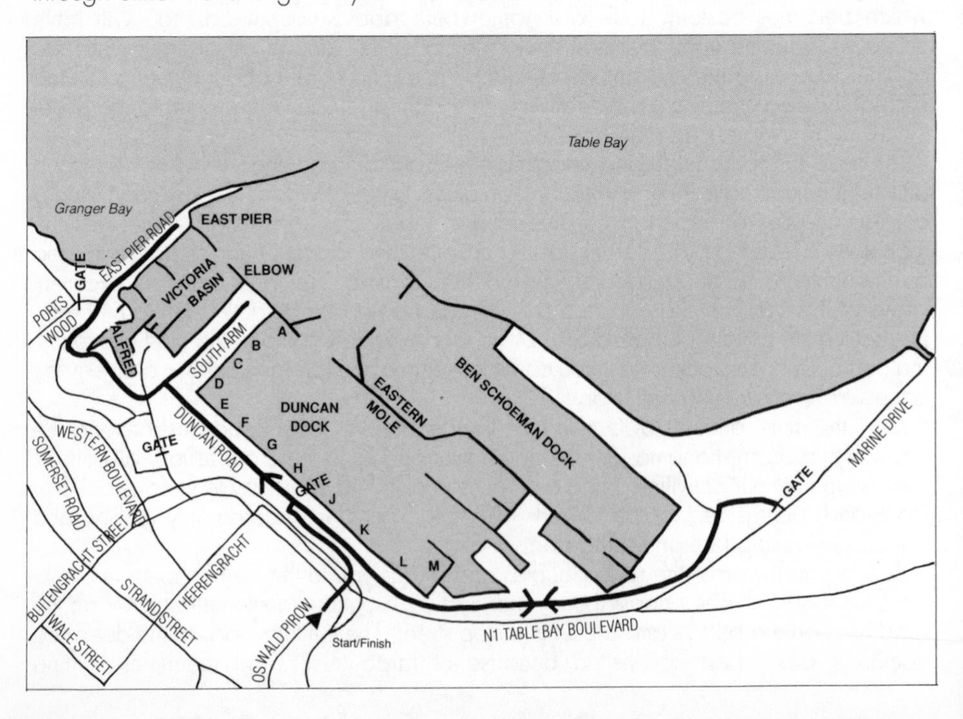

3 High Level Road to Kloof Nek

Features: An urban ride offering ever-changing high-level views of sea and city; lots of steepish but short hills. Traffic and braking experience is essential, but given this the ride is fine for single-filing families. Most of the route is well protected from southeasters. As far as security is concerned, when the city is quiet the section from starting point to the top of the first ascent might require alertness, so don't start it too late.
Grade and distance: A3; 13 km; 90 minutes.
Best times: Except during rush hours, the route is tolerable on working days. During tourist season some sections may be very busy unless you start early and enjoy a mountain sunrise but then the opposite side will be chilly. Sunset from the west side of the mountain is lovely although the suburbs may still be very hot at this time of day in summer. Avoid showery days because of wet brake dangers. Avoid northwest winds.
Special information: Make sure your brakes are in good mechanical order. The descents are short but a few are very steep. If you ride on a hot day take water.
Sustenance: Disappointing! The lower cable station has a small range of pricey victuals and there are sometimes ice cream vendors there. The Round House used to be famous for teas but the current owner is into *haute cuisine* and his fine offerings are not very suitable for consumption before the ascent to Kloof Nek. Kloof Nek Road has Central Supermarket halfway down, but the parallel Kloof Street has several restaurants and a Checkers store that is open very long hours.
Getting there: Park in Riebeeck Square, which is the area bounded by Shortmarket, Church and Buitengracht streets.
Doing the ride: Take in a scrap of history before you start: the old building in Riebeeck Square (first known as Boeren Plein) was South Africa's first theatre, built in 1800 and converted into St Stephen's Church in 1839. It is now being used for theatrical productions again. Now you may start: Ride 300 m down Buitengracht Street and turn left into Strand Street, which somewhere becomes High Level Road. The steep hill and bumpy road surface are somewhat compensated for by a fine view, which improves as you gain altitude. Stop at the top to catch your breath and absorb the view.

From the crest the road descends a little to traffic lights at the Ocean View Drive junction on the left (offering an alternative parallel route, but tougher pedalling). The road now becomes effectively narrower because of parked cars. Ride another 2,3 km, a stretch with several sets of lights. Take care along here; despite the narrowness of the road, speeding cars are commonplace and lights often disobeyed. Most of the streets to the right go down to Main Road in Green Point, Three Anchor Bay or Sea Point. The route crosses from Sea Point to Fresnaye at Duncan Road, the houses getting progressively grander as you approach the final 600 m of this very steep section, which ends at a T-junction where you'll be relieved to turn down right.

This is Fresnaye Avenue; you'll need your brakes. Turn left at the second stop street into Kloof Road and start a 500-m climb with the road (temporarily) widening near the top as you pass into the suburb of Bantry Bay. After it levels off there are steep cliffs to your right from which loose sand sometimes spreads across the road. At the top there's a sharp left bend with a mirror on a pole enabling motorists coming out of Nettleton Avenue to perfect their aim at passing cyclists, so do not be too distracted by the magnificent Atlantic view from Clifton to Llandudno.

With Lion's Head above you, ride down the twisty, bumpy descent for 1,3 km and, just short of Camps Bay High School, turn left into what is still Kloof Road – the straight-on part becomes Lower Kloof Road. Pass Stan's Halt youth hostel turn-off and the Round House restaurant, both places part of the historic property The Glen. The road is tree-lined and sheltered but very twisty and distinctly uphill; take care on the two hairpin bends. If you ever do this route in reverse you'll overtake all the cars on this section, but will need good brakes to negotiate the hairpins.

It's 700 m from the second hairpin to the top, Kloof Nek, with fine views across Camps Bay on one side and the city on the other. Take the second left turn around the traffic circle and regain your breath as you ride down wide, smooth Kloof Nek Road; look out for crawling buses being overtaken by recklessly driven cars. You might notice Bellevue Road on your right; it's reputed to be Cape Town's steepest hill and is used by masochistic riders for training.

Take great care at the bottom of the hill where you must brake hard and turn left at the traffic lights. The continuation of the road facing you is one-way *up* only, and there have been some horrific accidents here with vehicles continuing straight over *down!* Now turn first-right into Upper Buitengracht Street, which is one-way but has two lanes, and is somewhat uneven. Tamboerskloof suburb lies to your left and exploring it is a wonderful if painful way to develop your hill-climbing ability.

The road becomes two-way and drops the 'Upper' part of its name just before the traffic lights at Buitensingel Street. The historic Bo-Kaap is up on your left and apart from offering further hill practice it presents the cyclist's horror, cobblestones – familiar to those who live in Europe but mercifully scarce in Africa. After the Wale Street traffic lights you're within sight of your starting point.

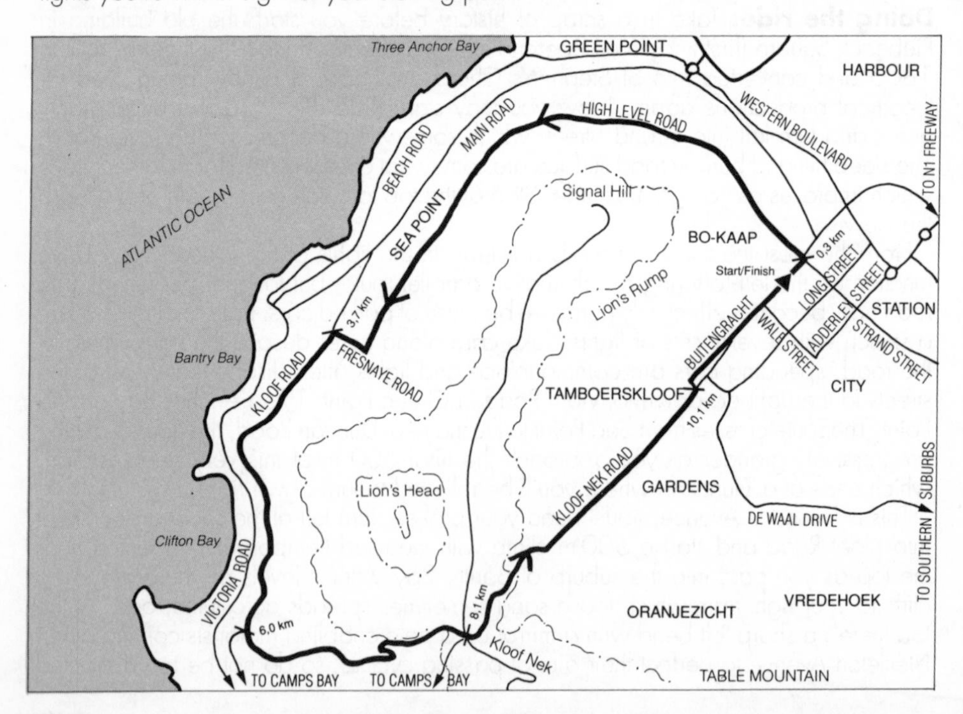

4 Signal Hill and Tafelberg Road

Features: Continual and ever-changing high-level views encompassing most of Cape Town. Mostly at a constant height but including some noticeable ups and downs. Much of the route is deserted during the week. Definitely not a route for unaccompanied women or children; the lower slopes of the mountain have many caves that are frequented by undesirables.
Grade and distance: B1; 19 km; 60 to 90 minutes.
Best times: Any wind is unpleasant because the mountain's profiles cause local strong gusting. On the other hand, windless summer days are extremely hot along the eastern and northern aspects. Cloud blowing in from the Atlantic can bring localized showers along the route. The best time is early morning, even if it looks foggy, because fog rarely rises to the level of the ride.
Special information: If you do this trip in summer, be sure to take plenty to drink. Drinking from streams this low down is not advisable. If you have one, take a small telescope or binoculars to get a closer look at ships at sea and the various goings-on down below.
Sustenance: You're out of luck unless you're prepared to pay the inflated prices at the cable station; even the ice cream tricycles try to rip you off there. Why not take some well-chosen *padkos* and have a breakfast picnic in one of the verdant mini-kloofs along Tafelberg Road?
Getting there: From wherever you are in the city, head northwest until you reach Buitengracht Street. Turn left and follow this road to Kloof Nek and leave your car in the parking lot just to the left; if it's full, go round the traffic circle into Signal Hill Road which has a large parking area 500 m along. For those without cars, there are (infrequent) buses to Kloof Nek, otherwise ride up – heavy going but quicker.
Doing the ride: Go round the traffic circle and set off due north along Signal Hill Road. It climbs, and at first very steeply, past the forest station. The road is narrow and twisty but tree-shaded and smooth and it offers ever-expanding views across the city and Table Bay. After about 500 m there's a large parking lot from where walkers can set off up Lion's Head, and part of the way is suitable for ATBs.

The road inclines up again and then runs more or less level. After 800 m there's a left turn to the Muslim shrine (kramat) of Tuan Guru and Mohamed Gason Haibie Shah. The road from here runs gently down but is heavily potholed; the view is quite outstanding but don't get so captivated that you ride into the very deep gutter. There are some steep drops to the right, with, in parts, a protective fence. Two kilometres from the shrine you'll arrive at Signal Hill, the lion's rump, which at 350 m is little more than half the height of Lion's Head.

This position gives you a commanding view nearly all the way round from the front of Table Mountain, across Woodstock, up the west coast into the blue yonder, then to the infamous Robben Island, and round to the sea horizons far off Sea Point. Spend some time here if the outlook is new to you, then ride 3,4 km back to Kloof Nek and go half way round the circle into Tafelberg Road opposite.

After 600 m along this narrow bumpy road take care riding round a climbing double hairpin bend. Depending on the time of year you may spot fine shows of yellow kreupelhout or pink *Protea repens* (suikerbos) nestling in their leathery-leaved bushes.

The road continues to climb until it reaches the lower cable station. During the peak tourist season look out for irritable motorists roaring off after hours of waiting in the immense cable car queue. Once you've passed that busy spot enjoy the good views left and back to Signal Hill, and beyond to Tygerberg and inland.

The road contours along the sparsely fynbos-covered spurs and valleys of Table Mountain, which looms above you. The biggest 'valley' is Platteklip Gorge, 1,7 km from the cable station, and carrying the Fresh River, a perennial stream which used to provide the city with all its water but is now mostly canalized or ignominiously piped. After heavy rains largish stones and occasionally rocks roll onto the road. Approximately 1 km from Platteklip you should see a notice on the right saying 'To Saddle and Oppel's Kop' which marks the hiking route to Newlands Ravine. Just beyond this is a tiny dam on a stream, and then a swing due north under the lee of Devil's Peak, with Saddle Ravine in the 'corner'.

Now the road turns eastwards and you experience the force of the southeaster, if it's blowing. This stretch is very exposed but gives clear views across the Cape Flats suburbs and also back towards Signal Hill. Most of Tafelberg road is in fact along the 350 m contour, level with Signal Hill. The final 1,2 km is rather uphill and open but if you're not knocked back by the southeaster the views are well worth the ascent. In winter, on any of those clear champagne days after a spell of freezing rain, this is a great spot for looking at the snow-covered Boland mountains. The tarred surface ends here, but if you're riding an ATB you can ride on another kilometre or so to King's Blockhouse, just above Rhodes' Memorial. Without that extra bit it's 6,1 km back to your start, and you can see if you agree with our count of 50 bends!

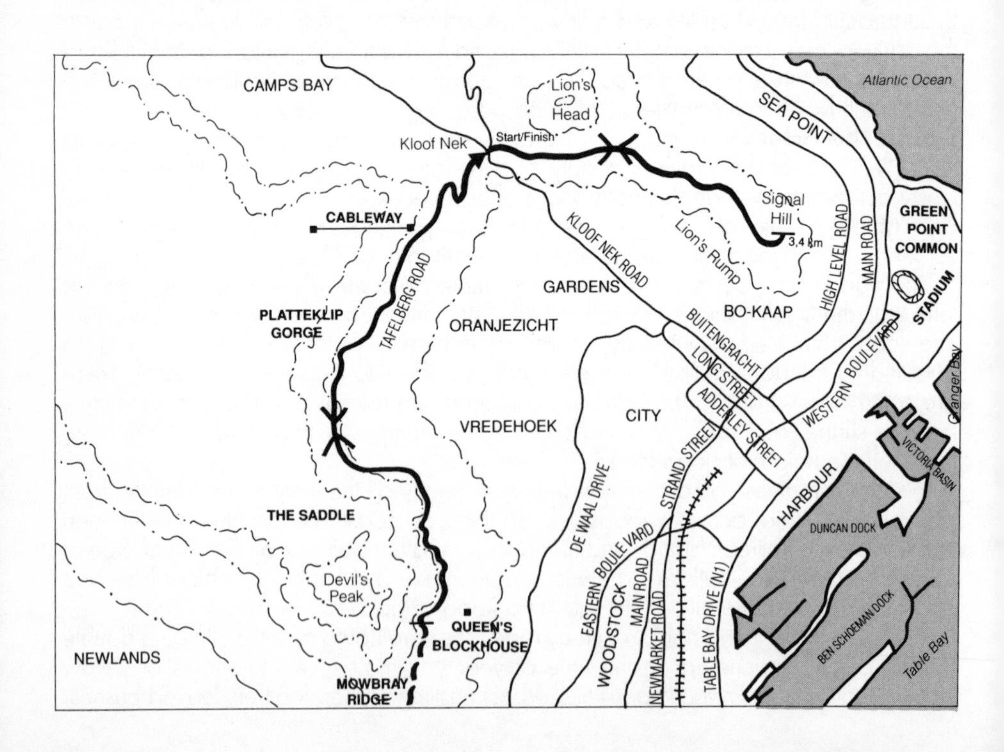

5 Green Point to Camps Bay

Features: A therapeutic ride through an area with a holiday atmosphere and no hills. It is almost completely sheltered from the southeaster in summer, but in winter after a great northerly gale spectacular breakers crash on to the shore. Security is good, and the ride is fine for families accustomed to suburban traffic.
Grade and distance: A2; 21 km round trip; 60 minutes riding time.
Best times: From late autumn to early spring there are few beachgoers and tourists so the roads, although busy, are not thickly congested. Choose either a weekday (between rush hours), or early on weekend mornings. On a late summer evening you can take in the sunset and enjoy the cool sea breeze.
Special information: Not so long ago, Green Point Common, where you park, was a tranquil cattle grazing area; it is now a sports and recreational complex. Recently there has been talk of 'intensifying its utilization', so enjoy it while you can! Although the route passes through one of the busiest and most densely populated areas of the country there's a cheerful 'buzz' about the place engendering enough goodwill to make the traffic tolerable. Sometimes you can watch cycle racing at the stadium. The track bikes used are super-light because they have no gears, no brakes, and no free-wheel; their speeds are phenomenal.
Sustenance: There are so many and such varied places to eat along the way that it would be unfair to recommend any in particular. Some, however, take shameless advantage of holiday-makers, so ask about prices before you order anything. Seagulls is often extremely busy but very sociable and excellent value; it is strategically situated near the end of your ride.
Getting there: Take the Table Bay Boulevard (N1) westwards and follow it round to where it becomes Buitengracht Street. Turn right at the second traffic light onto the Western Boulevard (M6). About 2 km on, drive clockwise round the traffic circle and take the third turning left out of it, then left again into Portswood Road. Park at Seagulls restaurant which is an isolated building next to the Green Point stadium.
Doing the ride: Set off the way you came, past the right turn from the circle, and follow Portswood Road to the left (as its surface deteriorates). There are high stone walls of historical importance, the one on the right enclosing the old harbour precincts and that on the left the City Hospital. Halfway down is the entrance to Fort Wynyard, a military museum of considerable historical interest. On the left after that are the grounds of Somerset Hospital, the first public hospital in Cape Town, which seems to be perpetually undergoing renovation.

If you keep straight and have the time you can enter one of the lesser-used harbour gates. This gate is very convenient for the excellent pub, Ferryman's, in the old part of the harbour. This section is now being massively upgraded as a tourist attraction. This pub was named after the recently discontinued 'Penny Ferry' by which seamen could be rowed across the entrance to the Victoria Basin instead of having to walk right round its periphery.

However, our ride resists the temptations that lie on the other side of the gate and bears left along Beach Road past it. You will, however, catch glimpses of parts of the harbour, the busy heliport, the Atlantic Power Boat Club, and then the General Botha Nautical Academy (which includes a catering school where you can have a fine dinner meticulously served by trainees trembling under the critical glare of their instructors). On the left you'll see the New Somerset Hospital, part of the Metropolitan golf course, and good views of Signal Hill and Table Mountain.

The road now becomes much wider and provides expansive sea vistas. There's a small parking lot and rocky beach, then a little way further the Green Point lighthouse, frequently mis-named Mouille Point (from the Dutch word *moelje* meaning 'mole' in the nautical sense – breakwater). In 1743 an unsuccessful attempt was made to build a mole out from the nearby promontory, Mouille Point, which shelters Granger Bay. More successful was the French cannon battery built in 1781.

The (pedestrian) promenade starts approximately here on the seaward side. There is also a small amusement park together with a miniature Blue Train and a constantly busy Putt-putt course. Three Anchor Bay is on your right – so named because of the three anchors which held the massive (and entirely futile) seaward defence chain stretched across the bay. There's a ski-boat slipway and an NSRI lifeboat station here; it's a nail-biting spectacle to see this small rescue craft pick its way through the huge swells and massive kelp beds during stormy winter weather.

Turn right at the lights, into Beach Road, and look out for the SABC building on your left (it has a big satellite dish). At this point you are on, or very near, the camp site of Capt. Sam Wallis, one of Captain Cook's officers. During the smallpox epidemic of 1776, Wallis decided to camp at Sea Point rather than expose his men to infection in Cape Town.

For the next 1 300 m there are six sets of lights and the traffic can be very heavy, although it is not usually speeding. You'll probably see dozens of joggers and other riders, but possibly the most entertaining sight is the diversity of pedestrians – every kind, from ultra-typical holiday-makers to quaint old eccentrics being exercised by their equally quaint little dogs.

You are now at the Sea Point Pavilion which contains various eateries of inconsistent standard. Next to it is the Sea Point pool, believed to be the largest sea-water pool in the southern hemisphere. The road divides about 200 m ahead, becoming one-way.

After another 600 m turn left into Queen's Road. Alternatively, either now or on your way back you can turn right then left onto a seaward parking lot, where you can look over the railings at a remarkable geological phenomenon. A descriptive plaque explains the uniqueness of this contact zone where liquid granite forced its way up from the bowels of the earth, then through the layers of sedimentary Malmesbury Shales before cooling and solidifying into a rock type called Hornfels. No less a personage than Charles Darwin travelled here especially to see this curiosity.

The President Hotel is behind you. Before being renovated to its present standard of opulence it was Queen's Hotel, hence the name Queen's Road, which at this point goes up a stiff little hill to a traffic island, just after which you turn right into Victoria Road (still M6). A landmark 400 m ahead is Bantry Bay café, on the left; the road along here is very narrow, bumpy and busy. Note the densely packed (outrageously expensive) flats clinging to the cliffside.

Don't miss the easily overlooked pedestrian traffic light about 1,5 km after the café. You're now in Bantry Bay, which was originally named Botany Bay because of the terraced herb garden established there by a Dr Liesching and Jean-Jacques de Ziegler during the 19th Century.

You'll now be high enough above the sea to enjoy excellent views across the (usually) blue Atlantic. About 600 m further is the main Clifton parking area which is hopelessly congested during summer and makes you feel rather superior because you have the good sense to come here on a bike. Another 600 m will take you past the Kloof Nek turn-off and the Camps Bay High School, with a large recreation area between you and the sea – an area turned into a grand carnival on Argus Cycle Tour Day, as the event ends near the top of the short hill which you now coast down into Camps Bay.

Camps Bay sportsground on the left is a pleasant place to lie down and cool off; otherwise chain your bike to something solid and go for a dip in the freezing sea.

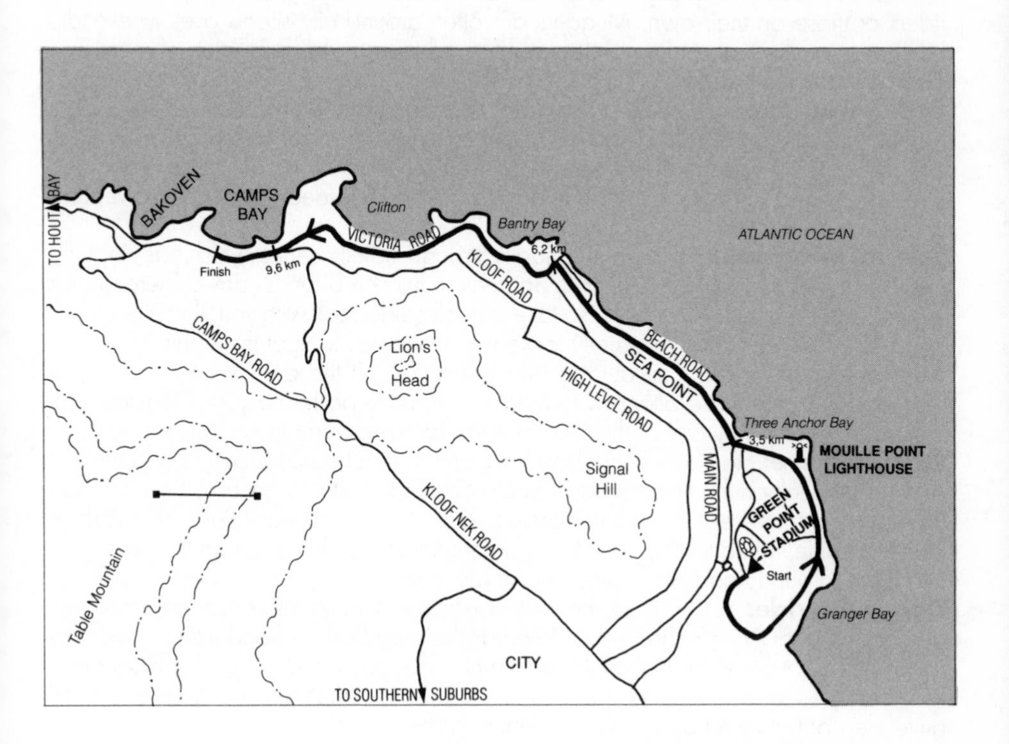

6 Rondebosch to Cape Town

Features: A ride that will interest mainly people who are unfamiliar with the area. It takes in many of the historical landmarks of old Cape Town and follows an almost level route, making it very easy for the weak unless there's a strong wind blowing. Parts of the route are through somewhat dilapidated areas which may worry timid riders or those on their own. Muggers are often around city streets over weekends, but mainly on the lookout for careless sailors and tourists with pocketfuls of money.
Grade and distance: A1; 16 km; 60 minutes.
Best times: This is definitely a Saturday afternoon, Sunday or public holiday jaunt – at all other times the traffic is far too heavy for enjoyment and safety. Early evenings are not a good time, mainly because of the likelihood of encountering inebriated pedestrians and/or motorists. Windy days should be avoided unless you're wearing goggles to protect your eyes from grit.
Special information: Part of this ride is through the city centre which has umpteen interesting sights which are difficult to appreciate fully on business days. There are far too many of these to include here, so take a small guidebook with you. If you're alone, make sure that your bike is securely locked up while you look at the sights.
Sustenance: Very few restaurants and takeaways in the city centre are open at weekends, except those attached to hotels. It's best to postpone your breakfast until you get back, then try one of the several establishments open in Rondebosch.
Getting there: Start from Rondebosch Common, reached by driving along the N2 and keeping left on the first exit past Groote Schuur hospital to get onto Settler's Way (N2). Take the next exit then immediately fork right onto Liesbeeck Parkway (M5). At the third traffic light after that, turn left into Park Road then left again at the next lights into Campground Road. Park under the shady trees.
Doing the ride: Set off back the way you came, turning into Liesbeeck Parkway, over the lights at Alma Road and on towards the busy Durban Road intersection.Pass under the N2 at the next lights, shortly after which the road loses its island and becomes temporarily two-way. Although the Liesbeeck River is canalized along here it is still quite pleasant, flanked by broad stretches of grass.

To your right is the historic old Valkenberg manor house, and adjoining it the Valkenberg psychiatric hospital, while on the left is the Hartleyvale soccer ground. The next traffic lights offer a route to Observatory, but carry on straight, passing Malta Park on your left and Liesbeeck Park on your right. Somewhere along here the road changes name to Malta Road to herald your entry into the Salt River industrial area where the road name again changes – to Albert Road.

Don't dismiss the agglomeration of small shops and businesses between here and town as a shabby run-down area. The buildings may be old but during the week this is a lively thriving district with quality products and services.

Before long you reach a traffic circle with several fairly busy branches, so take care. Ride across but note the broad road leading off right; that is Voortrekker Road (R102), important in some of our other rides. Sundry pedestrian lights precede the next major traffic lights which control the right turn to the harbour and Table Bay Boulevard and the lesser left turn leading to 'Old Main Road' (less well known as Victoria Road). After 1,2 km the road widens and acquires a centre island and a new name, Newmarket

Road (R102). Ride under some overhead bridges, and you will see the Good Hope Centre on your left and then the Castle, now in its 20th year of restoration.

You're now in Strand Street, with the station on your right and the Grand Parade on your left behind the bus terminus. Turn left immediately after the Golden Acre complex on your left (after passing under the overhead walkway). Get out your guidebook and take your time reaching the third set of lights after you turned; turn left again and find yourself in Darling Street, originally named Keizersgracht (when the whole of Adderley Street was Heerengracht). Cross Parliament, Plein and Corporation streets, noting the main Post Office and the Grand Parade on your left.

Carry on past the Castle – you are now in Sir Lowry Road. The Good Hope Centre comes up ahead, left; at the lights you intersect with Oswald Pirow Street which leads down to the N1 and the harbour. If the summer wind is blowing, watch out for heavy gusts from the right. The wind hits the mountain at an angle and seems to intensify as it bounces off and down. Once you're through Woodstock the effect diminishes.

On the face of it you now have to pedal through nearly 6 km of dreary deserted semi-industrial districts with lots of traffic lights. Not quite true; make time to do a few side trips and some window shopping. Note, for instance, the old-style hardware shops with their enormous stocks of old-fashioned goods. Ride up Searle Street and take a look at Trafalgar Park and its splendid big swimming pool.

Ride on into Rosebank, passing the twin-towered UCT residence on your right, then Woolsack Drive, the Baxter Theatre and the ghost of the famous student pub the Pig and Whistle, now, sadly, just a steakhouse. Turn left at the 'fountain' – the green cast iron object at the junction with Belmont Road. Ride down Belmont Road, over the railway bridge, across the lights at Liesbeeck Parkway, and then left at the next lights back into Campground Road and your car.

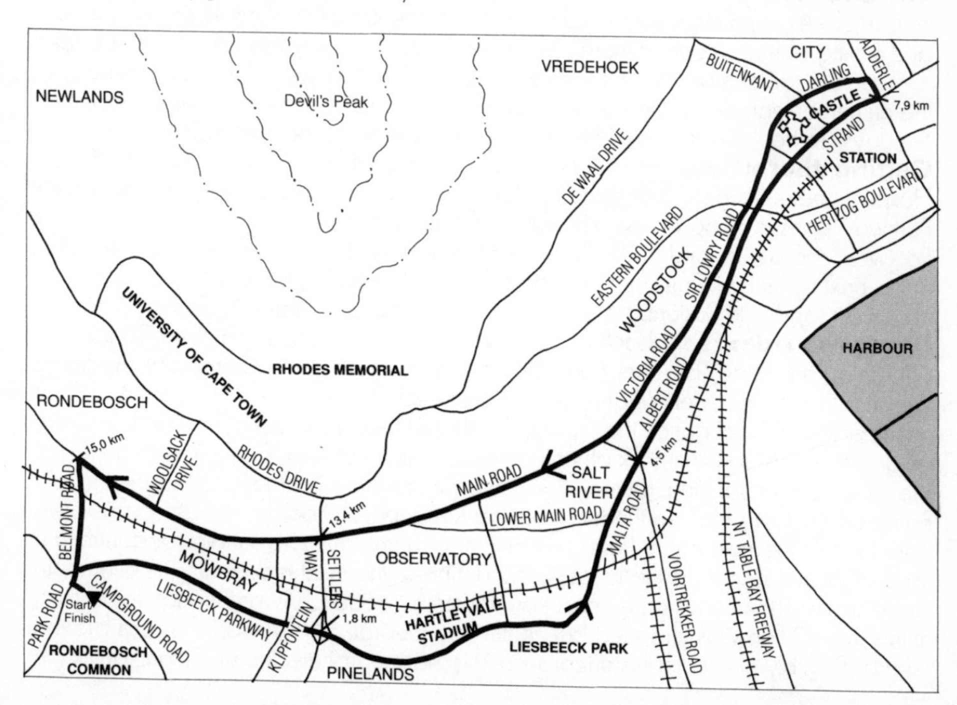

7 Rondebosch to Kirstenbosch

Features: This is an easy, gentle, mostly shady ride around a couple of long-established suburbs of 'colonial' Cape Town. If you time it right it's fine for a family outing, and you'll meet literally hundreds of other cyclists if you do it over a weekend or summer evening. Security is good.
Grade and distance: A2; 11 km; 30 to 45 minutes riding time.
Best times: Avoid rush-hour traffic, and also mid-afternoons when the numerous schools in the area disgorge their pupils. Winter is not a good season unless there's definitely no rain in the offing (Newlands is South Africa's wettest suburb). In the early evenings and on Sunday mornings large numbers of joggers and cyclists will be on the roads, but most people will enjoy that. Avoid the vicinity of Newlands rugby ground on Saturdays during the season.
Special information: Rondebosch Common was originally named *Ronde Doorn Bosjen* by Jan van Riebeeck, who had the area cleared for grazing in 1657. Despite the clearing, it regenerated much of its fynbos, some species of which are unique and the subjects of frantic efforts at conservation. Being so flat, the Common is a popular jogging circuit for the less fit, but it transforms into a high-speed track for the annual Rondebosch Common Kermesse, a demanding 40-lap cycling contest which attracts top registered and professional riders and is a fine spectator event.

Woolsack Drive, mentioned below, takes its name from the summer residence built for the famous author Rudyard Kipling by his friend Cecil Rhodes.
Sustenance: This is a very short ride, but if you like to include a stop for refreshments as part of the outing we recommend riding into Kirstenbosch National Botanic Gardens and eating at the restaurant there, where the prices are very reasonable. You'll need to reserve a table in advance if you go on a Sunday. On weekdays, consider any of the numerous eateries in the Rondebosch shopping area; some of these are open on Sundays. Kaffeehaus in Riverside Centre is very pleasant, but expensive.
Getting there: Take the N2 freeway, keeping left as it passes Groote Schuur Hospital (note 'Airport' signs). Keep left under three bridges following Liesbeeck Parkway signs leading off the freeway at the third bridge. Fork right onto Liesbeeck Parkway and at the third traffic light after that turn left into Park Road then left again at the next lights into Campground Road. There are parking lots a little way along on your right, opposite Rustenburg School at the edge of Rondebosch Common.
Doing the ride: Pedal back the way you came, along Campground Road, then right into Park Road/Belmont Road (the name changes somewhere near the traffic lights). Cross the next set of lights (start of Liesbeeck Parkway) and ride about 200 m; notice St Joseph's School on the right and Bishops Preparatory school on the left. Carry on downhill past Tannery Park office complex, which not surprisingly was formerly the site of a leather tanning factory. Go over the railway bridge and notice the old Rondebosch Town Hall on the left, now the Rondebosch library.

Turn left at the next traffic lights, which, considering this is a simple road junction, have what we suspect is the longest and definitely the most maddening sequence in Cape Town. The curious green cast iron 'fountain' (actually a water trough for horses) at this intersection was imported last century by George Pigot Moodie as a gift to the suburb. Possibly of greater historical interest is that the first electric street lamp in South

Africa was placed here, powered by a privately-owned steam engine generator.

Ride up the incline, noticing a cemetery to the right with, beyond, the new police station which replaced the quaint little double-storey station on your left at the crest of the rise. The road widens after the bend and passes the discreetly fortified Groote Schuur ('great barn') built by van Riebeeck and later converted into a residence known as The Grange. The ubiquitous Cecil Rhodes bought it, and after a calamitous fire in 1896 it was remodelled to Rhodes' liking by the famous architect Herbert Baker. Rhodes gave the place its original name and presented it to the nation as a residence for prime ministers. It is regularly but infrequently open for guided visits. Neighbouring Westbrooke, now the state president's residence, originally belonged to Judge William Westbrooke Burton who acquired it in 1800.

After passing the former Schweppes bottling plant (sited there because of the unpolluted 'Albion' mineral spring, still flowing), turn right at the traffic lights and storm the Klipper Road hill. At its crest it bears left into Newlands Avenue and passes the popular and sometimes controversial Foresters Arms. There is a demarcated cycle track along this tree-lined avenue (on the *right*), but use it with care as it leads past numerous bumps, blind drives and bollards, and, worst of all, past 'Forries' from which home-bound revellers sometimes emerge with alcoholic incaution.

Just before Forries notice on your left SACS, South Africa's oldest school, founded in 1829. Almost opposite are the sports grounds of Westerford School, followed a short distance on by a scout hall. Further on spot Avenue Café on the left, a well-stocked establishment which keeps long hours. Just before the next corner are two imposing white pillars, formerly the entrance to Newlands House, family home of the prominent Newton-Thomsons. The house was burnt down some years ago and a costly replica built as a government residence – currently of Foreign Minister Roelof ('Pik') Botha.

Cross the major intersection ahead (the lights include a cyclist phase) and wind along Rhodes Road. You're still in Newlands, originally named Nieuwland and serving then as a source of timber – much beautiful hardwood was cut down here, often for fuel. It became a fashionable residential area, despite the rain, after Governor Willem van der Stel built himself a country house there. Sense the mountain towering above you on the right; this prominent section is known as Fernwood Buttress, after the Fernwood Estate, remnants of which now constitute the parliamentary club visible through the trees on your left.

About 1 km ahead, after a puzzling slope that doesn't look like one, notice the small stone buildings on the left; this is where the Botanical Society holds its annual sales of indigenous plants from Kirstenbosch gardens. On the same side is the little stone church that served the village which once existed near this spot. Turn right into Kirstenbosch, with its expanses of welcoming lawns. You can either cycle through to look around and visit the restaurant, or else leave your bike in the racks at the gate.

Go back about 600 m along the way you came then turn right into Rose Street. Ride down a bumpy descent for 100 m and turn left at the stop street into Boschoff Avenue. In winter, little springs sometimes burst up out of this road surface and as a result it is bumpy and sometimes potholed. The circular open grass area further down on the left is kept nicely mown in summer and used occasionally as the parliamentarians' cricket pitch. Some 400 m further on turn right into Fernwood Avenue, which in autumn is strewn with chestnuts – their prickly overcoats can be unkind to tyres.

Follow this lovely shady avenue for about 500 m to the busy intersection at Paradise Road. The traffic light will not respond automatically to cycle traffic so press the button provided; then sit down and rest while you wait ages for the change. After crossing, stay with the left fork which crosses the Liesbeeck River and swings left again at the traffic circle a little way ahead. Just 300 m down, the route forks right, past the former Tech' Sports Club grounds (now Norwich Life grounds).

Cross the Cavendish Street traffic light and head down to the next lights at Main Road; note Pick 'n Pay on your right and, about 200 m further on on the left hand side, the splendid Newlands swimming pool. Numerous cyclists gather outside the pool on Sunday mornings and certain evenings to organize themselves into informal riding groups. This is very companionable, an easy way to meet new people, and can be instructive if a couple of more experienced riders are included in your group.

But for now, continue straight over the railway bridge (there's a yellow-painted cycling lane) and ride down past the Western Province Cricket Club grounds, and then the club main building (commonly referred to as Kelvin Grove – the original name of the main building when it was still a residence). Where the road swings right continue straight along a quiet bumpy *cul de sac* which is, in fact, a marooned section of Campground Road, the main part of which you turn left into at the end. You can stay in the road or cross over to the cycle track on the opposite side.

Half a kilometre ahead, just past a café, the track crosses back to the left side. Pass through the Sandown Road lights 200 m ahead, then ride another 500 m and turn right at the lights into Park Road just near where you started. There is a bicycle subway, mainly to help scores of pedalling school children, but we do not recommend its use at quieter times.

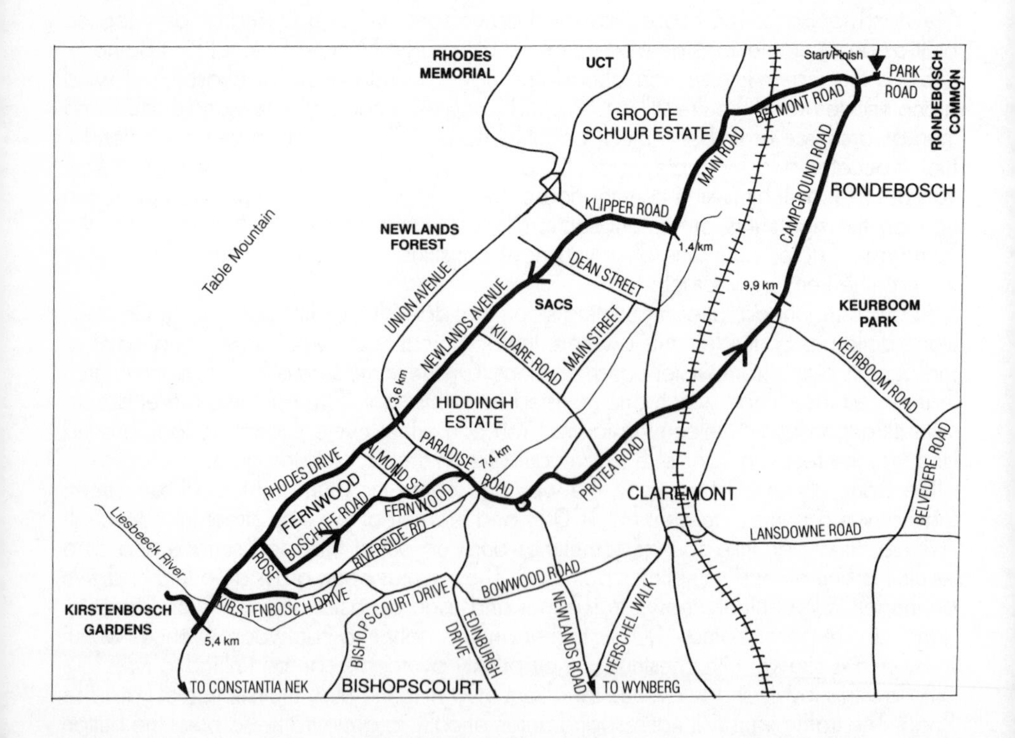

8 Rondebosch Circuit

Features: A short and very gentle ride around a pleasant old suburb. Plenty of scope to pedal down byways and investigate things. There are numerous historical features so take a guidebook. Safe and secure for families if they dodge the traffic peaks.
Grade and distance: A1; 10 km; 45 minutes.
Best times: Any season provided you avoid commuter and end-of-school rush periods. Also avoid Saturday mornings. Traffic is moderately busy at all other times.
Special information: Rondebosch Common was originally public grazing land before becoming a military camp. After the British occupation it reverted to pasture and perpetual public usage, technically under management by nearby St Paul's church.
Sustenance: Silwood Bakery has mouthwatering goodies (not cheap), and the superette mentioned in the ride description is also a good stop. There are numerous eateries to suit all tastes in Rondebosch 'village', many of them open on Sundays.
Getting there: Drive along the N2, then where it passes Groote Schuur Hospital keep right so that you can follow the M3 split southwards. Shortly after, take the exit just after the old windmill (Mostert's Mill). The sign reads 'Rosebank/University'. Turn left, go down Woolsack Drive, turn right at the traffic lights. Continue into Rondebosch and turn left into Belmont Road at the main intersection, noting St Paul's church up on the right. Cross the set of lights at Liesbeeck Parkway. Turn left at the next set, into Campground Road. Park in the shaded area of the Common opposite Rustenburg school. By train, get off at Rondebosch station, leave on the east side and turn left into Station Road, which soon intersects with Belmont Road.
Doing the ride: Go back along Campground Road, continuing directly across the traffic lights, past the group of shops on the left, one of which is Silwood Bakery. On the left some 300 m after that is Diocesan College, generally called 'Bishop's'. No-one seems to mind if the occasional cyclist takes a spin around the extensive grounds; notice the little chapel and the neat but unexpectedly small-looking buildings.

After that side-trip, ride another 200 m, across the Sandown Road junction, past Rondebosch junior school on the right and a small park on the left where events such as craft markets are held. The road to the left at the next traffic lights leads to Rondebosch Boy's High School (another optional side-trip). There is a demarcated cycle path along here, but use it with care.

About half a kilometre further along the low set-back building of Groote Schuur primary school allows for a fine view of Devil's Peak and Table Mountain. The next traffic light controls the Keurboom Road intersection which can be very busy. Another 200 m further on is the Groote Schuur High School. Ride 1,7 km to a very good superette on the right, with bakery. Over the next 500 m or so watch out for combi-taxis emerging from the Claremont station parking area ahead on the right.

Take extreme care approaching the Lansdowne Road bridge, which is fairly busy even over weekends. The Chris Willemse Home of Cycling is just over the bridge to the right – avoid it if you're an impulse buyer. Rather keep left, *not* crossing the bridge, and carry on down Lansdowne Road for 200 m where you'll notice the Villagers' rugby grounds and Brookside, home of the running club Celtic Harriers.

Notice the SANCCOB shop 100 m down on the left, and after another 100 m the well-stocked Olympic Cycles – less pricey than some of the other cycling shops.

Livingstone High School is on the right, then a right fork (don't take it), which is Chichester Road leading to the Kenilworth Centre shopping complex. Carry on down to the intersection with Belvedere Road, where there's a good bakery. Turn left into Belvedere Road and run with the southeaster if it's blowing.

Cross at the Keurboom Road traffic lights; a landmark here is the yellow playground loco. Notice yet another bakery and a cycle repair shop on the left. At the next lights Belvedere Road changes its name to Milner Road. There are lots of large, handsome houses around here.

The Kromboom Road crossing is 450 m ahead, with traffic lights, and then the road widens temporarily into two lanes. Next come the lights at Sandown Road where the route narrows again. Further on, to the right, notice the well-known 'Spook House', so named because its old German architectural style recalls the turreted haunted castles in fairy tale pictures.

Milner Road continues past Bishop's playing fields then unaccountably becomes a very wide dual carriageway, sweeping down through a slight dip before rising gently to the intersection with Park Road at a corner of Rondebosch Common. Continue straight, enjoying an unobstructed view to UCT, Rhodes memorial and Devil's Peak.

On your left you may find streams of joggers, runners and dog-walkers circling the Common. On your right is Vista Nova School for handicapped children, then the Red Cross War Memorial Children's Hospital. At the next corner of the Common, turn left into Klipfontein Road and 400 m down turn right into Sawkins Road which at some unmarked point becomes Campground Road and leads you back to your car.

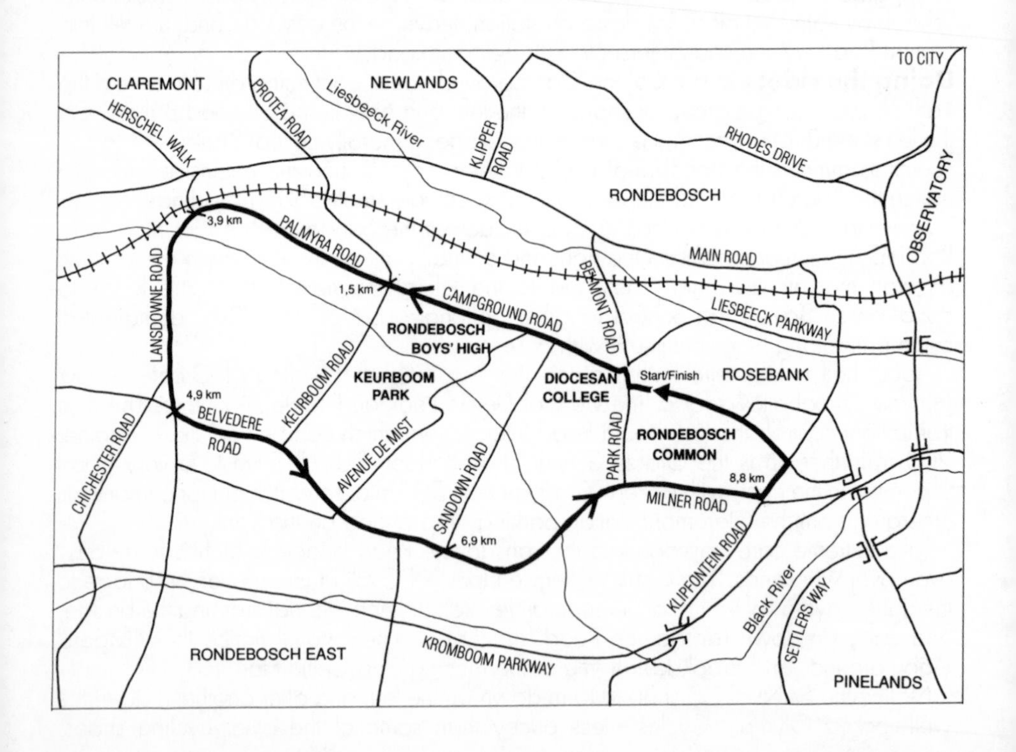

9 Kenilworth to Muizenberg

Features: This ride is almost level all the way, and at quiet times provides opportunities for practising sprints (you'll probably encounter some keen types doing just that). Good timing can give you a chance to watch the birds at Rondevlei Sanctuary. The area is exposed to summer and winter winds but whichever one impedes you in one direction will help in the other. Not recommended for families or inexperienced solo riders.
Grade and distance: A1; 29 km; 90 minutes riding time.
Best times: It's essential to avoid rush hours, including Saturday mornings. The traffic is heavy and fast-moving, and there are numerous low-flying combi-taxis. Road width varies continually, and the transition from road to shoulder is dangerously stepped along some sections. Windless Sundays are preferable.
Special information: This ride starts in lower Kenilworth, a suburb which originally developed around the farm Stellenburg where sporting dogs were kept for the Dutch officials of the time. It contains numerous very large old houses designed for the huge families customary a century ago. Not many of these buildings have any special historical merit and because of their burdensome upkeep they are steadily being demolished and replaced by flats and townhouses.
Getting there: Follow Table Bay Boulevard (N1) around the harbour periphery until, beyond the brick power station, you come to an interchange where you must follow the 'Muizenberg' signs to put you on the (M5) Black River Parkway. Take the left split onto Kromboom Parkway (M5) at the first 'Rondebosch' sign (golf course on left). Exit from the freeway at the sign 'Lansdowne/Claremont/Kenilworth', then turn right, over the bridge, then again right into the Access Park factory shops and Petticoat Lane flea market.

Train users should travel to Claremont (Harfield Road is a nearer station but a lot of trains don't stop there). Leave the station on the Claremont side, turn left and ride the short distance to the Lansdowne Road railway bridge. Turn right immediately after crossing then ride down Lansdowne Road to just beyond the Drop Inn bottle store. Fork right into Chichester Road which leads down across the Rosmead Avenue traffic lights and past Kenilworth (shopping) Centre.
Doing the ride: Head southwards out of Access Park through the traffic lights into Doncaster Road which skirts the Kenilworth race course. Pass Stodels nursery and continue to the lights at Rosmead Avenue; turn left. The road is uneven and rather narrow with a deep gutter but is tree-lined and pleasant. Half a kilometre along you will pass the fire station, then cross two sets of pedestrian lights (avoid this stretch on race days when it's seething with disappointed punters pouring across the road and/or driving away in a misery of non-concentration).

After 1,2 km you reach Ottery Road which marks the southern boundary of the race course and leads down to Youngsfield military base and various industrial areas. Another 600 m further is a stop street at Southfield Road; notice you are nearly parallel with the freeway on your left. Ride another 200 m and turn right into Basil Road. Measure a further 200 m and turn left into Churchill Road. Landmarks: Plumstead school on left; café on right.

Turn left into Dick Burton Road immediately after passing the school grounds, then

200 m more and turn right into Prince George Drive. This bit of navigation was to get you round the point where Kromboom Parkway peters out and leads into Prince George Drive – a comparatively busy road even at weekends. Another 200 m ahead is a bridge and some more lights, at which point the road quality deteriorates. The grand, unobstructed view of the peninsula mountain chain is some compensation for that.

About 1,2 km ahead is a left turn leading to Grassy Park, Zeekoevlei and Rondevlei – the latter is well signposted if you want to divert and watch the birds. It's a very attractive place to visit, with a modest entrance fee. The best time is very early (but then it's not open and you must watch through the fence), or at sundown when the birds return from foraging (but by then it's closed and again, so you must resort to looking in from outside). Some years ago two hippos were put into the area to clear the rampant grass in the waterways. They did this to such good dietary effect that a junior hippo was produced.

Half a kilometre after that turning notice the Gillray Boy Scout training centre on the left. Ride for 100 m to see Princess Vlei on your right, and the Princess farm stall (huge displays of fruit and vegetables, much of it from the nearby commercial growing areas of Phillipi and Ottery). All these vleis are interconnected and fed from various streams rising along the mountain chain. Unfortunately the streams are continually getting choked by over-growths of mostly alien weed, not to mention mounds of rubbish. These blockages threaten the levels and water quality of the vleis, as well as impeding storm water drainage.

Another 1 km along a widened and resurfaced section will bring you to the busy Retreat Road intersection, and another 1,5 km to the traffic lights at Concert Boulevard. A right turn here would lead to Retreat. The road surface is still good but the shoulders are potholed. After 1,4 km the road becomes a dual carriageway and takes you successively past Park Island and Eastlake Island, both parts of Marina da Gama (ride in and look around), ending at the traffic circle at Sunrise Beach. Turn right here.

Ride along Royal Road, cross the Sandvlei bridge and turn right. If you like, first detour left and have a snack at one of the places in Muizenberg Pavilion, where, nearby, you can also play Putt-putt or take a wet slide down the Super Tube (at a price). Ride along the edge of the grassy area next to Sandvlei and take Albertyn Road left to cross the railway line at the booms. Continue up to Main Road where you turn right.

Pass the Lakeside Bakery and carry on past the fire station on the left and the supermarket (good bakery; open long hours). Pass the Boyes Drive turn-off, swing right, pass the left turn leading to the Simon van der Stel freeway (M3) and Ou Kaapseweg. Half a kilometre on pass the Lavender Hill turn-off on the right, then a similar distance on pass Honeywell Road traffic lights followed by Tokai Road intersection (Pick 'n Pay on the left) and a superette (recommended) just after the lights. Now there's a short new widened section of road as far as Station Road (down to Retreat station) with Zwaanswyk school on your left and sports grounds for handicapped people a short distance ahead on the right.

Ladies Mile traffic lights are 700 m ahead, and another 700 m takes you past the Heathfield shops. Take care on the deceptively smooth road surface – there are some nasty slotted kerbside drain covers waiting to trap your wheel, as well as some sub-surface roots to give you a bump. No significant features along here – just the Diep River shops. Then comes Kendal Road, a bus depot, police station and bakery on the right, then the road goes down a dip before passing the Three Arts Theatre.

Approach the complex Gabriel Road intersection – left to Constantia and right to

Southfield and Grassy Park. The excellent Southern Cycles shop is 200 m ahead on the right; Timour Hall school on the left. Two more cycle shops only 100 m apart provide an interesting contrast – Speedy has fair prices, attentive staff and a limited stock range; Crosstique has high prices, uninterested staff and a good stock range.

From here you ride up the narrow and often extremely busy Wynberg main road, through no fewer than four sets of traffic lights to the crest of Main Road hill. Now coast down the gentle gradient through the Main/Summerley intersection, then, 100 m on, turn right (no lights) into narrow bumpy Kenilworth Road which for some odd reason seems to have a curious attraction for doctors and dentists.

Cross the railway at the booms, ride down to the bottom and find yourself confronting Rosmead Avenue again. Cross at the traffic lights and you're back in Doncaster Road. Ride 900 m to the lights at Chichester Road, then turn left into Petticoat Lane, the end of your ride.

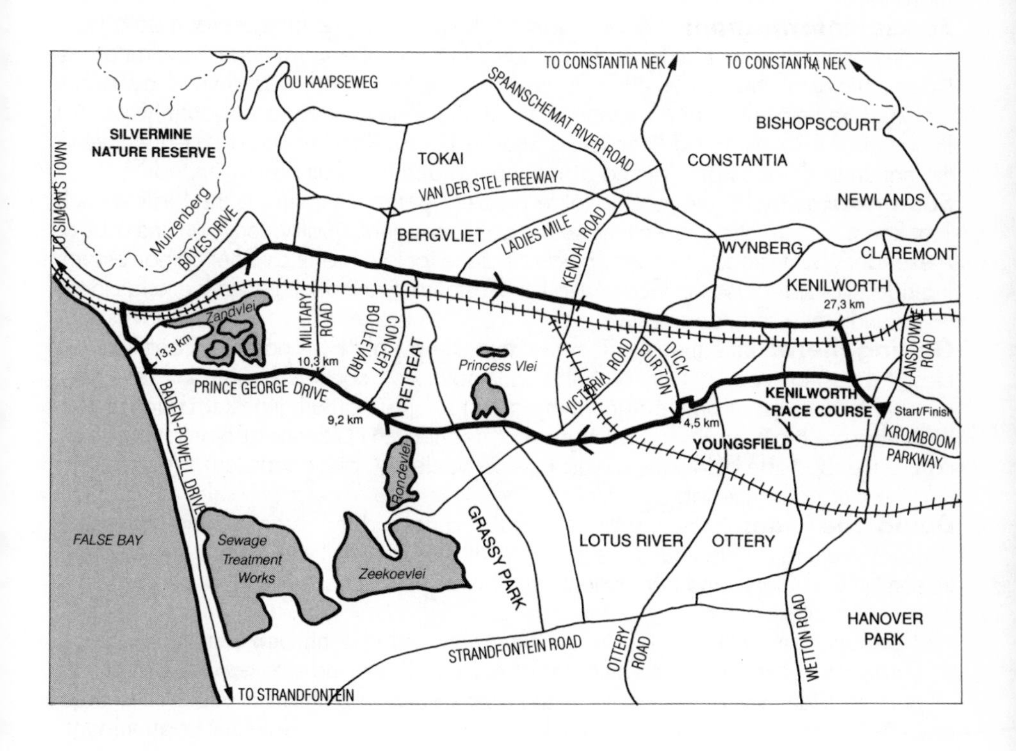

10 Kirstenbosch to Constantia Nek

Features: A circuit offering scenic shifts from natural fynbos mountains to the manicured gardens of gracious homes, from level suburban side-roads to stiff mountain climbs. Not ideal for families unless you pick a time when there is little traffic. The route is mostly shady, and security is good.
Grade and distance: B3; 16 km; 60 minutes.
Best times: In summer go early enough to catch the sunrise and/or to miss the heavy traffic of commuters and tourists along Rhodes Drive – but the lower areas will be chilly then (and probably misty at the end of summer). The southeaster is not a great problem on this ride. In winter, around midday is best (the sun drops behind the mountains by mid-afternoon).
Special information: The world-famous Kirstenbosch gardens have over 4 000 species of indigenous plants, and are thought to have been named after a one-time Dutch official at the Cape, J.F. Kirsten. However, the land was owned by British Colonial Secretary Henry Alexander early in the 19th Century and bought by Cecil Rhodes in 1895 as an addition to his Rhodes Estate. Rhodes willed it perpetually to the nation and it was proclaimed a national garden in 1913.
Sustenance: By far the most suitable place to get refreshments is the Kirstenbosch Tea Room which offers excellent value and consistent quality. Built on the site of Alexander's homestead, it's a very pleasant place for late breakfast after an early-morning ride. Consider also the Constantia Nek restaurant, although its service tends to be less friendly and rather inattentive.
Getting there: Take the N2 freeway, then keep right as it passes Groote Schuur Hospital so that you split off onto the M3 motorway south. About 9 km out, after passing the university on the right, turn right at the first traffic lights (Road sign: M63 Kirstenbosch/Hout Bay). Follow signs to Kirstenbosch/National Botanic Gardens. Park at the roadside below the lawns. Less conveniently, take a train to Newlands and ride the extra distance (about 4 km).
Doing the ride: Before setting off take a few deep breaths and do some muscle-stretching to help you tackle the steep Rhodes Drive hill which starts immediately. It's some 700 m long and bends gently southwards as it passes the Kirstenbosch plant nursery to your right.

At the top of the hill turn right at the T-junction and ride an only slightly less steep 450 m to the top gate of the botanic gardens, which is also the entrance to the director's attractively sited house. Opposite is Klaassens Road, from which you will emerge towards the end of the ride. Meanwhile enjoy a recuperative downhill coast through lovely shady trees.

After 1 km notice a left turn to the Hohenhort Hotel (marked) and the entrance, opposite, to Cecilia State Forest (no mountain bikes). A slight uphill is followed by another fine sweeping descent which will give you momentum to reach the Monterey Drive turn-off before you start slogging up nearly 1,5 km of incline.

Some two-thirds of the way up the road curves left past the Southern Cross Drive turn-off, then narrows and gradually levels out through a series of 'blind' bends. All the way along this stretch you can enjoy fine glimpses of distant False Bay and good mountain views of verdant Vlakkenberg (the mountain behind the Nek restaurant),

Constantiaberg, and the precipitous southern slopes of Table Mountain's 'back table'. Don't concentrate too hard on the sights though because you need to watch out for buses, trucks and boats on trailers shaving past you on the narrow bends – a very unnerving experience.

When you arrive at the traffic circle at Constantia Nek, turn sharp left and enjoy a 3,5 km downhill ride along the winding tree-fringed Constantia Nek Road (M41). Watch your speed because at certain times of the day there are a surprising number of heavy trucks and buses using the hill, not to mention a relatively new menace – speeding combi-taxis plying between Wynberg and Hout Bay.

Near the bottom you'll pass the Groot Constantia entrance and then the Old Cape Farm Stall with its costly delicacies. Pass Pagasvlei Road to the right and commence a short ascent, but cycle carefully because near the beginning is a large non-visible bump in the road. After the crest, carry on through the Parish Road traffic lights. Skirt Constantia (retirement) Village on the right and the attractive stone Christ Church on the left. At the next traffic lights (Spaanschemat Road) you can buy refreshments at the pleasant Alphen Farm Stall (café) or somewhere in the Constantia Village complex just before it on the right.

The next traffic lights are at Brommersvlei Road (which short-cuts back to Rhodes Drive) opposite the Constantia Club sports grounds. Barely 300 m on you pass through another set of lights where, if you turn left, you ride past the Alphen and Hohenhort hotels before joining Rhodes Drive. However carry on about 400 m, under the freeway and past Zonnestraal farm entrance then left up the steep, narrow and bumpy Alphen Hill Road passing Victoria Hospital.

Bear left after the lights at the crest of this hill and ride past Wynberg military base and the Lutheran church on the left, and the Diamond Centre and Dutch Reformed church on the right, at another traffic light. A left turn here would bring you to Wynberg military hospital, and a right turn to Maynardville – a pleasant public park formerly timber merchant James Maynard's estate, and developed into gardens by his grandson William Farmer around 1874. Farmer had the sense to employ a professional Kew-trained gardener. The gardens are used for open-air plays, notably Shakespearean dramas put on every summer, and annual carnivals.

Carry on straight (the road changes its name here to Waterloo), then bear left past Springfield Convent at the bottom. Pass through the next traffic lights (at the turn-off into Herschel Walk) and slog up the steepish 'Trovato Link' dual carriageway with Wynberg Park on your left. Just before the Link begins to bear right, turn left into Trovato Road (which runs through the park) then changes into Klaassens Road. You might spot the granite outcrop up on the right, the silhouette of which resembles a Hen-and-Chicks – the name of the old estate, which has now been built up. Living remnants of Van Riebeeck's famous almond boundary hedge (planted to help keep out marauding Hottentots) can still be found here.

The road is briefly level then has a short steep climb bringing you into Bishopscourt with its numerous costly mansions, some with extensive grounds, high security walls, uniformed guards and intimidating-looking dogs. Bishopscourt is well sheltered from the southeaster and because of its altitude it enjoys long hours of sunshine. It was originally named Bosheuvel but apparently gradually acquired the name of the Anglican archbishop's official residence.

At the first stop street, turn left (still Klaassens Road) and ride some 1 200 m past more huge houses, although you cannot see much of them behind their high walls and fences. Look out for another remnant of Van Riebeeck's hedge on the right; there's an explanatory plaque worth reading.

Emerge at the top gate of Kirstenbosch (where there's a drinking fountain specially erected for runners and cyclists), turn sharp right down Rhodes Drive and look out for high bumps caused by tree roots under the tar. At the traffic island turn left and speed down to where you started.

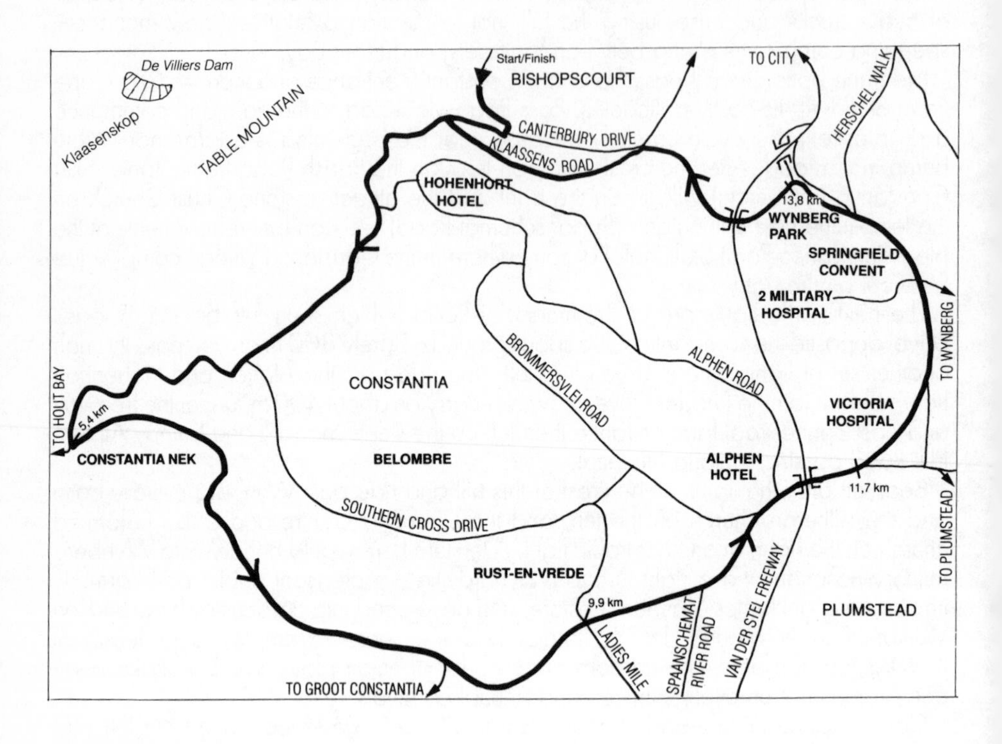

11 Constantia Circuit

Features: An undulating ride among the splendid homes and verdant estates of the Cape's first wine-growing area. Mostly shady and fairly sheltered from the southeaster in summer. Pleasant semi-rural atmosphere, with not much traffic if you pick your time carefully. Suitable for a family outing.
Grade and distance: A1; 17 km; 60 minutes riding time.
Best times: Summer afternoons, and early mornings in spring or summer (because parts of the route have heavy shopping traffic after 09h00, including weekends). Note that most museums and restaurants *en route* open at 10h00.
Special information: The whole route stays on the original 8 500-ha Constantia property on which Governor Simon van der Stel produced the Muscat d'Alexandrie wine that gained high favour at the royal courts of Europe in the 17th century. The present-day Nova Constantia, Klein Constantia and Buitenverwachting estates are parts of the original, but total only 150 ha in area. They still produce fine wines which can be bought on the spot.
Sustenance: There are several victualling places in the shopping centre, including takeaway outlets, or you can pick up *padkos* from the Alphen Farm Stall. There are two 'touristy' but pleasant restaurants at Groot Constantia manor, and an upmarket restaurant at Buitenverwachting – not entirely compatible with sweaty cyclists!
Getting there: Take the N2 freeway, then keep right where it passes Groote Schuur Hospital so that you split off onto the M3 motorway south. After about 13 km take the M41 'Constantia' exit. Pass two traffic lights and turn left at M42 'Spaanschemat River Road'. Constantia Village shopping centre is on your immediate right. Park anywhere.
Doing the ride: Set off westwards along the M41 Constantia Road you've just come along. It heads approximately towards the high radio mast on Constantiaberg. Cross a traffic light after 500 m, coast down a bit of a descent and take a mental note of Pagasvlei Road on the left, which you'll be coming back to a little later. Pass the recently re-located Old Cape Farm Stall on the left.

Carry on about 300 m and turn left at the 'Groot Constantia' signpost. The road then bears right and you ride about 1,3 km slightly uphill along an oak-lined avenue. Pass through the somewhat dilapidated historic gateway, disregard the side roads and bump along until you get to the grand old manor house. On the way you'll pass the top-class Jonkershuis restaurant on your right.

The manor house was built for Van der Stel and later modified by the famous architect Louis Thibault after Hendrik Cloete acquired the farm. Visit the house, now a museum, and buy the excellent pamphlet about the estate.

If you pedal off to the right you'll pass the architecturally controversial new cellars on the right and the original Cloete cellars (1791) on the left. The Tavern restaurant, if it has not been booked for a private social function, is a good place to have lunch.

Later, if you're not torpid from over-indulgence, ride back and take the Pagasvlei Road turn-off and suffer a bit of a climb. Keep your eye on the road names – Pagasvlei Road makes a somewhat illogical sharp right. A really grand view of Table Mountain, Constantiaberg and the Constantia vineyards opens out before you.

Pagasvlei Road ends at a T-junction where you should turn right into Klein Constantia Road. Notice the Huis-en-bos property which, although private, has a picturesque entrance road offering a glimpse of a thatched cottage.

Klein Constantia Road is bumpy but pedal on regardless, past Nova Constantia Road on the left, until you reach a fork. Here you can *either* take the right-hand prong which leads to Klein Constantia estate but involves some 500 m of steep gravel, *or* the left-hand fork which provides a more civilized surface leading to the aptly-named Buitenverwachting ('beyond expectation') estate. Please respect the various 'Private Property' signs along the way. All the buildings on this estate have been restored to their Cape Dutch architectural glory, and the grounds are beautifully kept. The restaurant is at the end of the road and provides a memorable eating experience.

You can go back the same way on to Klein Constantia Road and then turn right into Nova Constantia Road, which allows wondrous views of the Steenberg-Constantiaberg amphitheatre. Nova Constantia Road ends at a T-junction with Spaanschemat River Road. Turn right, and cheat the southeaster and possibly also the heavier traffic by turning left into Firgrove Road some 400 m on.

Pass the pleasant grounds of what might be your old school on the right (Constantia Reformatory), and roll on past some more fine residences. Now cross (by bridge) the M3 motorway, and find yourself in the green and orderly suburb of Bergvliet. A traffic circle lies ahead at which you turn left into Ladies Mile Road which aims you straight towards the back of Table Mountain, re-crossing the M3.

At the first traffic light turn right into the now-familiar Spaanschemat River Road which, about 1 km further on, will return you to the starting point. Cool off, if necessary, on the soft grass in front of the Alphen Farm Stall.

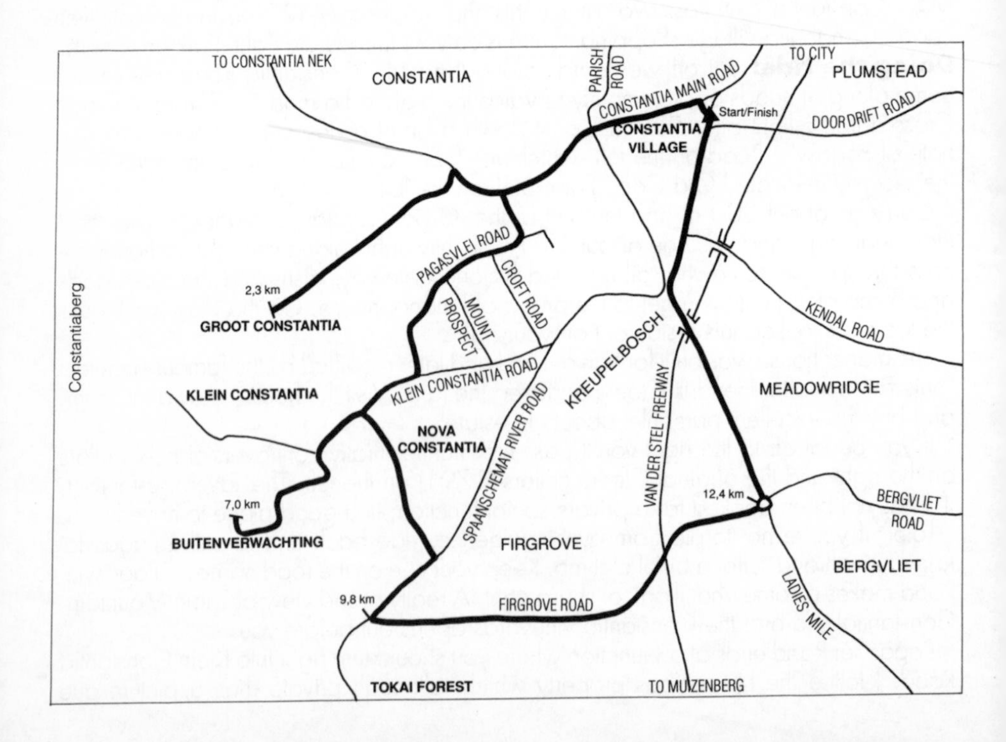

12 Tokai Circuit

Features: A quiet, mostly rural ride with minor inclines. Much of the route is partially protected from the southeaster. Rural sections are very popular with cyclists and runners. The ride is suitable for families and secure provided care is taken and bikes are not left unattended along the Main Road section.
Grade and distance: B2; 22 km; 1 1/4 hours riding time.
Best times: Avoid being on the Main Road section during commuter rush hours, Friday afternoons, or late Saturday mornings. In both summer and winter, the morning is the most suitable time.
Special information: On some weekend mornings you may be overtaken by swarms of cyclists or runners taking part in organized events. If this unnerves you simply pull aside for a couple of minutes to let the main mob past.
Sustenance: There are several food outlets in the Blue Route Centre, where you start and finish. Along the way, and depending on the season, there are some farm stalls selling fresh fruit (we don't include the Main Road vegetable shops). Some of them have fresh breads and home-made preserves for a roadside picnic. Unfortunately these stalls do not open early.
Getting there: Take the N2 freeway, then where it passes Groote Schuur Hospital keep right so that you can follow the M3 split southwards. About 21 km from town spot the 'Tokai/Retreat' exit; take this, then turn left at the stop-street and head down towards Main Road, noticing the extensive Blue Route Centre on your left. Choose any of the several entrances. If you don't have a car, take the train to Retreat (Simon's Town line), come out of the station and ride towards the radio mast on Constantiaberg. Turn left into Main Road, ride about 1 km and spot Pick 'n Pay on the right, across the intersection. Turn right at these lights, into Tokai Road, and start the route.
Doing the ride: Head westwards towards the mountains along a nice wide piece of road which passes under the M3 before narrowing and getting bumpy. Half a kilometre from the start, cross over the four-way stop street. Around March the farm stall on this corner has fresh Hanepoot grapes from the Steenberg farm on your left.

For the energetic there's an interesting detour and muscular challenge 300 m ahead if they take the left turn which leads 3 km up Swaanswyk Road, past some rather lavish residences, to the base of Prinskasteel. This name, formerly Prinseskasteel, derives from the Hottentot (Khoi) princess who, according to legend, was held captive by settlers in the nearby Elephant's Eye cave. A less exciting version of the legend is that she was the leader of the local tribe and used the cave as her headquarters. This detour is quiet and sheltered and offers wonderful views.

The less energetic should rather cross Swaanswyk Road and ride up the serenely quiet tree-lined single-lane De Waal Drive which leads past the Tokai picnic area 600 m from the crossing. Here stands the arboretum started in 1885 by Joseph Lister; it has a famed collection of mature indigenous trees. There is an interesting information office and you can get permission to pick mushrooms (at your own risk) in season.

Cross a small bridge 400 m on and reach Tokai Manor House after another 300 m. This traditional Cape Dutch style house with its lovely vine-covered pillars was built in 1792; its interesting history is summarized on the plaque attached to one of the gate posts. It is not open to the public, because it serves as a private residence for the principal of the Porter Reformatory in Constantia, which can be reached via the gravel road running off to the right of the house (as you face it).

The road to the left zigzags up into Tokai forest and is accessible to mountain bikers only. Many of the trees in the forest are alien, having been experimentally planted to see how they would grow in South Africa. There's even a stand of Californian Redwoods, which need something like another 500 years before they'll be considered mature enough for felling!

Retrace your path back to the four-way stop street. Turn right into Steenberg Road and ride past Pollsmoor Prison. This road has a coarse surface and is rather exposed to the southeaster. Nevertheless it's pleasantly rural and winds past a paddock with donkeys and Shetland ponies, then up a nasty little hill past a dairy farm and a chicken farm. At the crest, pay attention to the turn-off to Ou Kaapseweg, which you should consider riding up at some stage. It's a temporarily exhausting 3,5 km slope, and if the southeaster's blowing it can literally stop you dead near the top.

But that's not for today. Instead, keep straight, making good progress along the fine fast dual carriageway for nearly 2,5 km to the lights at Main Road. Take great care approaching the M3 on- and off-ramps – motorists here seem to have trouble seeing cyclists. Turn left at Main Road (signpost: 'Retreat/Grassy Park') and expect rather more traffic. Keep very alert for protruding manhole covers. After half a kilometre notice the sign 'Lavender Hill' pointing to the right; this offers a back way round to Marina da Gama.

A further 400 m brings you to the Honeywell Road intersection where you should look for the miniature spotted dog statue on the right. This oddity commemorates a famous old roadhouse, generally known as 'Spotties', which once stood here. One of its buildings was constructed as a giant spotted dog, the anatomical crudeness of which was somehow rather appealing. To your left is the Kirstenhof shopping centre.

Further on the road has been widened and re-surfaced, and with the southeaster now behind you there's some compensation for the traffic and the sequence of rather grotty shops scattered along the way. About 1,3 km after the Spotty you come to traffic lights at the junction with Station Road – going down to Retreat Station. On your left is the well-known Zwaanswyk school, and a bit further on to the right, the Protea sports grounds for handicapped people.

The suburb of Retreat takes its name from the position taken up first by the Dutch and then by the British forces at the Battle of Muizenberg in 1795. After this battle the British occupied the Cape. Much later the area was established as a permanent staging point for British troops being moved to and from the East. There were two camps, Pollsmoor and Westlake, both names perpetuated in the district, one as a prison and small suburb, the other as a sanatorium and golf course.

Turn left at Ladies Mile, 700 m ahead, and ride up a wide quiet road through the attractive suburb of Bergvliet. A collection of shops on the left about 1,3 km along includes a good café and a pleasant restaurant. Carry on until you reach a circle next to Bergvliet school; keep straight, pass over the M3 freeway, then turn left at the Spaanschemat River Road traffic lights. Wind down a fast but bumpy section; near the bottom there is sometimes a stall selling fresh strawberries in the season. Pedal up a short stiff hill past a Muslim cemetery; notice the right-hand Klein Constantia Road fork which leads to the Buitenverwachting and Klein Constantia farms.

Ride another undulating 1,6 km, past Nova Constantia turn-off and Uitsig farm stall (only open during grape harvest). Enjoy good views of Constantiaberg before bearing left and down into a delightful tree-lined and more sheltered stretch of the road, which rises slightly uphill as it leads through the Tokai forest. This was first planted in 1883 but the present stands of timber are young and immature. You'll see many people riding and dog-walking here, even during the week.

When you reach the four-way stop street, turn left and cruise down Tokai Road back to the Blue Route Centre.

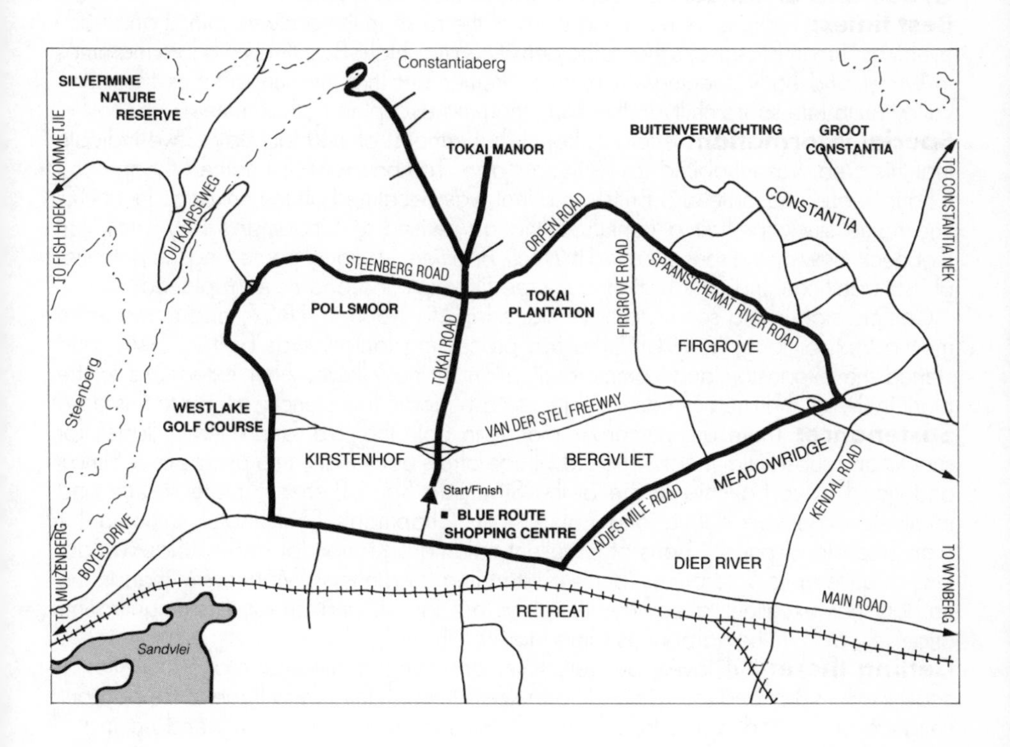

13 Hout Bay Circuit

Features: This is a short but varied ride with many opportunities for detours along the way. It is suitable for families and secure, provided you time your ride correctly.
Grade and distance: A2; 13 km; 45 minutes riding time.
Best times: Traffic is heavy along parts of the route in the early mornings and early evenings. In tourist seasons the traffic density is also high. Best times are late mornings in winter and early evenings in summer. Remember that the sun reaches Hout Bay valley quite late so it's chilly in the early morning except in high summer.
Special information: Artefacts from what remains of the Hout Bay Cave indicate that this area was inhabited 2 000 years ago. The bay was first named Chapman's Chaunce after the mate of a British ship that was becalmed off the entrance in 1607. The name stuck for half a century, although revised to Chapman's Bay, until Van Riebeeck, new on the scene, called it *'t Hout Baeitjen*, no doubt perceiving the potential of its magnificent indigenous timber – greedily exploited and never replaced.

Commercial fishing seems to have started in Hout Bay in 1867, and manganese mining (not for long) in 1909. The fish processing factory was built in 1947 and started the expansion and commercialization of the village. After extensions to the plant in 1959 the area became subject to a periodic foul stench, as it is to this day.
Sustenance: There are numerous places in both the 'old' and 'new' villages for snacks and substantial meals. The old village offers particularly fine pizzas at St Elmo's and good value franchised fare at the Silverado Spur. There's a more sedate and relatively expensive coffee and cake shop. Chapman's Peak Hotel is noted for giant-sized (and priced) pans of excellent calamari. Kronendal serves 'olde-worlde' teas at quite up-to-date prices (but is outstanding for dinners). Mariner's Wharf in the harbour has excellent takeaways (helpings are large), and an expensive grillroom. Snoekies, also in the harbour, is famed for its fish and chips.
Getting there: It is lovely but very time-consuming to drive all along the Atlantic coast to Hout Bay and following Victoria Road through the new village to the harbour entrance at the end of the beach. (Don't drive past otherwise you'll end up in the commercial harbour, which is not an ideal starting point.)

Alternatively, follow the N2 freeway, keeping right where it passes Groote Schuur Hospital so that you split off onto the M3 motorway south. Turn right at the first traffic lights, signposted 'M63 Kirstenbosch/Hout Bay'. Follow the signs for 16 km over Constantia Nek to the bay. Just before reaching the old village look out for Princess Road on the right, signposted 'Harbour'. Follow subsequent harbour signs.

Train travellers should go to Wynberg (on the Simon's Town line); outside the station is the terminus for infrequent but regular buses all the way to Hout Bay harbour. Unless you travel at reasonably quiet times, you won't be allowed to put your bike on the bus. Combi-taxis serve this route very well and are more flexible about carrying bikes – but it depends entirely on the driver.
Doing the ride: Ride away from the harbour back along Victoria Road for about 400 m, then turn right into Princess Road; note the signpost 'Fish Hoek via Chapman's Peak'. The road is slightly potholed and often sand-sprinkled. The road crosses the Hout Bay river, known to have sheltered hippos in ancient days, then 250 m ahead joins Hout Bay main road (M6/M63). Note the signpost 'Constantia/Wynberg' as

you turn left here. On the right, alongside the set-back entrance to the Hout Bay Hotel, craft markets are set up on weekend mornings. About 200 m beyond the hotel gateway is a right turn, which you should take if you want to visit the excellent little museum. It is imaginatively run, with frequent special events, and contains carefully arranged displays dealing with the long and fascinating history of Hout Bay. It's open during the day, but not on Sundays and Mondays.

Pass historic Kronendal house/restaurant on the right. The original house (its form detectable in the rear portions of the present building) was built for Willem van Dieden and Pieter van der Westhuizen shortly after 1681. The present form resulted from alterations by Johannes van Helsdingen in 1800. It is a national monument.

Carry on past the 'City' turn-off on the left as the road improves in width and surface quality. Pass Glenellen riding school on the left, and a cemetery on the right (many interesting inscriptions on the headstones). To the left, alongside a briefly level section, is the Disa Aquarium with its displays of tropical fish.

You'll soon pass the Oakhurst Farm Stall. The road along here is sheltered and shady but there are bumps from tree roots and the shoulder is inconsistent in width so that the distance between the yellow lines can remain constant. For some odd reason buses on this section overtake cyclists then immediately cut across them to pull off the road to pick up passengers.

Just when the steady climb begins to seem wearisome you can turn left into Longkloof Road opposite the entrance to Groot Moddergat, now an exclusive weekend retreat for well-heeled guests, but formerly part of the original Kronendal estate. A short, very steep, descent takes Longkloof Road over a low bridge which is sometimes flooded in winter by the raging Hout Bay river – referred to in old maps as the 'Palmiet' or 'Disa' at this point. Turn left into Valley Road which, after an initial uphill, is a long descent. Look out for riders (horse, not bike), especially during evenings and weekends. Recently a series of stop streets has been established in this road, irritating for the motorist but welcome if they are successful in thwarting the foolish speeding which takes place along here.

On the right is a large forested estate and all the way down on the left are houses. Some, but by no means all, are very attractive, and most have paddocks with horses. The valley is wide and pretty with grand views across to Constantiaberg and, almost dead ahead, Karbonkelberg and Little Lion's Head.

At the second stop street you can see The World of Birds on the right. This is a wonderful place and a credit to its almost obsessive founder and director, Walter Mangold. There are more than 300 species of bird in the sanctuary, many entirely free to fly away but choosing to remain where they are so well cared for. Many sick or injured birds have recuperated here, helped by an enthusiastic team of young volunteers. There are also some small mammals from various parts of the world. The place is extremely well worth visiting and supporting.

Along the right hand side of Valley Road, among the extravagant new houses, are a few historic homes or farmhouses, dating back more than a hundred years and of considerable architectural interest – Sans Pareil, Victor's Kloof, Fairview, Fern Grove and Nooitgedacht. At the last stop street, turn right (you're back on the M6 route again), ride for 400 m and take the slip road to the left at the traffic lights. This is Victoria Road, and while it is exposed to sun, wind and traffic it is wide and smooth and lets you have an invigorating fast descent into the new village, where there are several victualling possibilities and a cycle shop.

Stay on this road and you'll end up where you started. If you have time (and a chain to lock your bike) you can ride on past Mariner's Wharf into the commercial harbour to look at the cannons of the West Fort, built in 1781 or 1799, and then maybe buy something from the Fish on the Rocks kiosk. You can buy crayfish and other sea products in the harbour, but don't expect anything to be cheaper or fresher than in retail outlets.

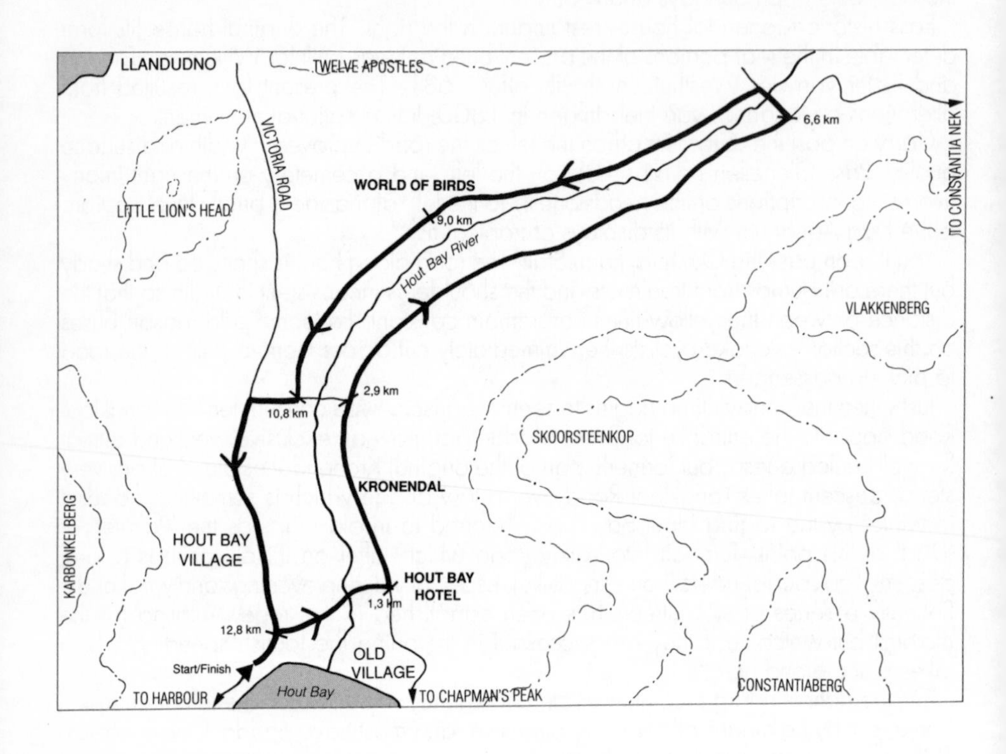

14 Hout Bay to Camps Bay

Features: A popular and interesting sea-and-mountain ride, with one major hill, which can be done from either direction (depending on the wind). It can be timed so that you can enjoy the sunsets, and is suitable for families if all members are confident about the rather narrow and crowded road at the Camp's Bay end. Suitable for the timid as there are usually many other cyclists on the road.
Grade and distance: A3; 12 km each way; 40 minutes riding time each way.
Best times: A summer evening is most suitable if you want to see the sunset, but roads may be congested with holiday-makers. Otherwise mid-morning after the early traffic has diminished and mist has lifted. Miserable if a squally northwester is blowing.
Special information: If you intend watching the sunset from one of the better vantage points you're likely to complete the ride in the dusk, so your bike should have lights and you should wear a reflecting garment. Those interested in geology should note the transition from Table Mountain Sandstone to granitic intrusions (decomposed) along the way.
Sustenance: Mariner's Wharf, where you start, has splendid takeaways but it would be unwise to start your ride after consuming a lot of food. Rather return, change into appropriate clothes and have dinner in the (rather pricey) restaurant. Consider tea and a snack at Suikerbossie Restaurant (the route is downhill after that). The new (northern) part of Hout Bay has a café and coffee shops. Camps Bay has several well-known eateries such as Blues, Zerbans, Flamingo, etc.
Getting there: Get onto Table Bay Boulevard (N1, next to the harbour) in its northwesterly direction. Follow it where it swings left and merges with Buitengracht Street (southwesterly), then turn sharp right at the second traffic light to get onto the Western Boulevard (M6). Follow this road through its various twists and turns and name-changes (but it's the M6 all the way) to Hout Bay harbour (signposted). Park inside the harbour entrance near to Mariner's Wharf.
Doing the ride: Before leaving or after returning have a look round the harbour, area which is picturesque and usually quite active. Leave the harbour entrance along Victoria Road (the way you came) doing your best to avoid blown sand, which is unfriendly to chains and gears. Look out for occasional potholes.

Note the yacht club on the beach and the Princess Road right turn which goes to Hout Bay's 'old' village. Victoria Road rises past a variety of shops, including a cycle shop, then makes a short steep incline to traffic lights at the junction with the road to old Hout Bay, Constantia Nek, Chapman's Peak, etc. But carry on across the intersection and start the steep 2 km climb up Suikerbossie hill.

To your left rises Little Lion's Head, and to your right is a fine mountain view up Hout Bay valley and Orange Kloof to Constantia Nek. As you crest the hill there's a sudden spectacular view of the sparkling Atlantic, and the tempting right turn-off to Suikerbossie tea room/restaurant which offers warmth and shelter from the wind.

There's a welcome fast descent along the wide three-lane road, but don't miss the views. Below, Llandudno clings to the hillside and you can see the remains of the *Romelia*, a tanker under tow which was blown onto the Oudeschip rocks during a gale in 1977. Sandy Bay's topless beach is partially visible, and the mountain rising above it is named Karbonkelberg. Now you swing round a right-hand bend and enjoy a surprise view of distant Robben Island and, on a clear day, the far-off West Coast. Landwards the Twelve Apostle range stretches towards Lion's Head.

The next right hand bend opens the outstanding view of Lion's Head itself, Clifton, Camps Bay and the cable station atop Table Mountain. Entrance to the popular Oudekraal beach is a little way on, to the left. Another 700 m further on you will see (at low tide) the cut-down wreck of the *Antipolis,* which was being towed in tandem with the *Romelia* and suffered a similar fate.

Note the fine isolated house on the right; it was formerly a farm house – the farm Oudekraal owned by the Van Breda family. A number of landslides have occurred on the next few kilometres of road, and retaining walls have recently been built to prevent this happening in future. Notice the seaward-side parking lot usually occupied by sea shell and curio vendors, and, approximately opposite, a gate leading to the grave of a Muslim holy man. Nearly a kilometre further on the road narrows and acquires pavements and flanking bungalows. You are in the suburb of Bakoven, named after the shape of a large rock which most people find very difficult to pick out! This stretch is level but winding and sometimes very busy.

Next, pass the Theatre on the Bay, police station and tidal pool before a slight descent to the Camps Bay beach and shopping area. Formerly the Argus Tour used to finish at the shops, but because of traffic chaos the route was extended up the short final hill adjoining the Maiden's Cove/Bachelor's Cove recreation area to the left.

Finish anywhere you like here and ride back the same way. If you had the southeaster behind you on the way it will only blow really hard near the top of Suikerbossie, and you may find you have to pedal quite hard to get *down* the hill you may have struggled up earlier.

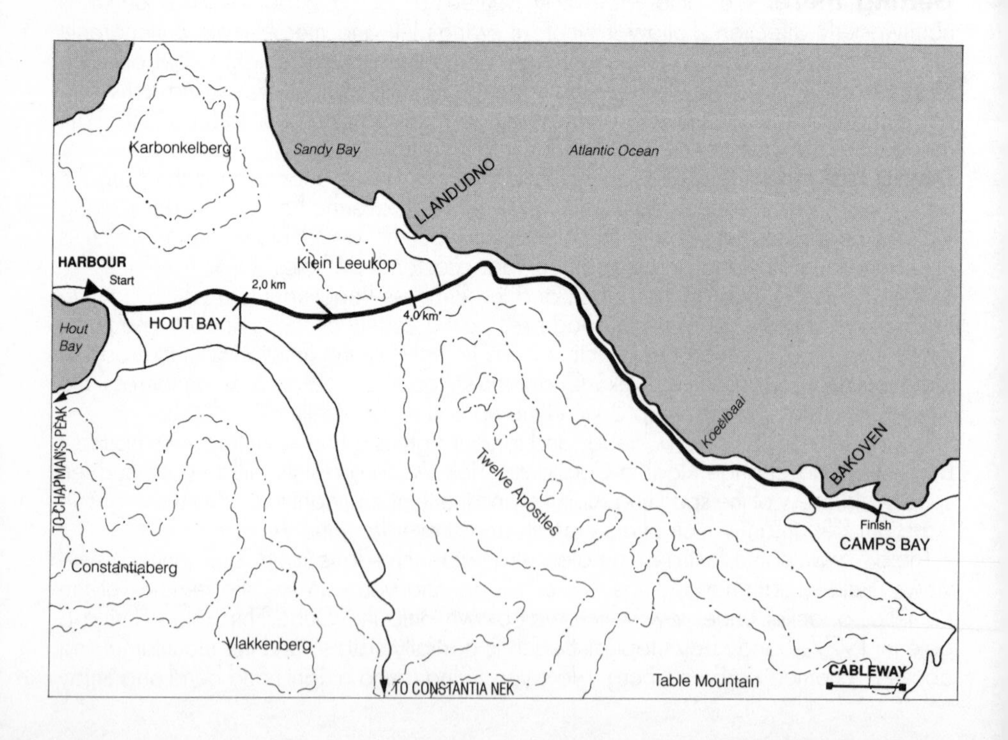

15 Hout Bay to Sun Valley

Features: A grandly scenic ride with continually changing seascapes. The return trip needs planning if you want to see the sunset without riding back in the dark. It is quite suitable for families if you avoid commuters and the peak times for motorized sightseers. One idea is to make two parties, with two cars, each starting from a different end, meeting in the middle for the sunset and then riding on to pick up each other's cars. A safe ride for all ages accustomed to cycling.
Grade and distance: A3 – but B3 if you ride the return trip; 12 km each way; 45 minutes each way.
Best times: To enjoy the sunset from the best vantage point, the period from late spring to early autumn gives you sufficient twilight to complete the ride or return the way you came. Alternatively do the ride earlier and content yourself with merely thinking about the sunset while you have drinks on the Chapman's Peak Hotel verandah. The tourist rush starts surprisingly early, so morning riders should aim to complete the trip early. Commuter traffic is not heavy on weekday mornings.
Special information: If you go for the sunset, use a reflective garment and a good taillight to make sure you don't get run down as it grows dark. Helmets are advisable, especially after rain, as quite a number of small stones (and occasionally big ones) fall off the sheer cliffs. Exuberance must be restrained on some of the downhill sections as a cornering error could send you right over the edge.
Sustenance: If your timing is right, the ideal is to end up on Chapman's Peak Hotel verandah for sundowners and calamari. Earlier in the day there's a wide choice of feeding establishments in Hout Bay's old village – such as the Silverado Spur, St Elmo's, Hout Bay Hotel grill, Kronendal (for afternoon teas or excellent dinners), and various coffee/tea/cake shops. If you don't do the return ride you can carry on to the Noordhoek shopping centre or even to Fish Hoek; both centres have numerous restaurants/takeaways.
Getting there: Drive along the N2 and bear right where it splits to become the M3, continuing to its first traffic lights about 9 km from town. Turn right at the signpost 'Kirstenbosch/Hout Bay M63', and follow these signs to Constantia Nek and then down to Hout Bay. Do not turn right as you approach, but continue approximately straight, past Kronendal on your left, then through the village to Chapman's Peak Hotel immediately before the start of the hill at the far end of the village. You'll probably have to park at the beach opposite.
Doing the ride: The first section is also the steepest – leave the hotel in the direction you came (on a coarse, rather narrow surface), then turn sharply left, where the road levels out somewhat. Notice the famous bronze 'constipated leopard' perched on the rock near the sea down on your right – actually a very good sculpture done in 1963 by the late Ivan Mitford-Barberton to commemorate Hout Bay's once-resident leopards.

From the sharp turn, ride past the Flora Bay holiday bungalows down on the right, and after 200 m spot Military Road on the left. This was built by the French for access to the East Fort which they erected in 1781 during their short occupation of the Cape while allies of the Dutch against the British. The strange concrete platform on the right is part of an uncompleted, time-share development. The East Fort itself can be reached down a short rough track to the right (signposted). The cannon barrels are still lying there and the site gives a lovely view across to the precipitous Hangberg (Sentinel).

Notice the derelict jetty far down on the right. Manganese and iron had been identified in the southern peninsula in the 18th Century, but serious mining (which didn't last long) was done only in 1909, just above the road you're now on. The shafts are easily found and visited, and there are still thousands of tons of ore stacked up ready for despatch down the long-vanished chute to the jetty.

The road flattens out now and widens. If the southeaster is blowing you'll find it comes howling down some but not all of the valleys you pass, depending on its prevailing angle. Be ready for a sudden surprise blast! The road winds very pleasingly along here, steadily ascending, with three major picnic spots on the right and numerous smaller ones elsewhere. Notice a track leading down to the Round Table holiday camp, at a place named on old maps as Rondeheuvel. Notice also a small waterfall at road level tucked into a left corner near the second large picnic spot; this is a perennial stream and very potable.

The views change continually, improving as you gain height. The last stretch to the viewsite gives you a tail boost from the southeaster. Walk down with your bike to drink in the view and perhaps to wait for the sunset. Panning from the right you can see most of your route winding in and out of Constantiaberg's western slopes, then Orange Kloof at the head of the Hout Bay valley, then across to Little Lion's Head, Karbonkelberg and Hangberg with Duikereiland (Cormorant Island) just below it – but no duikers, only seals! Further out to sea off Duikereiland you can see the treacherous Vulcan Rock breakers. If the southeaster's blowing strongly you'll see what sailors call 'willy-waughs' here and there in Hout Bay – points of violently disturbed water and spray where the down-jetting wind hits the sea surface.

Hout Bay was originally named Chapman's Chaunce, later becoming known as Chapman's Bay, after the name of the mate from the British ship *Consent* which, under Capt David Middleton, landed a shore party with John Chapman in 1607 – nearly half a century before van Riebeeck arrived. The original ship's log entry is on display in the Hout Bay Museum. But 200 years later, Van Riebeeck's name *'t Hout Baeitjen* had gained favour and the name Chapman's Bay was transferred to the sweep off Noordhoek Beach to your left. Another half a century passed before the high peak behind where you now stand was also named after Chapman.

The road you arrived on was completed in 1919, following a bright idea put to the Divisional Council by the Cape Peninsula Publicity Association, and firmly encouraged by the then Administrator of the Cape, Sir Frederic de Waal. The next section you ride along was far more of an engineering achievement, although it took advantage of the contact zone between the hard Cape Granite and the softer overlying Table Mountain Sandstone. This section was started from the Noordhoek end and only connected with the Hout Bay side in 1922.

The descent is very spectacular with sheer multi-coloured cliffs towering above you and some extremely sharp bends which have unseated several downhill cyclists in various competitive events. Take great care, especially if there's a winter wind accelerating you; keep a look out for stones in the road and for oncoming vehicles cutting the corners. Just past the small stone hut on the right, there's a perennial spring feeding a convenient face-level natural bowl in the rockface on the left; its water is delicious. You'll spot it easily because of the surrounding greenery.

About 1,5 km down from the viewsite another left-hand bend will suddenly reveal Noordhoek Beach stretching away to Kommetjie. The road now begins to go uphill again, and you might find the going harder because of the southeaster, which you may now meet head-on among the loops of Little Chapman's above Monkey Bay. At the crest of this mini-hill you get a fine view of Noordhoek and the whole valley through to Fish Hoek in the distance.

The head of the rustic Noordhoek valley, up on your left, is mostly part of what was formerly the Chaplin Estate, and is currently the source of intense acrimony between Serina, which wants to mine the kaolin deposits there, and local residents and environmentalists who want to preserve the unspoilt nature of the valley.

The road winds down to the beach turn-off, which also leads to a newish restaurant named The Red Herring, which has a good reputation. There are still a couple of farms in this area, mostly for keeping horses. The atmosphere is pleasantly rural with no hint of the nearby sea.

The road now bears right, widening, and faces the full force of any southeaster – but at least it's level. Ride along, gradually entering the outskirts of Noordhoek, which consisted, until quite recently, of holiday houses but is rapidly becoming suburbanized. The origin of the name is uncertain; it could be from the Dutch equivalent of 'north glen' or from the Norwegian *glen-Noors*. The area was granted in 1743 by the governor-general of the Netherlands East Indies, Baron van Imhoff, to Johanna Russouw, widow of Burgher Councillor Frederick Russouw.

You have a choice of finishing at the BP service station about 3 km ahead, just before the junction with Ou Kaapseweg (our distance measuring point) where there's a small supermarket and bakery, or you can turn around and go back the way you came, or even cycle on as far as Fish Hoek.

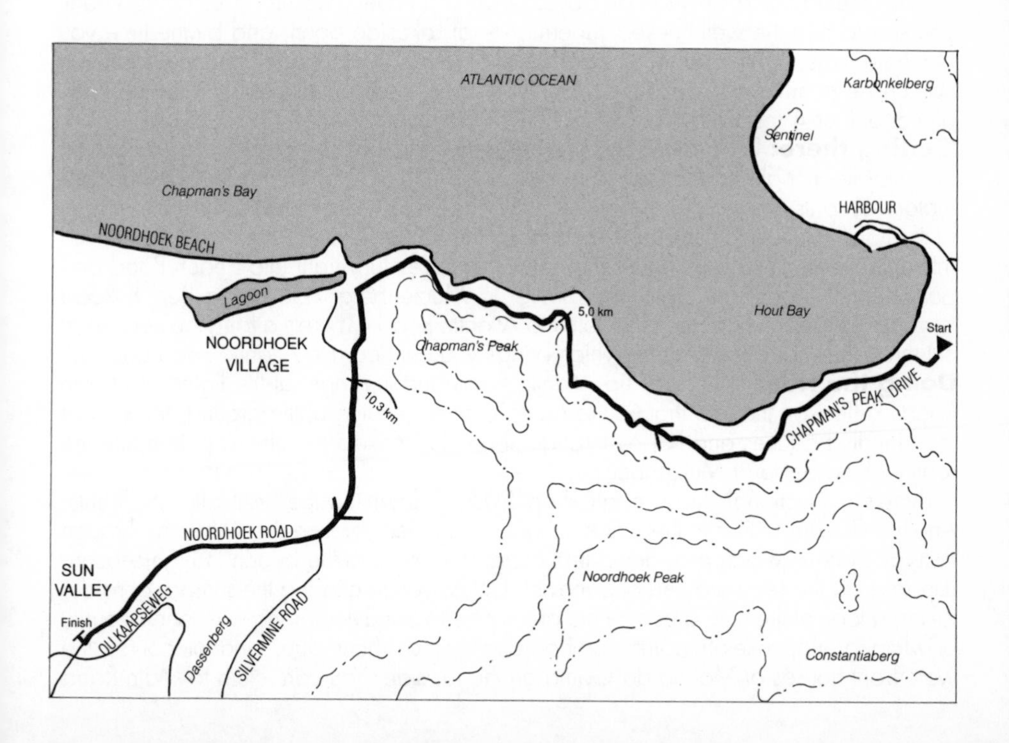

16 Boyes Drive Circuit

Features: This ride provides some spectacular views of the False Bay coastline and the ocean. It is suitable for families if the coastal road section is negotiated out of peak traffic hours. Security is assured during recommended times.
Grade and distance: A3; 14 km; 45 minutes riding time.
Best times: Preferably pre-rush hour(s) on summer mornings – Sundays are ideal. If you are especially early you can take in the sunrise and complete most of the ride before the southeaster reaches its full force. Evenings, if not windy, are pleasantly quiet but most of the route will then be in full shade. The same goes for winter afternoons, although winter mornings are fine after rush hour.
Special information: Riders with mountain bikes can include a beach jaunt if the tide's out far enough for a band of firm sand to appear. Not recommended if the beach is busy (when ATBs can be a menace) – there may well be a regulation against their use. East of Sandvlei mouth would be more suitable for mountain bikers, but this stretch is much lonelier so its security is not assured.

There are a couple of steep descents on the circuit; beginners should take care. The Main Road coastal section has umpteen manhole covers, many of which project or recess sharply. Hitting one can have devastating effects on your bike and your person, so try to avoid them. If you do the circuit really early, consider riding carefully along the seaward sidewalk (illegal, but unlikely to land you in Pollsmoor).
Sustenance: Early morning rides usually mean you must carry your own – but a picnic breakfast at a view-site on Boyes Drive is a novel pleasure. If it's not too early you should find the well-stocked supermarket at Lakeside open, and by the time you get there, also the Red Parrot pizza shop in St James. If you ride in the afternoon you can chose from several options at the Muizenberg Pavilion – possibly even an early dinner at Pier 4 restaurant.
Getting there: Drive along the N2 freeway, then where it passes Groote Schuur Hospital keep right so that you can follow the M3 split southwards. Take the M3 motorway to its uttermost end. Turn left. Drive down to Main Road (M4) and turn right at the lights. Drive into Muizenberg as far as the traffic lights at Atlantic Road. Turn left into Atlantic Road to pass under the railway bridge. Turn right into Beach Road and park near the pavilion. Train users travel to Muizenberg, ride along Beach Road towards the beach huts, then turn left into Atlantic Road. (There's a fairly obvious short cut through a narrow sidestreet which brings you out near the Atlantic Road bridge.)
Doing the ride: Ride back up Atlantic Road and turn right at the lights into Main Road. Reflect on the fact that you're riding over a genuine battle ground; thinking of the friendly beaches and happy throngs of holiday-makers it's difficult to imagine the reality of the Battle of Muizenberg in 1795.

There's a functional cycle repair shop 200 m down on the right after the lights. Another 200 m further is the junior school, on the left. Notice the right-turn, through railway booms, which provides a less congested route to the beach in high season; it leads past the seaward end of Sandvlei. Unless you're chasing the sunrise, consider taking a look at the nice green picnic areas next to Sandvlei, along with tennis courts, bowling green, take-off points for boardsailors, a yacht club, and of course the waterfront houses of Marina da Gama on the far side. You can return to Main Road by riding the wrong way up Uxbridge Road (it is partially one-way) from near the Imperial Yacht Club.

Had you stayed on Main Road you would have noticed the steep winding short cut up to Boyes Drive. Now ride 300 m past the Uxbridge intersection and you'll very likely enjoy the delectable aromas from Lakeside Bakery on your left. Then comes a post office on your right, followed, 400 m on, by the fire station. Another 100 m on is the supermarket mentioned earlier – good value and open long hours.

Boyes Drive begins 300 m ahead on your left, at the Almondbury Restaurant. George Boyes was a Simon's Town magistrate who almost single-handedly motivated the building of this road. Traffic was not a problem in those days (the 1920s) so the reason for his enthusiasm for this quite costly project is not clear. The drive starts with a mild but long ascent, steepening as it swings left, where it may begin to catch the adverse southeaster. Notice the lead-off to Westlake Club on your right.

Roughly 1 km from its start, Boyes Drive levels out and gives you high wide views of Sandvlei (in summer it is usually sprinkled with boardsailors moving at amazing speeds). Marina da Gama, built on the vlei, is an unusual and attractive concept which had a second phase that was never begun, and unfortunately probably never will be because of costs. Phase Two was to have linked the canal system to the sea to provide, apart from many more buildings, a marina and all-season access for seagoing craft.

The road sweeps along for nearly 2 km, past the steep short cut mentioned earlier, then up a slight rise to give a commanding view right along the Muizenberg beaches towards Strandfontein and Gordon's Bay. Next, the road dives down and up again quite steeply (high-speed motorists are not unusual along here) past some attractively positioned houses. There are benches along the pavement for people wishing to contemplate the view, which is even better near the top, and includes the coastal panorama towards Simon's Town. If you had planned a roadside breakfast and are now deterred by the wind, don't worry, because further round the road is quite sheltered.

There is a long, winding but shallow descent from here on, with view upon view unfolding, each interestingly different, although you may have to ride on the pavement to see properly. Consider that serious official thought is being given to turning Boyes Drive into a four-lane highway to relieve congestion on Main Road.

Notice the numbers of walking paths leading up the mountain, and the thoughtfully provided pull-offs for parking. These are lovely walks through the fynbos, and some include safe and accessible caves. Next time you're out this way, why not cycle to the start, then include a mini-hike with your ride? Kalk Bay harbour looks especially attractive from up above, resembling the picturesque little harbours widely found in Europe. (The name 'Kalk', meaning chalk, comes from the former necessity to make building lime by burning sea shells in large kilns, of which some have left traces, e.g. at Seaforth and Buffelsbaai.)

Boyes Drive ends opposite the little beach at Kalk Bay. From midday onwards it is often possible to buy fish in the harbour, straight off the boats, and for a small extra sum you can have it gutted and filleted. The harbour entrance is halfway up the Main Road rise to your right. If you're not into buying fish, then turn left at the Boyes Drive traffic light and ride along past Kalk Bay station (consider a midday Sunday fish braai at the Brass Bell).

There are various landmarks along here – historic St James church and its associated

Star of the Sea school, and St James Hotel with the Red Parrot in what looks like a former garage below it. There are several fine tidal pools, and the small Dalebrook beach is always very sheltered – but totally choked with visitors over fine weekends. Several intriguing little streets up to the left can be explored at your leisure, but most have very steep inclines. Kalk Bay is full of interesting characters, some of whom are writers and artists. One such was the late Robert Ardrey, best-selling author of *The Social Contract* and *The Territorial Imperative,* who considered Kalk Bay the most delightful spot in the world.

Did you notice the unexpected and attractive mosaic on St James post office? If so, take a look at its counterpart on the Muizenberg post office. When you pass Rhodes Cottage museum and Natale Labia museum you'll know your circuit's nearly over, but before you pack up, take a good look at the Muizenberg station, completed in 1913; its Edwardian style and unique clock tower are rare in a public utility. There has been talk of letting the station's upper floor as a restaurant.

Back at the Atlantic Road traffic lights, turn right and return to your car.

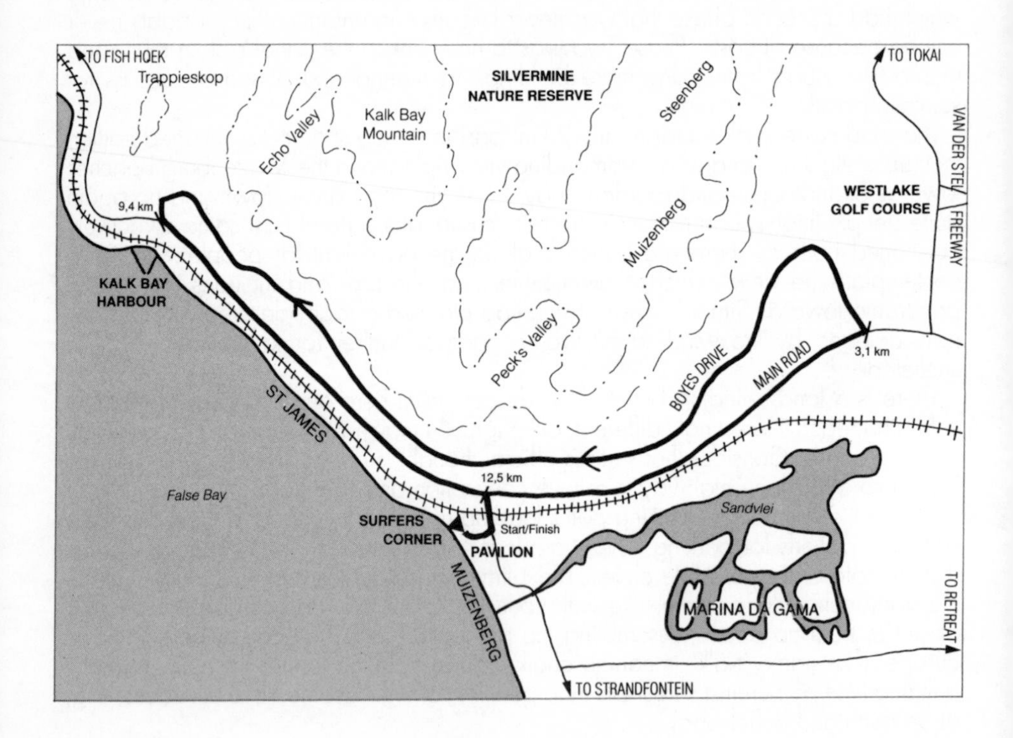

17 Ou Kaapseweg and Silvermine

Features: An exceptionally scenic and varied circuit involving a long hard climb, but ending with a wonderful extended sweeping descent through unspoilt fynbos-carpeted mountains. A nice family ride for those able to tackle the hill or willing to wait at the top while the less fit walk up. Most of the route is quite lonely during weekdays but popular with fitter cyclists and runners over weekends.
Grade and distance: B3; 27 km; 1 hour 45 mins.
Best times: Any time as long as you miss the commuter traffic along the coastal road section. Avoid strong southeaster weather because this wind blows much harder near the top of the long climb – and surprise gusts can be dangerous. Avoid doing the most arduous parts in the heat of the day.
Special information: Ou Kaapseweg was once the route used for hauling wagons to the southern peninsula. The coastal route, which looks so easy nowadays, was in those days both too rocky and too sandy – wagons attempting it were frequently bogged down or overwhelmed by the tide.

Fish Hoek, part of the route, was an established Dutch East India Company fishing spot in the late 17th century, and after his resignation as governor Simon van der Stel collared the fish supply contract. He is believed to have built a house for the fishermen of 'Visch Baai' in 1699 near what is now Clovelly, which may have been spoken of in those times as the 'Hoek' of that Visch Baai. During the first British occupation of the Cape, Lord Charles Somerset built a road across the quicksands of the bay and later granted Andries Bruyns land there for vegetable farming.
Sustenance: There are numerous good places to eat in Fish Hoek, for takeaways and sit-down meals, such as the Copper Creek Spur and François (corner of Beach/Recreation roads). There's also a fair choice in Kalk Bay and Muizenberg. But eating before tackling a big hill is not a good idea, so we recommend waiting until you return to the starting point, where there are food outlets in the shopping centre. In high summer carry water, which you'll need after the hill; but there are clean roadside waterfalls for at least half the year.
Getting there: Drive along the N2 and take the right-hand split onto the M3 which you follow to its uttermost end, then turn left into Steenberg Road (M64), then right at the traffic lights into Main Road (M4). Follow this coastal road through to the far end of Fish Hoek, turn right at the traffic circle, then follow this Kommetjie Road (M65) to the four-way stop street. Turn right and drive down to the turn-off to Noordhoek. Park near the BP garage on this corner. Even if you know the way, don't come over Ou Kaapseweg – you might get discouraged! Train users can arrive at Fish Hoek and take one of the many and frequent combi-taxis – or ride to the start.
Doing the ride: Set off back (southwards – Ou Kaapseweg Extension) but turn left at the traffic lights into Frigate Road, then take the first right into Corsair Way. These Sun Valley roads are smooth and in good condition. Pass playgrounds on your right, then cross the stop street and carry on along this suburban street.

When you reach the traffic lights, cross over and enjoy a smooth-surfaced ride as far as the lights at the top of a rise. The road becomes bumpy after this but descends pleasantly for 1,7 km to the traffic circle. Turn left, past a good supermarket/bakery on the left, and across the traffic lights (turn right here if you need a swim). You're now in Fish Hoek's main road, which can be very busy. Look out for elderly folk who step into the road without checking that the coast is clear.

Take care: some of the manhole covers protrude quite far from the surface of the road. Look out for Regal Cycles on the left, and an excellent fish-and-chip shop on the right next to a service station. Cross over a pedestrian traffic light (again, watch out for old folk). After the shops the new unaesthetic police fortress is on the left, then there is a smooth run (beloved by speed-trappers) to the 'hoek' as the road passes the left-turn to Clovelly and swings sharply into Kalk Bay.

You might hit the southeaster for a short distance here, but once you get round the approaching left bend running past the Kalk Bay harbour entrance you'll be fairly well sheltered. The village has been associated with fishing since the early 1700s but, surprisingly, the first breakwater was built only in 1919 and the harbour completed only in 1939. June/July sees the most activity at the harbour – this is normally the height of the snoek season.

About 300 m beyond the traffic lights at Boyes Drive turn-off is the Kalk Bay station and its famous Brass Bell Restaurant. With Dalebrook beach and tidal pool on the right, cross the St James boundary at Quarterdeck Road. Next come the Star of the Sea school, railway station, St James Hotel and Red Parrot, and then you cross the boundary with Muizenberg somewhere after Hector Road. Look out all the way along for manhole covers.

Your next landmark is Rhodes Cottage museum – well worth a visit. The newer Natale Labia museum follows, then the remarkable Post Huys – restored some years ago but already in need of maintenance. Notice the Edwardian-style station on the right (a national monument), then ride on past some pretty gardens on the left, through the lights at Atlantic Road. Lakeside bakery is 2 km ahead, and another 600 m further is a supermarket with a fine bakery.

Turn left at the next traffic lights and ride up smooth wide Steenberg Road towards the mountains. Cross the aborted M3 motorway, and continue past the Lakeside golf course. The road becomes somewhat steeper and curves to the right giving you perhaps a short-lived push from the southeaster. Turn left at the 'Ou Kaapseweg M64' sign, select your lowest gear (even if you don't need it yet) and start a wicked climb. About 1,1 km ahead there's a hairpin bend which has claimed many an incautious descender.

After the hairpin you will feel the southeaster, which will progressively worsen as you climb and as you tire. This hill is not terribly steep but is 3,5 km long and can be demoralizing for all but the super-fit. At certain times of the year the morning sun shines parallel with the gradient and straight in your eyes, so ride on the other side of the road to avoid being run down by sun-blinded motorists behind. Take great care at the bend at the top, which places you at right angles to the prevailing summer winds. A sudden gust can knock you over if you are not careful.

Now you've conquered the Steenberg, and the view all around is quite magnificent. On the right ahead there's an excellent view-site with parking, and a little further on is the main entrance to Silvermine Nature Reserve which, for a 2 km side-trip, provides an idyllic spot for a lakeside breakfast.

The land to the left has a concentration of plant species that for months on end have clusters of white flowers which make them look snow-covered. After the summit is reached the route bears left past the southern (minor) entrance to the reserve. This entrance gives access to Higher and Lower Steenberg peaks and to the lovely picnic waterfall near the head of Silvermine River, which runs into the sea at the Clovelly corner. After the entrance the long descent begins; it can be very fast but the road has a coarse surface and the shoulders are potholed in places.

Near the top, (and before you gain speed) look over on the left – black eagles can sometimes be seen soaring in the early morning just above the rough outline of Wolfkop where they may roost (the mountain doesn't seem remote enough for a nest).

About 2,2 km from the summit, just after a long left bend, spot the 'Zilvermyn' notice pointing to an old prospecting shaft at the roadside. All that can be seen today is an insignificant hole with water in the bottom. It's not clear if any silver was ever found, although there is a record of Rijckloff van Goens, governor-general of the Netherlands East Indies, visiting the 'silver mine workings' in 1682 with Simon van der Stel.

In the dip at the bottom of the hill is a crossroads. A right turn here would take you past Silvermine retirement village to Noordhoek; left is a bad sand road leading to the Clovelly Country Club through an area of alien bush sprinkled with squatters who eke out a precarious existence selling braai wood at the roadside. Climb out of the dip and treat yourself to a fine view across Noordhoek beach to Kommetjie and the Atlantic. There's a left hairpin followed by another lengthy and quite steep descent down to the right turn for the service station and mini-supermarket from where you started off.

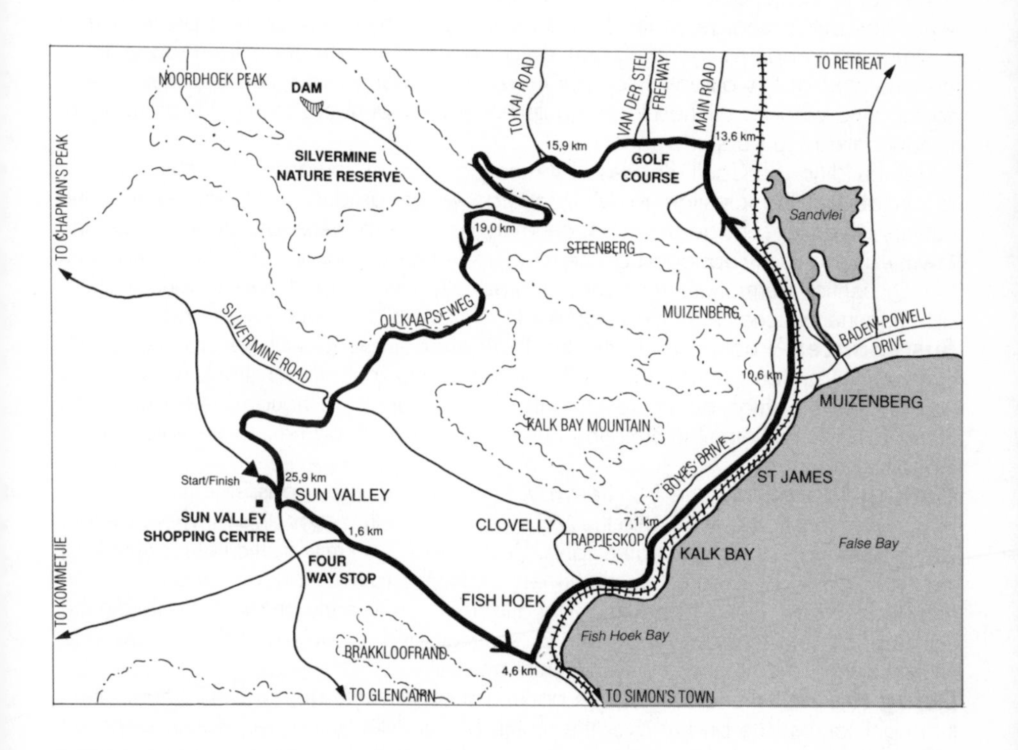

18 Muizenberg to Strandfontein

Features: This is a very short ride with no hills. It provides an opportunity to challenge the southeaster head-on in summer, and/or to practise sprint and interval training while enjoying bracing fresh air and refreshing yourself with a swim at the end. The route is congested in summer and a little lonely in winter, and is not ideal for families.
Grade and distance: A1; 16 km; 30 to 60 minutes, according to the wind.
Best times: Wind or no wind, there is heavy and inconsiderate traffic along here in summer, particularly at weekends, unless you ride at first light when the sight of the sunrise provides compensation for shortage of sleep. Strong winter winds seem to acquire a peculiar gustiness along this stretch and make cycling irritating and potentially dangerous. Wind-free winter afternoons are often very pleasant, but remember the sun sinks early.
Special information: If you normally ride an ATB, you can deviate onto the beach at numerous points along here. When the tide's out there are often long stretches of firm sand a few metres above the water's edge. Avoid struggling through deep sand – the sand sticks to your wheels, from where it falls onto your chain and gears.

The name Muizenberg may derive (records don't agree) from that of Wynand Muijs, who was put in charge of the fortified cattle post there (established pre-1740). It became known as *Muijsenburg* (not -berg). At that time, the road from Cape Town degenerated at this outpost into a narrow track among rocks and marshes so that southbound wagons still had to be hauled over the Steenberg mountains along what is now called Ou Kaapseweg.

The building of Cecil Rhodes' little cottage round towards St James brought respectability and prestige to Muizenberg, which gradually blossomed into the country's premier seaside resort – it certainly has superb, very safe beaches. But the town was eventually upstaged by the wind-free Atlantic beaches of Clifton, and, with few influential permanent residents, it gradually deteriorated into a forlorn state, although the beaches remained popular for day visits by beach lovers and surfers.
Sustenance: At both ends of this trip there are complexes with several restaurants that keep long hours (Strandfontein Pavilion and Muizenberg Pavilion). Muizenberg now has several high quality restaurants of good repute, although we haven't tried them. Consult the helpful Information Bureau in Atlantic Road next to the library, near the railway bridge.
Getting there: Take the N2 freeway, keep right where it passes Groote Schuur Hospital so that you split off onto the M3 motorway south. Follow this to where it ends, turn left then right at the next traffic lights. Drive about 3,5 km to traffic lights controlling the Atlantic Road junction. Turn down left, under the railway bridge, and then right, into Beach Road. Plenty of parking is available if you're early or late enough (but the parking lots are chock-a-block during summer and at weekends). The train to Muizenberg is the natural and convenient alternative.
Doing the ride: Cycle out of the parking area towards distant Devil's Peak, then turn right, across the bridge over the mouth of Sandvlei, into Royal Road. Continue along this road, which, later in the day, is often lined with fish vendors. Half a kilometre from the bridge is a traffic circle connecting Prince George Drive on the left and Sunrise Beach on the right. Go halfway round and continue along the coastal road, which is

called Baden-Powell Drive from this point onwards.

Just over 250 m along you'll pass the entrance to the Coastal Park on the left, and then, after another 800 m, a parking lot on the right with a takeaway kiosk which seldom seems to be open. About 3 km from the Sunrise circle is an entrance to the sewage processing works. By telephoning the City Engineer's Department you can get permission to enter the area for bird-watching. The large settling dams (which are not malodorous) attract numerous species of resident and migratory birds.

The road curves gently to the right until it is barely 20 m from the beach, and you'll see a row of low pillars erected in a wholly futile attempt to stop sand blowing across the road. From here you get inspiring views across False Bay to Cape Hangklip and Cape Point. In olden times, ships from the East sometimes turned northwards after passing Hangklip, thinking they had rounded the Cape. They then found themselves trapped in this 'false' bay, unable to sail free against the southeaster.

Along the next 4 km just about all you'll see inland are fynbos dunes, which, in summer, are frequently set on fire by wind-blown cigarette butts carelessly tossed out of car windows. The dunes are particularly high near where the Pelican Park area is being developed. When you reach the traffic lights, turn right and ride the short distance down to the Strandfontein Pavilion which has extensive modern facilities, including very good takeaway outlets.

If it's still early enough for the roads to be quiet, and if the southeaster's blowing, try some speed trials on your way back. If your bike has a cycling computer fitted you may be astonished to find that during a burst of real effort you can get up to speeds of 60-70 km/h – at least while the wind's behind you!

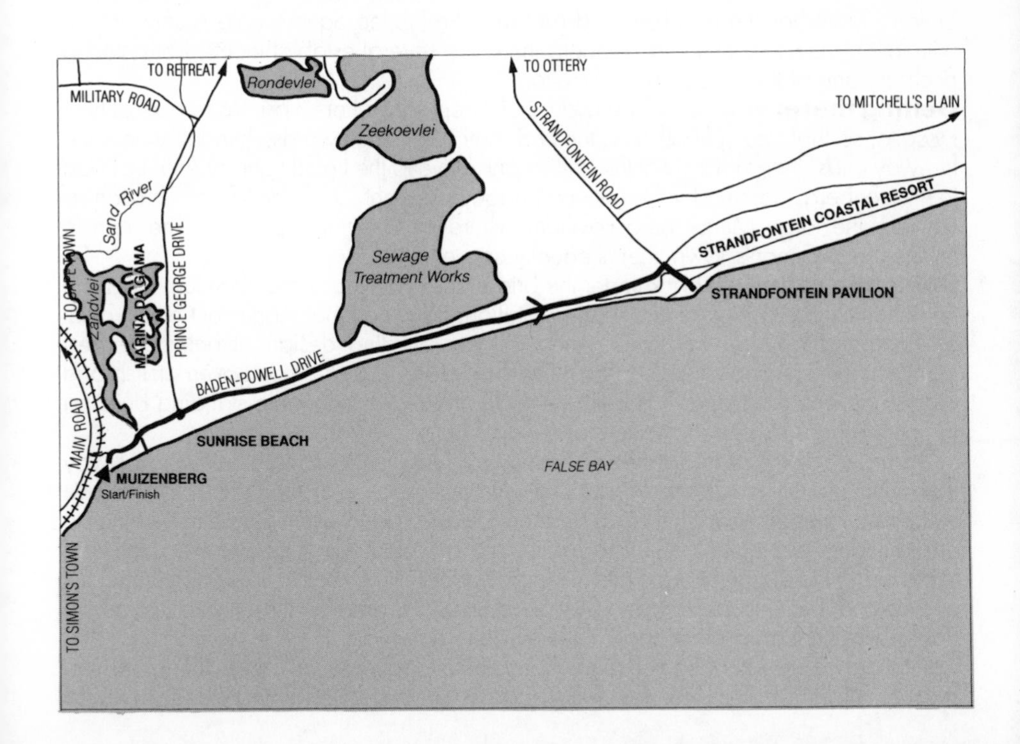

19 Muizenberg to Simon's Town

Features: A very easy ride with numerous historically interesting things to see. If you go at the recommended time there should be a wonderful sunrise. Security is good and the ride is suitable for families, provided you pick a time when traffic is light and look out for obstructions on the road surface.
Grade and distance: B1; 24 km round trip; 60 minutes riding time.
Best times: This is a magnificent, if slightly chilly, early morning ride for most weekends other than winter, when it's too dark to do the ride before the traffic gets heavy. The St James/Kalk Bay section is not much affected by the southeaster, but the section from Clovelly onwards will make fairly stiff going against a strong summer wind. Evenings are not so good – there is heavy holiday traffic in summer and in winter the light goes early.
Special information: The road from Muizenberg to Clovelly is quite narrow with high kerbs, almost invisible bumps, much broken glass in the gutters, and numerous manhole covers projecting above or sunk below the surface – if you hit one hard you may buckle a rim as well as burst a tyre. If you ride when it's quiet you can stay well away from the kerb and be free to pick your way past the obstructions.
Sustenance: Numerous acceptable possibilities. Consider the excellent Sunday midday fish braai at the Brass Bell on your way back. There's the Copper Creek Spur in Fish Hoek and fine takeaways (and sit-down meals) at François in Fish Hoek. Glencairn has Dixies, a Dutch/Indonesian restaurant (which we have not tried). Simon's Town has the excellent Lord Nelson. The Jubilee Square café is satisfactory, with lovely views. Back in Muizenberg there are several establishments, from pleb to posh; try one of the places in the Pavilion.
Getting there: Take the N2 freeway, then keep right where it passes Groote Schuur Hospital so that you split off onto the M3 motorway southwards. Turn left where the freeway ends, then turn right at the traffic light. Drive to the traffic lights at Atlantic Road in Muizenberg; pass under the railway bridge; turn right into Beach Road as soon as you see the large Muizenberg Pavilion, where there's ample parking. The train to Muizenberg (Simon's Town line) is equally convenient.
Doing the ride: Ride back under the bridge the way you came, then turn left at the traffic light. Take a look at Muizenberg station; it's a national monument and typical of the grand days of rail travel when railway building design attracted the best architects. Almost opposite is De Post Huys, built in 1673 by the then governor, Ijsbrand Goske, as a lookout post. It is believed to be the oldest habitable standing building in South Africa; it's open to visitors at certain hours.

On the left, on the seaward side of the railway, runs the pleasant pedestrian walkway from Muizenberg to St James. About 400 m from the station on the right is an attractive building with (real) Spanish tiles; this is the Natale Labia museum where interesting art displays are held quite often. The Labias are a well-known Cape family, Countess Labia being the daughter of the late mining magnate Sir J.B. Robinson. (Another famous and colourful mining personality, Sir Abe Bailey, is buried on the hillside just below Boyes Drive approximately above where you're now riding).

Another 400 m will bring you to the Rhodes Cottage museum. This building was the seaside retreat of Cecil Rhodes, whose presence is credited with having launched

Muizenberg early this century as a holiday resort for well-heeled inlanders. Rhodes died here, and the museum, open daily, contains many fascinating items associated with this remarkable man.

Pass St James station on the left, formerly the site of a very old Roman Catholic church built mainly for the pioneering Filipino fishermen of Kalk Bay, too many of whom had drowned while sailing or rowing across to Simon's Town for church on Sundays. After the railway was extended beyond Muizenberg a great emotional and tactical battle was fought to get the railway authorities, who found the church in the way of their planned new station, to rebuild the church on an alternative site, which, eventually, they did.

Notice the St James Post Office; like its Muizenberg counterpart it has a lovely mosaic on its outside wall. St James has a small wind-free beach and a nice tidal pool, packed so full in summer that it's hard to see the water. Further down on the right is the four-star St James Hotel, once owned by a son of John Paul Getty, the American oil tycoon who was one of the world's richest men in his day.

The next station is that of Kalk Bay, which is unique among South African railway stations in having a privately-rented (and extremely popular) public bar and restaurant complex – the Brass Bell – from which delightful vistas of the Kalk Bay fishing harbour soothe the patrons.

The people of Kalk Bay are remarkable, being blends of indigenous South African groups with immigrant Spanish, Portuguese, Dutch and other European nationalities as well as Filipinos. If you detour into the harbour when the fishing boats are coming in you'll hear an extraordinary semi-Afrikaans dialect and may notice that the fish are still auctioned in 'bobs', (slang for shilling), as they were when sterling was still the South African currency.

A short distance beyond the station there's a traffic light to control the route to Boyes Drive, and then the harbour entrance halfway up the next hill. Opposite is a Bible college and then you'll be round the corner with, if it's blowing, the southeaster briefly behind you. The road is wider and clearer here and you'll undulate past the Clovelly Station, which the railway authorities are gradually closing down, to the fury of local residents. It used to carry a notice forbidding fishing from the platforms – surely the only railway station in the world to do so!

Ride round the long wrongly-banked left bend, scene of innumerable vehicle crashes, into the straight section leading past the new slab-sided brick police station on the right into Fish Hoek – a little town that exemplifies how underplanned ribbon development can spoil the potential of a beautiful location.

There's a bicycle shop (Regal Cycles) on the right-hand side of the main road as you ride through. At the far end, you can detour to the left at the traffic lights to enjoy the beach, which, in its little corner, is sheltered from all but the most violent southeasters. Our ride continues through the lights and bears left past the traffic circle, up a short hill, and levels out next to the sea just short of Sunny Cove station. There are fine views across False Bay to the Hottentots Holland mountains while up above you is Elsies Peak; no one seems to know who Elsie or Elsa was.

If it's blowing, the full force of the southeaster may now attack you as you ride along a good surface marred by occasional large bumps, towards Glencairn. Notice the sheer-sided old quarry on your right. Rock from this quarry was used widely for building in these parts, mostly for the attractive stone buildings of Simon's Town – but not for the harbour wall, the blocks for which were quarried above Simon's Town itself. Read the 'salient dates' information on the roadside billboard announcing Simon's Town on the left, just before the road enjoys a brief down run.

Notice the right turn, a long and tiring uphill through the Glencairn valley. Beware of strongly blowing sand as you pass the small Glencairn beach much favoured by skilled boardsailors when the summer winds are blowing. Pass Glencairn Hotel (right), ascend a minor incline, note Glencairn station on the left, Dixies restaurant on the right, then the cemetery, followed by the fish oil refinery from which, in winter or on still days, an appalling stench emanates. If the tide's low, notice the large lump of metal just offshore; this is the cylinder block of a naval collier, *Clan Stuart,* which dragged its anchors and was wrecked in 1914 or 1917 (accounts vary).

At the next traffic lights you have the option of turning right into Dido Valley Road and visiting (if it's not Sunday) Topstones, which claims to be the world's largest producer of polished gemstones, and Mineral World, its associated gift shop which runs a 'scratch patch' where visitors can rummage for gemstones.

Meanwhile ride straight on and past the naval gun emplacement, which nowadays is used only (and seldom) for training. The Fire Station and Traffic Department are on the right as you cruise along the wide smooth road past the station and into Simon's Town proper. Turn back anywhere you like, or consider picking up a brochure from the Information Office next to The Residency on the left so as to take an instructive wander through this historical town.

On your way back, if you rode very early, you may see great numbers of keen cyclists training or racing along this much-favoured stretch.

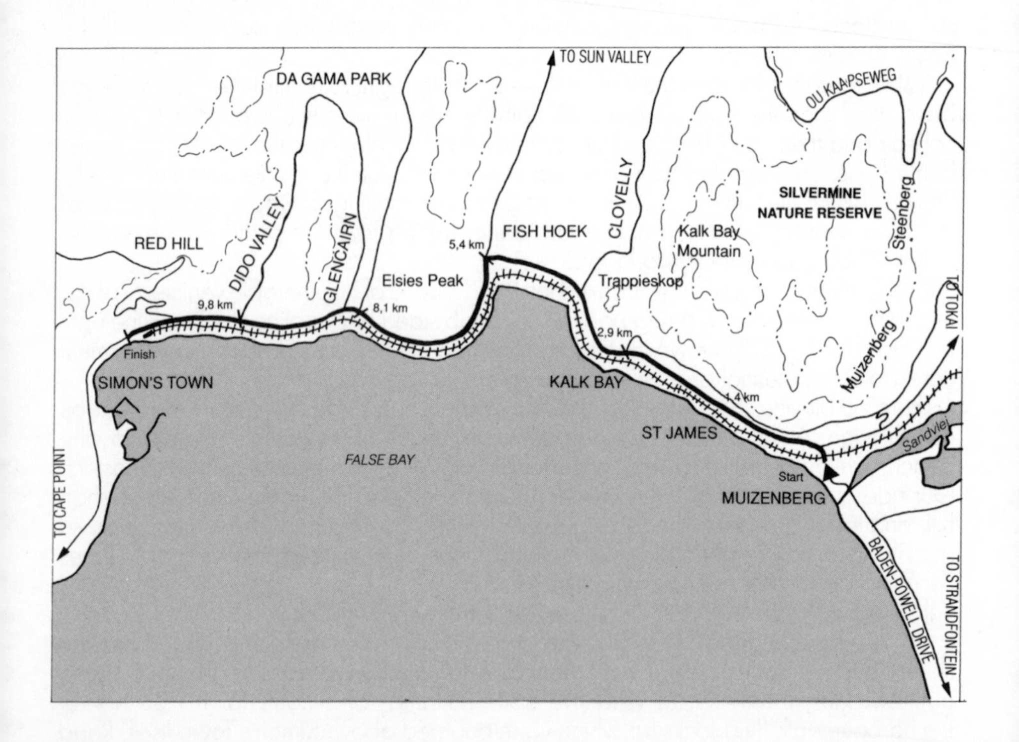

20 Glencairn to Scarborough

Features: This is quite a tough ride; extremely scenic, but with two daunting hills, one of which can be made much nastier by the southeaster. Not a good setting for conversations on the move, so better suited to solo riders or perhaps to two people of matching physical ability.
Grade and distance: C3; 30 km; 90 minutes to two hours.
Best times: Commuter traffic is not a great problem here. Early summer mornings are ideal, enabling you to take in a marvellous sunrise, beat the heat, and endure the southeaster before it stiffens later in the day. Alternatively, you can start in the late afternoon and enjoy the sunset. However, this may mean that you have to travel the last few kilometres in the dark.
Special information: When you ride up (or down) Red Hill you may have to dismount if you meet a truck or bus on one of the several hairpin bends. These long vehicles need the whole road to effect the change of direction, and occasionally an inexperienced driver gets stuck diagonally across the road.

Be cautious about taking photos in the Red Hill area. Although the naval installations are well known to thousands of national servicemen, taking photographs is strictly forbidden and an innocent tourist who does so can be arrested. The authorities are understandably sensitive: some years ago, not long after the Navy's super-secret underground nerve centre at Silvermine had been commissioned, East German television broadcast an informative 'tour' of the installations!
Sustenance: You're on your own! There are no restaurants or cafés along the route. If you set off in the early morning, Camel Rock restaurant will not be open by the time you pass. Your best bet is Dixies, a pleasantly sited Dutch/Indonesian restaurant just past the end of your ride. You can extend the ride to include Kommetjie and its shops, but there too nothing will be open if you're riding early enough to see a summer sunrise.
Getting there: Take the N2 freeway, then where it passes Groote Schuur Hospital keep right so that you can follow the M3 split southwards. Where it ends, turn left and drive down to Main Road. Turn right and follow various Muizenberg/Fish Hoek/Simon's Town signs along the (M4) coastal road. Park in one of the beach-side areas near Glencairn Beach (the next beach after Fish Hoek). Going by train is actually easier – just buy a ticket to Glencairn (Simon's Town line).
Doing the ride: Set off southwards from Glencairn, supposedly named after an immigrant Scot from Glen Cairn who was fond of wandering around the area playing his bagpipes. Ride towards Simon's Town, up a short hill, past the station, noting Shelley Beach and the tidal pool. If you came by train or parked near the station you will already have passed Glen Road, which leads past the hotel (friendly bar customers, often including interesting old salts retired from the navy) and up the Glencairn valley.

Dixies is on your right (there is a public telephone if you need one). Ride past the cemetery and the malodorous Marine Oil Refinery (somewhat shortsightedly displaying its association with a well-known food group). Notice the wreck of the *Clan Stuart* offshore. Climb slightly, cross the Dido Valley traffic lights, ride past the naval gun emplacement, and appreciate your last 400 m of easy riding for some time.

Turn right at the 'Scarborough via Red Hill' sign. The first 500 m or so is bumpy and pretty steep, to the first of several hairpin bends. After that it's 400 m to the next hairpin (left turn). If you need to rest here the interesting view of Simon's Town will occupy you. Renew the attack; after 400 m the road takes a sharp left turn over a stream, and there is a tumble of rocks and bush on both sides of it.

Struggle on uphill for half a kilometre, to a right-hand hairpin that offers a fine view back towards Muizenberg. There is a sharp right bend 500 m further; don't wobble into the deep storm-water gutter against the rocks.

Keep an eye on the time – you don't want to miss the sunrise after all this effort.

There is a 900 m stretch, consistently steep, before the final hairpin (left) but even this is not yet the top. The best viewing spot for the sunrise is on the left, but another 1,7 km of uphill riding is needed to reach the top. Here, for the price of a great buffeting if the wind's blowing hard, you'll be rewarded with a truly splendid panorama over the Atlantic and across the Cape of Good Hope Nature Reserve to Cape Point (which, by the way, is not the southernmost tip of Africa, as so many visitors assume).

After all your hard work you can now enjoy a nice fast 2,5 km downhill, but be careful of the sharp bends, rough surface, and the possibility of an early driver thinking it's safe to take up the whole road for cornering. The last left-hand bend is particularly steep, but after that the gradient eases as you approach the junction for turning right towards Scarborough. It's still downhill enough to ride at a good speed; pass Koggelfontein road maintenance depot, then continue your downward sweeps for some 800 m into Scarborough.

The first left turn is 400 m into the village and leads to the beach and a public telephone. The beach end of this road is very near the northernmost tip of the nature reserve, at a point known as Schuster's Bay – doubtless because Schuster's farm and Schustersrivier lie close by. Another 400 m will bring you to the famous Camel Rock, with its namesake restaurant opposite.

From 450 m beyond the village the road becomes bumpy, narrow and cold with frequent early morning mists. The mountain side is known as Misty Cliffs, and tiny plots there change hands for incredibly high prices considering their remoteness and complete lack of services. However the solitude, clean beach, glorious sunsets, magnificent surfing and boardsailing seem to be compensatory attractions. Notice the scattered Witsand holiday houses on the beach side of the road. Across the bay are the jetty and dismal little buildings for the Die Eiland crayfishermen.

Over the next 1,6 km the road rises steadily and moves a little inland, passing a picnic spot to the left which gets choked with busloads of happy patrons over fine weekends. A little way ahead you'll come to a junction where you must turn right into Slangkop Road, probably named after Slangkoppunt and its famous lighthouse at nearby Kommetjie (which you can reach by turning left at this point).

Slangkop Road rises for half a kilometre to a vantage point giving impressive views across to Noordhoek and Hout Bay. The road is wide but coarse-surfaced, and there is a fast 2 km descent to the T-junction with the Fish-Hoek/Kommetjie Road. Turn right here and perhaps encounter the southeaster head-on. This often contrary wind is demoralizing for the tiring Argus Cycle Tour participants battling along this rather dreary stretch of road from Kommetjie.

The Ocean View turn-off lies 500 m ahead on the right. Pass by this then keep grinding along the gum-tree-lined stretch for 4,4 km to the four-way stop street. The last 700 m of this section is slightly downhill and gives you a chance to gather strength for the next long hill. Turn right at the stop street, towards Glencairn. It's a long hill, nearly 2 km, and you will find the ascent very hot in summer. If the southeaster's blowing, the strength of it increases towards the top – here it may be so strong that it stops you in your tracks. Notice on your way up the land scars made by the controversial Serina kaolin mining establishment.

For your reward you now have a 3 km run down the Glencairn valley, very fast and exciting if the wind allows it, and the road is wide and smooth with no surprises. Up on the left is Elsies (or Elsas) Peak, more than 300 m high, which separates you from Fish Hoek.

Before you get too far down the hill you'll see Da Gama Park, a housing project on the plateau atop the mountain and originally developed for S.A. Navy personnel. Also on the right, but lower down, you can spot the buildings of the original farms Welcome (not Welkom) and Oaklands, established by the well-known Brand family (the family of Johannes Brand, a one-time president of the Orange Free State, although he was born near Richmond, not in Glencairn!).

At the bottom of the hill turn right and head for car and home – perhaps after a swim from the safe and uncrowded Glencairn Beach.

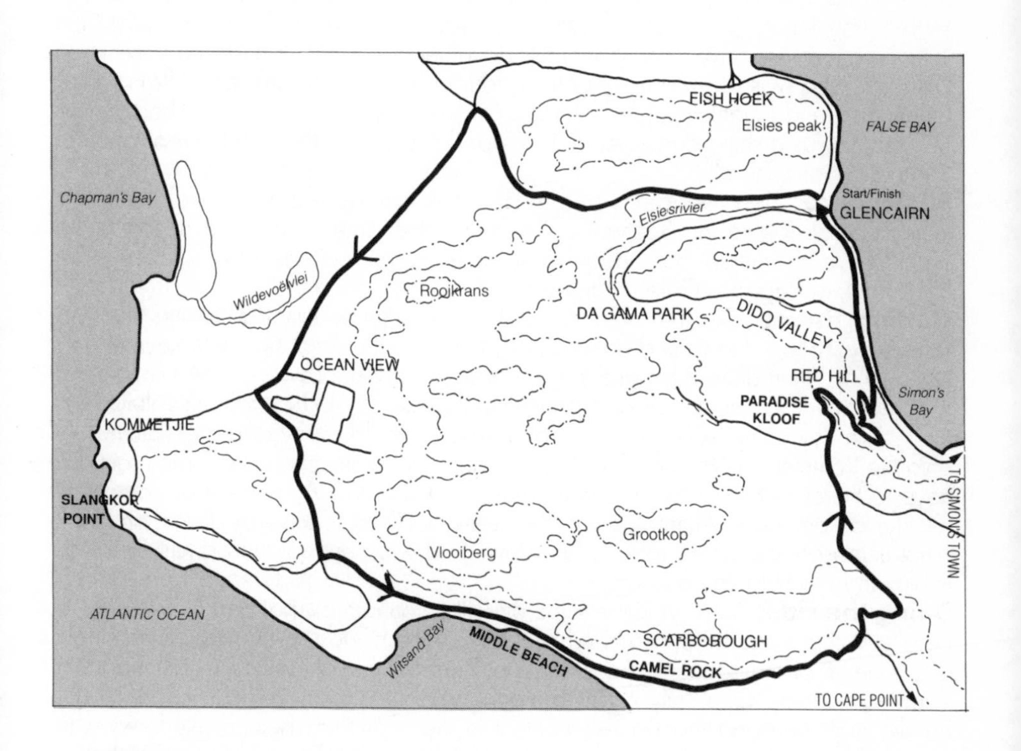

21 The Imhoff/Slangkop Circuit

Features: Not many cyclists ride this pleasant seaside circuit which is largely sheltered from the southeaster and offers glorious sunsets. Kommetjie is a quiet district so this ride suits riders unaccustomed to traffic. Parts of route are lonely, especially during the week, and so the ride might not be suitable for timid solo riders.
Grade and distance: A3; 12 km (not including detours); 45 minutes riding time.
Best times: A strong northwester provides the only unpleasant conditions for this ride, although if you can get there before the wind starts to blow strongly, while the cold front is still offshore, the cloud effects can be stunning. Over summer weekends the Soetwater stretch is filled with milling crowds and hired buses, but at most other times the whole route is quiet.
Special information: Kommetjie village developed comparatively recently on a large tract of land originally granted in 1743 to widow Johanna Russouw by her suspected admirer, the governor-general of the Netherlands East Indies, Baron Gustaf Willem van Imhoff. Some records refer to Russouw's widow as Christina Diemer, but this name seems to have been that of her daughter or daughter's husband (Christiaan Diemer?) who was given a neighbouring farm, still known as Imhoff's Gift. In 1802 Johanna's granddaughter married John Osmond, an astute opportunist who had arrived in False Bay as a ship's carpenter in 1899 and eventually acquired the reputation of 'King of Simon's Town'.
Sustenance: Over weekends and in the peak holiday season several indifferent kiosks operate along the Soetwater stretch. At other times you should resort to the superette or to simple but adequate establishments such as Mike's Continental Restaurant, or Papados Cafe in Kirsten Road.
Getting there: Take the N2 and split to the right where it becomes the M3 motorway. Follow it to its end at Steenberg Road. Turn right at sign 'Ou Kaapseweg M42/M64' then drive 2 km and turn left at sign 'Ou Kaapseweg M64'. Follow this road right over the mountains and down into the Fish Hoek/Noordhoek valley. Pass the Pick 'n Pay complex on your right and drive to the four-way stop street. Turn right onto the Kommetjie Main Road (M65) and drive to Kommetjie; park. Train users will have to travel to Fish Hoek and then take an Ocean View bus (few) or combi-taxi (plenty) to Kommetjie. Alternatively cycle the extra 10 km (each way) from Fish Hoek – not unreasonable as the road is fairly level and whichever of the prevailing winds is blowing will help you one way.
Doing the ride: Press off in the same direction you came. The road curves around parallel with the seashore then winds steadily up the hillside, presenting increasingly good views of the sea and the Slangkop Point lighthouse, which is an important shipping beacon. Originally it was a marine wireless station, established in 1910, but the high iron and manganese content in the mountains behind interfered with transmission and the installation was moved in 1937 to the Cape Flats. The lighthouse was commissioned only in 1919 (non-maritime records give the dates 1913 and 1914); it is a prefabricated steel tower identical with the one on Dassen Island and has a 16,75 million candlepower light which is second only to Cape Point among southern African lighthouses.

Slangkop itself, up on your left, is only 177 m high, but it presents some dangerous bends for *descending* cyclists and is therefore closed to motor traffic for the Argus Cycle Tour. The crest of the road is reached 1,5 km from the village and then winds comfortably down a fairly narrow and very coarse-surfaced road with several well-sited pull-offs for viewing. Notice the strange bands running out from the shore – these are caused by strip-harvesting of kelp for conversion into fertilizer and agar. On weekdays you can often see divers going in at low tide to chop off the kelp along the sea bottom. The severed plants float to the surface and the incoming tide washes them onto the beach for gathering and processing.

About 1,7 km from the crest the road levels and bends left to provide a fine view southwards down the peninsula past Scarborough. At the upcoming crossroads turn right into Wireless Road (there is another Wireless Road in Kommetjie itself). After 250 m on the level the road (much smoother here) goes downhill, gradually turning westwards until, about 1,25 km from the crossroads, there is a left turn. This takes you down to a bumpy gravelled parking lot offering good views of the coastal road along Witsand Bay towards Scarborough. From here you can walk across to the dismal looking buildings and jetty of the crayfishery at Die Eiland – nearly washed away in 1973 when a winter spring tide was forced higher by a strong westerly gale.

Return to the Wireless Road junction and consider a 3,5 km detour (each way) into Soetwater (Sweetwater) recreational area. During the week and out of season the gates are unmanned, but at other times the place is open for long hours at a small entrance charge. There are neatly clipped hedges to keep sand off the nice smooth road, which is provided with extensive parking areas and kiosks. There is a small beach section amid the rocks and a good tidal pool (freezing cold). At the far end there is a caravan park and then gates (permanently closed) leading to the lighthouse and back along rough Lighthouse Road into Kommetjie.

Instead of or after the detour, head back up the Wireless Road hill and cross over the Witsand Road intersection into Slangkop Road. The surface here is quite rough but wide, and 600 m takes you to the crest alongside Kleinberg on your right. From here, although only 140 m up, you get fine views across to Hout Bay, the Sentinel, Chapman's Peak, and Constantiaberg. The road descends along a moderate gradient to join the Kommetjie Main Road you drove along. About halfway down the hill is the turn-off to Ocean View, named after an old farm located just to the right, back where Slangkop Road begins.

Turn left at the junction, which is approximately in the middle of the original Imhoff's Gift farm. Some of the later farm buildings are set back a little way on the north side of the road – have a look as you drive home. The southeaster will blow you nicely along through the gum-lined road into the village. Turn right into Kirsten Road (the second one at right angles) and go down to the Benning Road T-junction. Turn left and pass the end of Long Beach where you can watch the surfers. You might see a couple of really daring ones challenging the world-famous Outer Kom break if you have binoculars. Notice the old milkwood trees, carefully protected by law and local pride.

You now have to turn left into Gladiolus Road, right into Afrikaner Road, then left into Beach Road which you can follow around 'Die Kom', Dutch for a shallow pan – hence 'Kommetjie' for the natural tidal pool which is the central feature of the village and offers a somewhat warmer dip (in summer) than the sea. Notice the sad little plaque on one of the benches – it commemorates Petty Officer 'Willem van die Diep' Smith who perished in the inexcusable fair weather collision between the naval vessels *President Kruger* (which sank) and *Tafelberg* a few years ago.

The road curves left into Van Imhoff Avenue which intersects the main road about 300 m down, approximately where you started from. If you still have time and energy, an interesting detour is to go back into the village and find Rubbi Street running up to the right. At its end is a tiny stone chapel built in memory of Giuseppe ('Joseph') Rubbi, an Italian immigrant of fine character who established a well-known building business in Cape Town. The chapel is always open and with its commanding views across Chapman's Bay is a serene place for meditating.

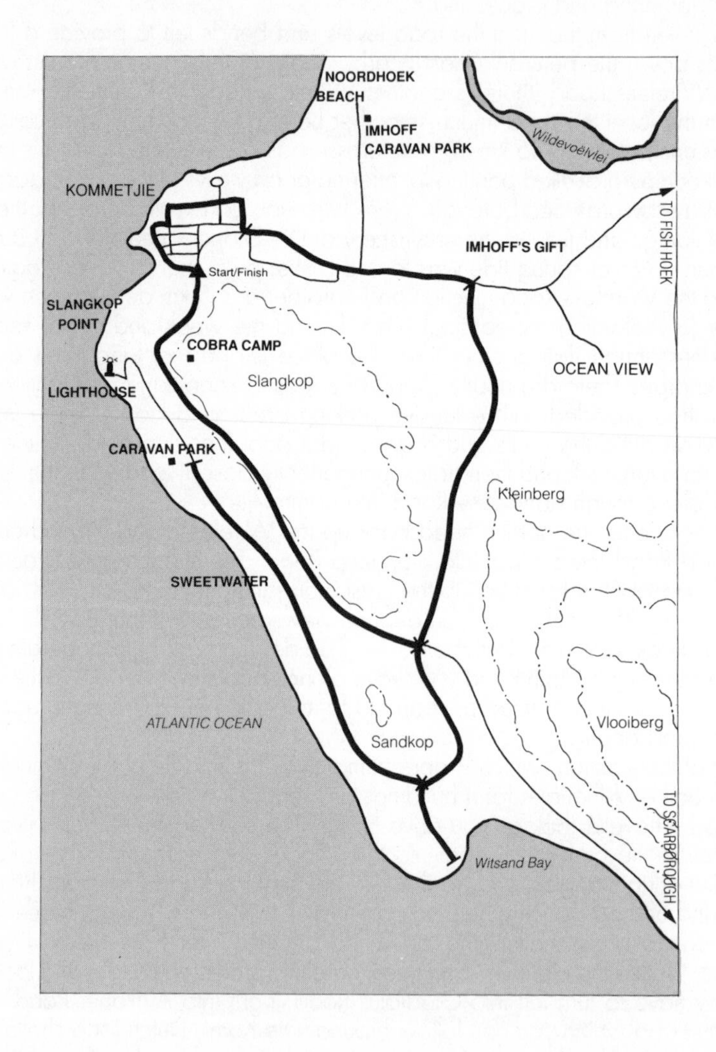

22 Simon's Town and Smitswinkel Bay

Features: A bracing hilly ride (but not all uphill) which provides you with a chance to enjoy historic Simon's Town and many fine False Bay views. The wind is usually blowing in one direction or the other. Family members should be fairly well matched in fitness. Some steep descents – not suitable for novices. Very convenient for access by train.
Grade and distance: C3; 28 km; 90 minutes riding time.
Best times: In clear weather, early enough to watch the sunrise over False Bay, preferably in summer so that you can enjoy it before the traffic increases. Avoid severe southeasters or winter northwesters.
Special information: Popular circuit for keen cyclists training; watch their technique. If you wish, you can take the opportunity to browse after breakfast in the outstanding and richly historic Simon's Town Museum. Some steep descents; check your brakes.
Sustenance: Several good and pleasant places in Simon's Town after your return, including Lord Nelson, Blue Lantern, Jubilee Square tea room.
Getting there: Take the N2 freeway, then keep right where it passes Groote Schuur Hospital so that you split off onto the M3 motorway south. At the end of it, follow signs saying successively Lakeside, Muizenberg, Fish Hoek, Simon's Town. Park just before the Simon's Town station in the Long Beach parking lot (seaward side).
Doing the ride: Leave the parking lot or the station and turn left towards the town. Either after your ride, or some other time, you should walk through this old naval port with a guidebook (obtainable from the Information Centre). Many of the buildings are national monuments, and even those that aren't are often steeped in history.

Many of the buildings have explanatory plaques on their street-facing walls. If you're not rushing along to catch the sunrise, stop and take a look at some of these.

Just after the station you'll pass the grand old green and white Admiralty House and, 150 m further on, Studland on the right. The latter is South Africa's oldest surviving purpose-built wine house and was put up by winemaker J.P. Eksteen in 1797 (the present name was acquired nearly a century later). Read all about these places in the guidebook. Further ahead on the left is The Residency, which you can take a closer look at by turning down towards the Information Centre and museum.

The long wall on the left of the main road protects part of the naval base. Behind the wall you can see St George's, the oldest Anglican church in southern Africa; it was established on the upper floor of a naval mast-storage house and is open to visitors. The road descends past the naval base entrance and passes the ramp leading to the Town Pier, where one can sometimes see the big-game sport fishing boats landing their catches.

The small modern building on the left is the post office, and next to it is Jubilee Square with its statue of Able Seaman Just Nuisance, a Great Dane which gained world-wide fame among naval men during World War II for his ability to escort inebriated sailors back to base.

The long wall on the right about 100 m further on fronts a building which was originally the naval hospital. Slightly further on is the entrance to the naval dockyard. If you detour left at the end of the naval wall you'll find the Martello Tower museum. It was built in 1796 and may be the only such tower in good condition surviving in the world. Nearby, up on the right, is a cemetery with hundreds of intriguing headstone inscriptions indicating the sad results of daring and disaster in centuries past. On the seaward side of the road almost opposite is the naval roll-of-honour memorial.

The crest of the next rise in the road gives the first of many sweeping views of False Bay and is also the start of a bumpy section. If you're unlucky, it's also where the southeaster starts to buffet you. If you're keen on snorkelling there are numerous interesting rocky inlets worth exploring between here and the point just before the road finally turns inland.

Cruise along the next 2 km noticing the golf course, Blue Lantern restaurant, Oatlands holiday camp and the Cape Times Fresh Air Camp at Froggy Pond. After these the road begins to rise steadily with mixed smooth and bumpy sections.

Just after the Black Marlin restaurant comes a steepish descent to Miller's Point where there's a skiboat launching slip approximately on the site of Edmund Miller's whaling station, built in 1828.

For almost another 2 km the road offers some good occasional views of Cape Point and is undulating or flat, giving you a chance to gather strength for a short stiff climb to Partridge Point followed not long after by a kilometre-long climb past Smitswinkel Bay to the Cape Point Nature Reserve turn-off. The bay is said to be named for the Bellows and Anvil rocks, but as these are far away (off Cape Point) this seems improbable. An official British naval chart of 1795 shows 'Great Smith's Winkle Bay' and 'Little Smith's Winkle Bay'. Quite possibly Smith and Smith junior had separate farms here and gathered shellfish (periwinkles**?**).

Partridge Point is possibly the best place from which to view the False Bay sunrise. Smitswinkel Bay marks the boundary of a marine reserve encircling Cape Point almost to Scarborough on the other side of the peninsula. This stretch is lonely in the early mornings but its only real potential danger comes from baboons. They appear from nowhere if you look like you're going to picnic. Never feed them – it encourages them to grab picnickers' food, and they can be dangerously possessive if one tries to grab it back.

The Smitswinkelvallei climb is a strategic stretch for Argus Cycle Tour participants. The top riders try to break away from the rest of the pack here, hopefully shaking off the less fit to gain a psychological advantage by the time they reach the 50 km mark at the top of the hill.

Once you're over the top, and if you've been wearied earlier by the southeaster, the wind will help you on the ride through the gum-tree-lined George's Valley for more than 8 km to the Scarborough/Red Hill junction. There's a growing vista of the Atlantic Ocean beyond the nature reserve on the left, and a few old and rather bleak-looking farm houses on the attractive mountain slopes of Klaasjagersberg to the right. In order, the farms are Bonne Attente, Wychwood, Shirwill and Happy Valley.

From the Red Hill junction you're in for a hard climb up a rather rough and twisty road. However it's wide, shady and sheltered from the southeaster – but not from the winter northwester. The gradient eases after about 2 km then runs down some 1,7 km to the first of Red Hill's hairpin bends. But pull off just before this to a lay-by on the right which gives a magnificent view across False Bay with a miniaturized Simon's Town below you. Had you done the ride from the opposite direction this would have been the best spot for a view of the sunrise, but it's a long steep ascent that is somewhat off-putting in the pre-dawn gloom.

Ride down Red Hill with extreme caution, especially if midday is approaching. The road is quite narrow, very steep in places, has several acute hairpin bends and is surprisingly heavily used by buses and naval trucks.

Turn right at the bottom of the hill and follow the main road past the Fire Station and Traffic Department to your starting point.

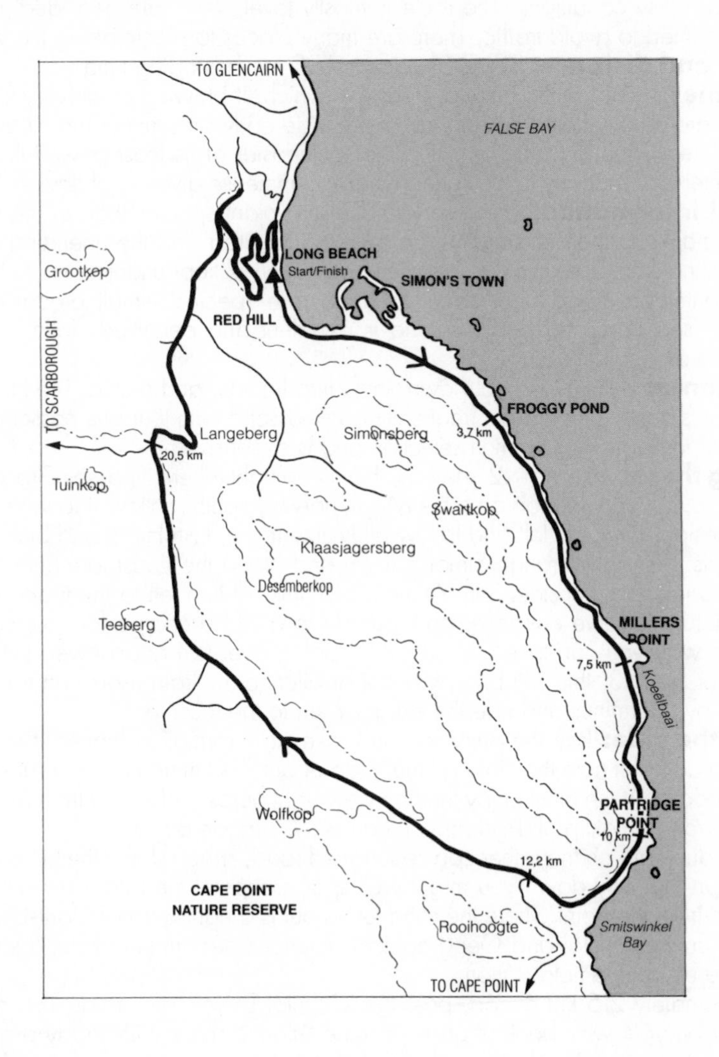

23 Cape Point

Features: A peaceful refreshing ride – ideal for those who spend the week in crowded, noisy conditions. The route is mostly level, very safe and ideal for family groups if timed to avoid traffic. There are many places to picnic along the way.
Grade and distance: B2; 27 km total; 100 minutes riding time.
Best times: Avoid traffic and southeasters, which, if blowing at all (very frequent in summer) are usually fierce hereabouts. If you ride early on summer mornings you will beat the heavy tourist traffic and find the southeaster at its least powerful. Best is a calm winter day, or early in the spring when an immense diversity of flowers appears.
Special information: The reserve has more plant species than in the whole of Britain. Thanks to the comparative isolation of the area and the unending efforts of volunteer 'hackers' the invasion by alien vegetation is kept under control. There are various antelope (buck), mountain zebras (a rare species), small predators and a wealth of sea and land birds. Fishing is excellent and permitted. Take lightweight binoculars along with you.
Sustenance: Best to take your own, including liquids, and picnic. The Homestead restaurant is cosily situated but frequently packed solid with tour bus passengers. The kiosk near the point has a small selection and is expensive.
Getting there: Take the N2 freeway, then keep right where it passes Groote Schuur hospital so that you split off onto the M3 motorway south. Follow it to where it ends near Lakeside, then turn left and follow all Muizenberg, Fish Hoek and Simon's Town (M4) signs. Go right through Simon's Town and along the coast to where the (only) road turns inland up a steep hill. At the top of this hill turn left to the Cape of Good Hope Nature Reserve entrance; park outside to avoid a charge for your car. If you know the way you can take a short cut by going over Ou Kaapseweg (M64) from the end of the M3; this will bring you out at Glencairn. Train users can travel to the Simon's Town terminus and ride the extra 12 km to the reserve.
Doing the ride: Pay the entry fee and take an information leaflet; if you intend making a day of it note the closing time. Ride about 700 m up the moderate gradient of Rooihoogte. At the crest enjoy the fine view right across False Bay from Smitswinkel Bay to Cape Hangklip. If it's clear you can see Gordon's Bay.

Taking due care on the rather coarse-surfaced road, speed down the hill to the plain below. On the way down you might well spot groups of the larger animals. A little further on from the point where the road levels out is a right-turn to Olifantsbos, where the UCT Environmental and Geographical Sciences department owns a substantial old house used as a field station.

Approximately 2,5 km ahead, pass the 'Circular Drive' sign. If you like, go down it now or on your way back. It goes past the Atlantic shore with shady picnic spots (which tend to get claimed very early on nice days). You may come across the curious sight of zebras or other large 'wild' animals grazing right next to the beach.

Back on the main road, just short of 1 km along is the left turn to Bortjiesdrif beach. Another half a kilometre will take you past the Homestead restaurant and, 300 m further on, an information centre and field museum – which seem to be closed more often than not. About 500 m on is the left turn to Buffelsbaai which is a pleasant spot with safe swimming. If you go to this beach, marvel at the little hand-pumped borehole which yielded fresh water only a few strides away from the salty sea!

Some 250 m ahead is a right turn to a replica Dias Cross, not far off the road; the original was erected in 1488 by Bartolomeu Dias after he had successfully rounded the Cape. The next 1 km takes you up a bit of a slope, where you can enjoy good views of the Atlantic and False Bay. Then, at rather more than a kilometre on, is a right turn leading to the Cape of Good Hope (but you have to leave your bike or car and walk quite far to reach it). There are actually three promontories for ships to pass: Cape Point (east), Cape Maclear (middle) and Cape of Good Hope (west).

The famous Rooikrantz fishing ledges (the water right below them is very deep) may be reached by taking the left turn-off about 400 m further on. Another left turn a little further down the road leads to the Environmental Education Centre.

A short hill curves along the contour below Da Gama Peak and is followed by a sharp 500 m uphill to the Cape Point parking lot. Here you can post a letter and buy souvenirs and refreshments. Walk up to the toposcope which shows the directions and distances of surrounding landmarks. If you feel like testing your fitness, try to ride up what may well be the steepest hill in the western Cape. Otherwise walk up or take the specially low-geared Flying Dutchman bus.

Notice the old lighthouse tower at the top of the hill; it was completed in 1860 because of the large number of shipwrecks that had occurred along the coast.

Alas! No one had realized that the light would be hidden in the mist whenever it was most needed! It took no less than 54 years, plus the major disaster of the *Lusitania* wreck, among lesser founderings, before the present lighthouse was built 123 m lower down. The Cape Point light, half-a-million candlepower, is believed to be the most powerful in the world.

Return the way you came, with detours if you have the time and energy.

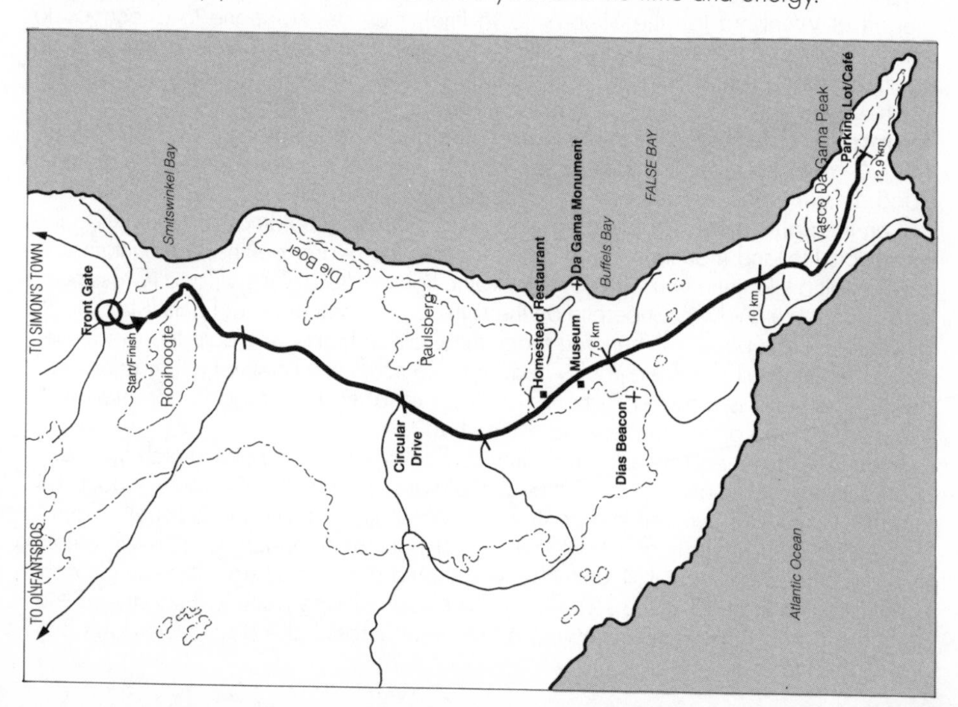

24 Ottery to Mitchell's Plain

Features: A level but mostly suburban ride offering stupendous views of the whole peninsula mountain chain and opportunities for sorties to the beach. Not recommended for youngsters. Security cannot always be guaranteed.
Grade and distance: C1; 33 km; 90 minutes riding time.
Best times: Timing is critical. On weekdays the roads are very busy, and at rush hours definitely dangerous. Midday, on any day other than Friday, is a fairly good time but Sundays are preferable. In summer, mornings are best – before the southeaster picks up. If the wind is blowing hard then avoid this trip because of beach sand blowing across the road and getting onto your chain and gears.
Special information: If you go over a weekend the beach resort area will be extremely crowded. There is a considerable potential security risk so do not leave your bike or carry-bag unattended – locked or otherwise – while you swim or go for snacks. Women should not ride unaccompanied.
Sustenance: Mnandi resort has good takeaways but is closed in winter except at weekends. Strandfontein Pavilion also has good value takeaways.
Getting there: Take the Table Bay Boulevard (N1) and head eastwards round the harbour, passing the brick power station on your left and following the 'Muizenberg' signs at the interchange to get onto the Black River Parkway (M5) which splits left near Rondebosch and changes name to Kromboom Parkway. Take the first 'Ottery' exit which brings you onto Ottery Road. Drive about 3 km and arrive at the Ottery Hypermarket where there is plenty of parking at all times. If you are travelling by train, get off at Wynberg (on the Simon's Town line), then ask someone to direct you to Prince George Drive (nearby but difficult to explain in print). Cycle about 200 m southeast along it and dog-leg back to Ottery Road. This will add only about 2 km each way to your ride. The Cape Flats line has a station at Ottery.
Doing the ride: Leave the Hypermarket area and continue along New Ottery Road for 1,6 km in the direction you came, then turn right (southwards) into Strandfontein Road. Pass the police station on the left and Makro (where the Sunset drive-in used to be) on the right. There is a pleasing view across the smallholdings on your left to the Hottentots Holland mountains, and on the right to the nearer peninsula mountains.

After half a kilometre you will reach the traffic lights at (Old) Ottery Road. Cross over, ride 1 km, note Midway Superette on the right, cross another set of lights (Klip Road), and follow the S-bends. When you reach the Golden Horseshoe café the road loses its well-maintained shoulder. You're heading due southeast now, which may be bad news if the wind is blowing, although a little way ahead the road is bordered with trees, which help dissipate the wind somewhat.

About 200 m ahead note the right turn to Zeekoevlei, a popular stretch for water sport with several boating clubs, although the water is distinctly unsavoury. About 3,4 km after this turn-off, turn left into Spine Road which is signposted to Mitchell's Plain.

The road along here is good but look out for patches of beach sand blown onto it by the southeaster. About 1,4 km further you should see a small sign 'Kus' on the right pointing out a short cut to the sea. There is a good vantage point 2,2 km ahead – a slight rise and an open area allowing a fine view across False Bay to Gordon's Bay and Cape Hangklip.

The Mitchell's Plain water treatment plant lies 1 km ahead on the left, and a further 800 m on are the traffic lights of Weltevreden Road. A left turn will lead you to the airport and eventually to Bellville, but a right turn (note sign 'Coast') gives you a wide smooth surface down to the bridge *under* Baden-Powell Drive, the main coastal road. Ride another 200 m and turn right into Lukannon Road. Had you continued on straight you would have arrived at Mnandi resort which has a tidal pool, picnic areas and many other facilities.

Provided it's not covered by wind-blown sand, Lukannon Road is a pleasure to ride on – wide and smooth with a cycling shoulder thoughtfully provided. It runs gently down for about 600 m to a parking lot at the beach, from where you happily bowl along nearly 2 km with the southeaster behind you. However, the part of the road that skirts the Lukhanan pumping station is very bumpy – bear this in mind and slow down. Just 300 m further on pass a right which leads under the bridge back towards Mitchell's Plain, emerging at the 'Kus' sign mentioned earlier.

Another 500 m or so down the road is a parking lot with ablution facilities. The next landmark is the Blue Waters resort and holiday cabins; note the right-pointing sign indicating Mitchell's Plain centre. A stop street comes up 2 km further on after you've passed a Putt-putt course. If you turned left you would come to the splendid Strandfontein Pavilion, which has comprehensive facilities including a reptile park.

However you must start your ride back by turning right and crossing over Baden-Powell Drive at the lights 200 m ahead. About 1 km further on you'll return to Spine Road, from which you retrace your route for about 9 km to where you left your car.

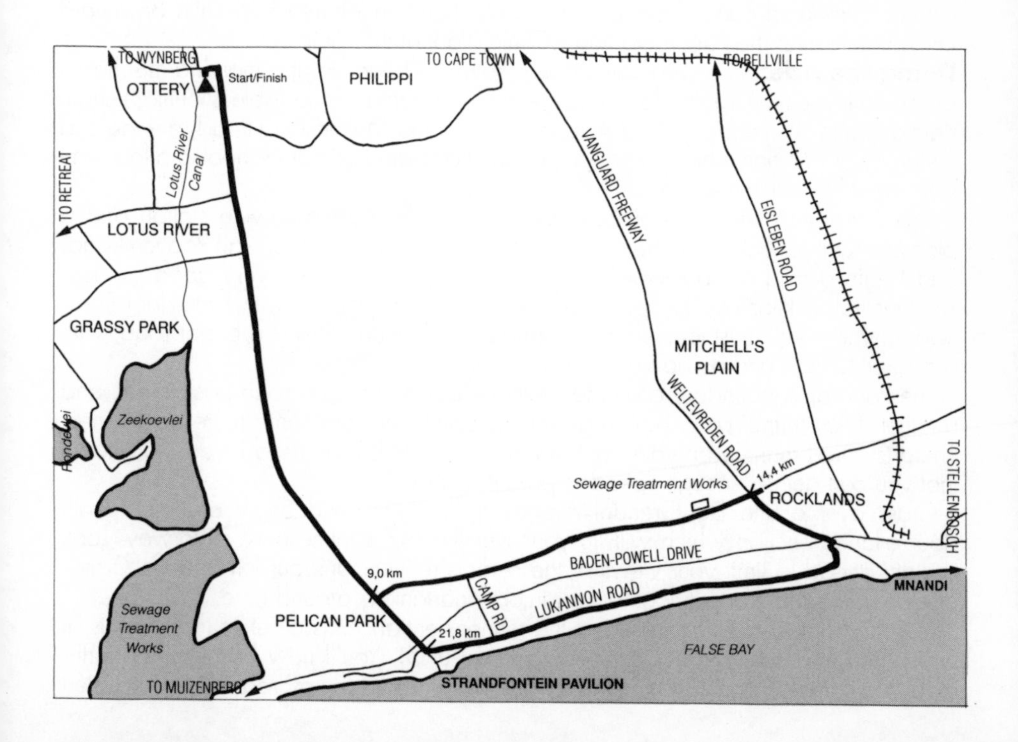

25 Panorama to Table View

Features: A ride through open unshaded areas with almost continuous grand, sweeping views that give you an enormous sense of freedom. The disadvantage of the openness is exposure to wind, no matter where it's blowing from. Gentle hills only. A populous but seldom congested area where families can ride in safety. A few sections are bordered by coastal bush which might just harbour ne'er-do-wells.
Grade and distance: B1; 16 km; 45 minutes riding time each way.
Best times: Spring and autumn usually provide periods of extended calm weather, at which times your only concern is to avoid the usual rush hours. At other times, go for early mornings before whatever wind there is intensifies.
Special information: Panorama is a relatively new suburb, forming part of the municipality of Parow, named after Captain Johann Parow whose ship was wrecked in Table Bay in 1865. He decided to settle in the Cape instead of returning to his native Prussia.
Sustenance: There are various nondescript cafés along the route where sweets and cooldrinks are available. We recommend waiting until you reach Table View where there's a nice roadside bakery. In Bayside Centre there's a range of eateries for all likely needs. Some are open every day; we haven't sampled them.
Getting there: Get onto Table Bay Boulevard (N1) and head eastwards round the container ship terminal of the harbour. Stay on this road, heading towards the Tygerberg hills. Travel until you spot Exit 7 signposted 'M14 Parow/Plattekloof'. Exit left into Plattekloof Road; drive about 1,5 km then turn left into Rothschild Boulevard immediately after the Panorama Medi-Clinic. Park at the clinic.
Doing the ride: Ride westwards down Rothschild Avenue. If a morning mist hasn't obscured it you'll be treated to a magnificent 'panorama' of the Table Mountain chain right down to Muizenberg. After 400 m turn right into Malmesbury Road, a wide and well-surfaced section which takes you past the Panorama primary school to a four-way stop street half a kilometre ahead.

Cross straight over and continue another 500 m, past a service station and a pleasant Kwiksave shop, to the next stop street. Turn right, into Gert van Rooyen Road, and begin a mild climb towards the Tygerberg hills along this very good surface. Another half a kilometre further on you will reach the junction with Plattekloof Road again, where you must turn left; note signpost 'Milnerton'. This is a busier road, with a poorer surface and a wide uneven shoulder.

The Panorama boundary coincides with the powerlines you soon pass under, and another 1 km further on is Bothasig – at this point there are some more powerlines. There is an oil refinery on your right; it's an ugly sight but the road here is so smooth that you can get up enough speed to pass it quickly.

Cross over at the De Grendel Avenue traffic lights and enjoy a nice smooth double-laned section which will lift you over the N7 Malmesbury motorway. Look straight ahead to limit your views of the Fedmis refinery on your left and the Caltex one on your right. Keep a look out for trucks and tankers around here.

Less than half a kilometre beyond the refinery entrances is a set of traffic lights at which you must turn right, into Koeberg Road (M5). You'll now be heading north, away from Table Mountain. This is a wide, dual carriageway road, but keep alert because some of its traffic will be moving exceptionally fast.

Pass the Killarney Hotel and turn left into Blaauberglaan (M14) at the lights. Ride for 400 m after turning at the lights and you will find yourself crossing the Dieprivier feeding Rietvlei, once planned to become the greatest small boat harbour in the southern hemisphere.

You'll notice stables on the right, but the main attraction is the fine view to Table Mountain across the waving reeds of Rietvlei. If you're into bird-watching this is a rewarding spot. For a brief 200 m the road reverts to a single lane with sidewalk before blossoming into a new super-smooth dual carriageway. Half a kilometre along is a small shopping centre marking the entrance to Table View. There's a small bakery on the left (recommended). The suburb of Flamingo Vlei is on your left.

Now there's a slight but sustained climb for just over 1 km to the crest of a hill, from which you can get a glimpse of the Atlantic. Another 1 km will bring you to the peculiar but no doubt scientifically designed intersection leading into Bayside Centre.

You can return to Panorama the same way you came, or consider an interesting detour requiring you to leave Bayside Centre and ride past Pick 'n Pay along the Otto du Plessis coastal road (R27). This will take you past Rietvlei, where, you can sometimes watch radio-controlled model boats and, just beyond the vlei, radio-controlled model aeroplanes. If you're unlucky enough to be riding in a rising southeaster, at least enjoy the spectacle of the boardsailors racing across the wind-exposed vlei.

Ride 5 km along this road then turn up left into Race Course Road just after the bridge crossing Dieprivier (the exit from the vlei) which feeds Milnerton lagoon. This turn will take you back to Koeberg Road. Now turn left into it and ride past Ascot race course and Montague Gardens for 4 km. This will bring you to the Caltex/Fedmis complex where you turn right and return the way you came.

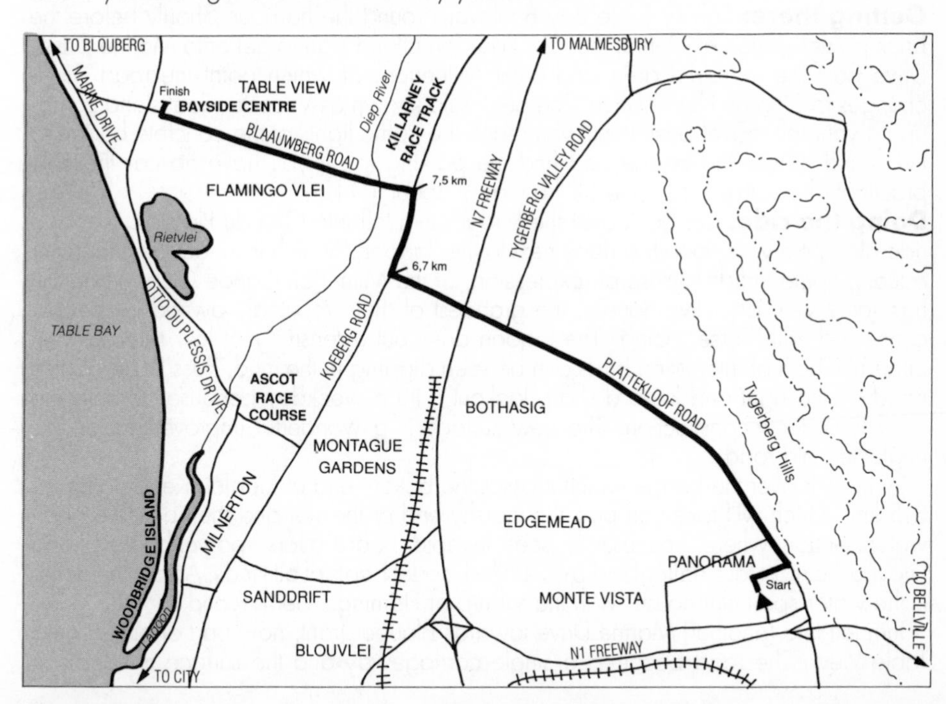

26 Milnerton to Blouberg

Features: This is an easy ride from Milnerton to Blouberg and back, with splendid views of Table Bay, and no stiff hills – but the possibility of strong winds one way or the other. Traffic is not dense unless there's a surfing event in progress, in which case the outward route is likely to be very congested with drivers and pedestrians not used to looking out for cyclists. Not a recommended ride for unaccompanied children or solo riders.
Grade and distance: C1; 38 km; 90 minutes.
Best times: In summer the southeaster tends to stiffen during the day so a morning ride is preferable. During the week the route is usually quiet. In winter the onshore wind, even if it's not carrying rain, can be chilling unless you're dressed against it.
Special information: The southern end of Woodbridge Island used to be dominated by the (now-restored) De Villiers Graaff mansion, but over the last few years it has been 'developed' into a concentration of graceless semis. Nevertheless, the beach has not deteriorated and offers good ATB riding and wonderful beachcombing after a winter storm. The view across the bay is hackneyed but nonetheless beautiful. Similarly the beach is fine for ATBs or strolling at the Blouberg end of the ride.
Sustenance: For this out-and-back ride the natural thing to do would be to lunch at the Wooden Bridge – the restaurant adjoining the golf club at your start. Booking is essential. Otherwise we suggest calling in at the Bayside Centre on your way back – it has several very acceptable eateries. On the Table View beachfront is a fine restaurant, Sunset Boulevard.
Getting there: Follow Table Bay Boulevard round the harbour. Shortly before the brick power station exit left at the R27 Paarden Eiland sign to get onto Marine Drive. Drive past the industrial area and enter Milnerton, at which point the road name changes to Otto du Plessis Drive. The peninsula known as Woodbridge Island comes up on your left; travel past it until you reach the traffic lights at the concrete bridge to the island. Cross the bridge and find the parking lot. If you have no car the only practical alternative is to cycle all the way – about 10 km.
Doing the ride: Go back over the bridge, turn left into Otto du Plessis Drive, and ride along the very smooth surface next to the 'lagoon,' which is in fact the Dieprivier estuary, home turf, to misuse an expression, of the Milnerton Canoe Club. Milnerton has some very attractive houses, the grandest of them reputedly owned by people connected with horse racing. The lagoon dries out extensively at low tide but then large numbers of interesting birds can be seen digging in the mud. Pass Race Course Road on the right and keep a sharp lookout if it's a weekday because currently the road is under reconstruction. The new surface is a wonderful improvement on the neglected old road.

Swing left over the bridge which crosses the bottom end of Rietvlei. Keep riding for 3,5 km, which will take you past the marshy end of the vlei and then past the open water section where one usually sees intrepid boardsailors, power-boaters, and (maybe the most fascinating) radio-controlled model boats of all kinds. Across the water is the water sport clubhouse, with the suburb of Flamingo Vlei beyond.

Turn left into (another) Marine Drive towards Bloubergrant, now part of burgeoning Table View. The road becomes a single carriageway and the surface is rough; in winter it is often covered in sand by the northwester. Pass the traffic lights for the M14 back to Table View proper. You're now next to the sea and there are some shops on the right. Notice the measured kilometre set out here; it provides an opportunity to check your bike computer.

Much of the shoulder along this section is very rough because beachgoers park along it. The actual turn to the beach is 2,2 km from the traffic light just mentioned, immediately before a steep little hill. At the top of the hill you'll have fine views across Table Bay to Robben Island and Table Mountain. The next 4,3 km undulates gently and the speed limit rises, so keep on the lookout for speeding cars. This section is quite deserted but allows for peaceful riding all the way to Melkbos. Pass the Melkbos Cultural Centre then notice the detour to the beach about 700 m ahead.

The little bay has historical significance, being the site of the British landings in 1806, followed by the rather trivial Battle of Blouberg. The road now curves around to the right, inland, and you pass left turns leading to the 'town' and caravan park before arriving at the stop street of the R27 West Coast Road. If you were to turn left you'd be only five minutes ride from the Koeberg nuclear power station. However our route requires a right turn at the stop street.

The ride back is all along the R27 which, if you don't have a big head wind, is surprisingly pleasant, with rolling farmlands and a more or less constant view of Table Mountain. Fortunately the shoulder is in good condition along here; you may have to use it because slow traffic obligingly (but illegally) rides astride the yellow line to let more speedy traffic pass. If you ride in the evening the sunsets are nearly always marvellous here, but take very great care not to be run down from behind.

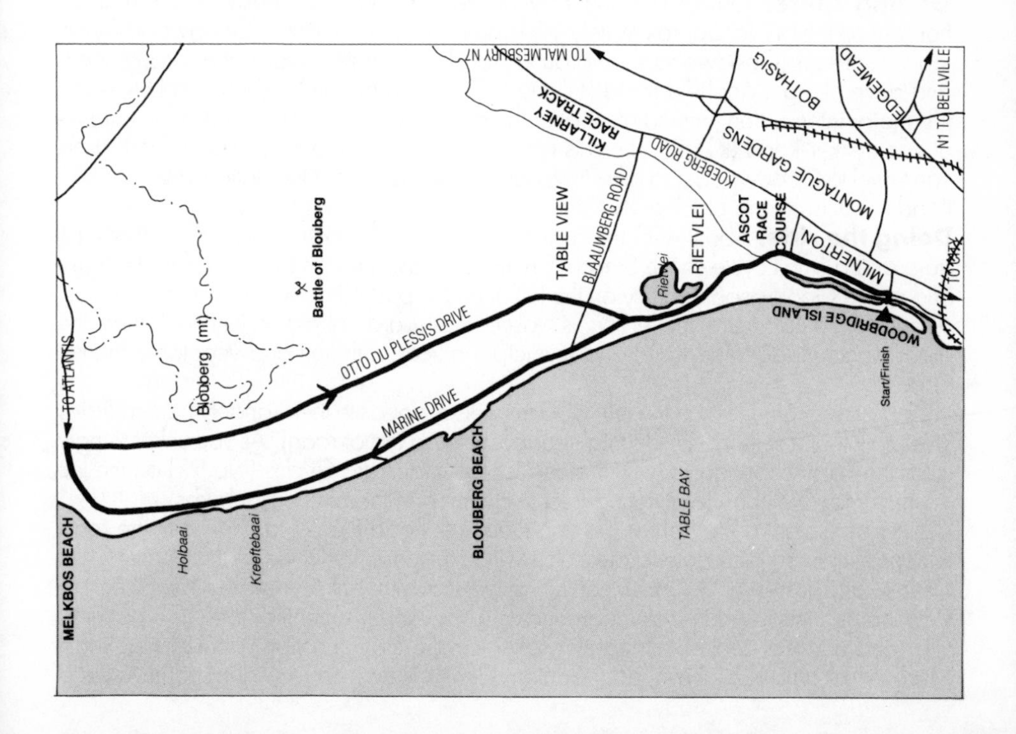

27 Goodwood to Bellville

Features: This is the only legal and direct through-route by which southern suburbs cyclists can reach the main northern suburbs and points further east. There's a high concentration of resident cyclists and of bicycle shops along here. Security is not a problem.
Grade and distance: A1; 18 km; 60 minutes.
Best times: Unless you want to visit the cycle shops, avoid working hours because this road is extremely busy and has numerous intersections. At other times it is pleasantly quiet, not being a convenient through-route for motorists. The route is mostly built-up and runs across the prevailing wind direction, so unless there's a massive gale windiness is not a factor. The early morning is a good time for this ride – the sunrise tends to show built-up areas at their best.
Special information: Because of the numerous intersections the route is rarely used for cycling events; however, the famous Rapport Tour usually incorporates a stage starting or ending along here. There are also occasional 'street miles' (standing start flat races – find out the dates from cycling clubs).
Sustenance: There are quite a few cafés along the way, but the route is short and level so you shouldn't need refuelling. However, if you're from another area, why not try one of the restaurants noted for their competitively priced sumptuous Sunday dinners? Try the Pepper Pot (197a Voortrekker Road) for gigantic helpings, or the Lobster Pot (Voortrekker Road, opposite the magistrates' court in Bellville.)
Getting there: Get onto Table Bay Boulevard and drive eastwards round the harbour on the N1 for approximately 11 km to the exit for the N7 to Goodwood/Montague Gardens (Goodwood showgrounds road). Turn right towards the showgrounds and drive along Wingfield Road (still the N7), which becomes Vanguard Drive. The first major intersection (immediately after the cinema complex and Libertas Hospital) is at Voortrekker Road (R102). There is a parking area outside the hospital. Train users can travel to Goodwood and take any road northwards out of the station to Voortrekker Road – it is only one block away.
Doing the ride: About 400 m eastwards along Voortrekker Road is a good 7/11 store and a small cycle shop, Smitco, on the left. Pass through two sets of traffic lights and notice Goodwood's library on the left, then the post office with public telephones. About half a kilometre further on is Vasco Boulevard, a major junction, then the Goodwood magistrates' court and municipal offices with fruit and vegetable market opposite.

City Cycles comes up on the left, 400 m ahead, opposite the strangely named Elsies River Halt (not a station, as you might suppose, but a major road). As you unknowingly cross the Parow boundary 300 m along look out for Astra Cycles (No 97) on the left – which may well be the all-round best cycle shop in the northern suburbs.

A major turn-off to the right is Jan van Riebeeck Road (M12); at this point the road widens, but its surface deteriorates. You will soon pass the lawns of the Parow Civic Centre, and just over 1 km further on is the Parow Centre (look out for Checkers Warehouse); this is worth looking around as it has various amenities such as a bowling alley and a fitness centre. Immediately after it is the main junction with Delarey Road which offers a route to the airport. Sanlam Centre is next on the right and includes a

Totalsports branch; Parow Cycle House is nearly opposite.

The West Street traffic lights are the landmark for Tygerberg Commercial School on the left. Stellenbosch University's commerce faculty is reached by turning left into Mike Pienaar Boulevard immediately after the railway bridge. You are now officially in Bellville and the Louis Leipoldt Hospital is on your left, somewhat dwarfed by the immense Tygerberg Hospital complex visible down the hill to your right. A caravan park and sport grounds follow on the right, where the road narrows and becomes bumpy.

You enter Bellville main shopping area about 900 m ahead and encounter a major intersection with Durban Road (R302) opposite the magistrates' court. The Home of Cycling is a little way down Durban Road – a good shop with well-informed, keen staff. There are several cafés of varying quality among the shops. The impressive premises of Bellville High School will soon appear to your right, followed by the spacious and well laid out grounds of the Bellville Civic Centre.

You can go a little further if you feel like it, but the area becomes industrial and loses any appeal it might have had. Return the same way – remembering that one always sees things missed, and different aspects of the same things, when one takes a reverse direction route.

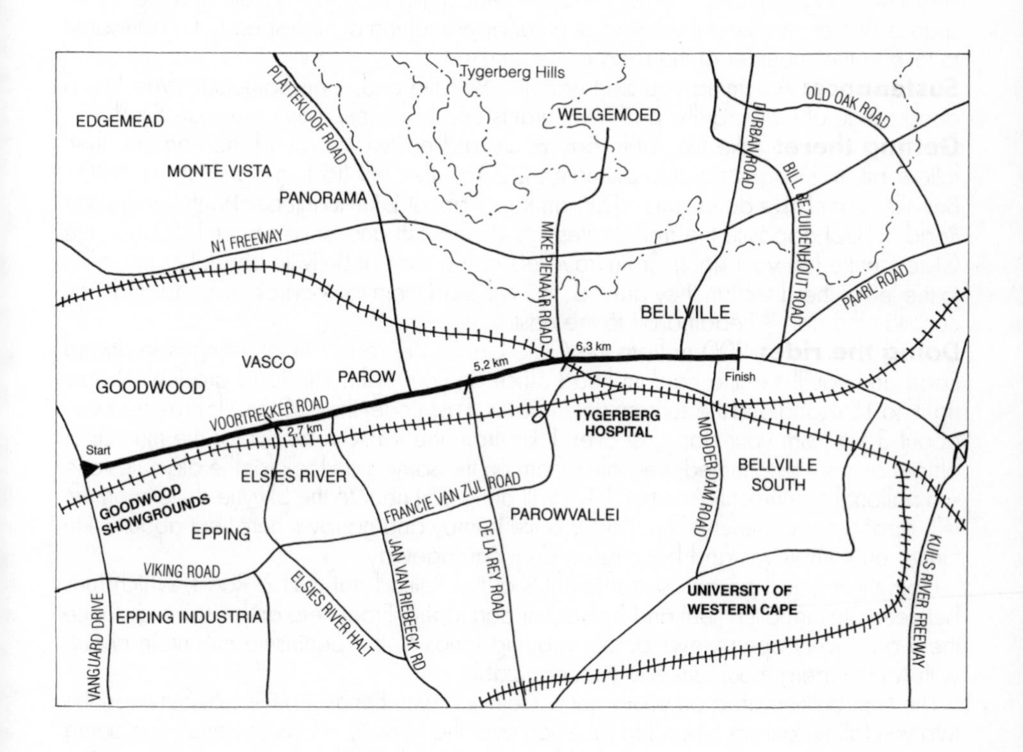

28 Bellville to Somerset West

Features: This is a nice level ride, and fast if the wind isn't strong. Most people will have to ride back again which will not be a problem if they do the outward direction against any wind. The rural views are very pleasing, especially in late spring and autumn. A useful road to know because it is the best legal route for Capetonians wishing to cycle eastwards (cyclists are not allowed on motorways). Not recommended for solo female riders. Some sections are suitable for cycling two abreast.
Grade and distance: B1; 31 km each way; 100 minutes riding time for the outward trip.
Best times: The Bellville/Kuils River section is moderately busy during the week, but otherwise the trip is fairly traffic free. Extreme wind is unpleasant, but windless days will allow smog and/or fog to creep over the Cape Flats to spoil the view.
Special information: Getting familiar with this route may be useful if and when you decide to participate in fun rides, some of which regularly include sections of this ride. A word of caution: although (and maybe because) weekend traffic density is very low along this route it is not unusual to encounter motorists travelling at horrifying speeds. When you hear the sound of a car approaching at high speed, it is advisable to take to the shoulder of the road immediately.
Sustenance: Assuming you start from the Bellville end, then Somerset West has a good range of cafés, grills, posh restaurants and bakeries, many open on Sundays.
Getting there: Take the Table Bay Boulevard eastwards round the harbour, then follow all 'N1' signs for approximately 22 km. Exit left (to turn right) at the 'R302 Bellville' sign. Drive down (this is Durban Road) about 2 km to intersect with Voortrekker Road (R102) opposite the magistrates' court. Turn left and drive about 1,5 km to the Civic Centre (on your right). Train travellers can get off at Bellville and take any street to the left of the direction they arrived; this will lead them to Voortrekker Road and they can start the ride – heading off to the east.
Doing the ride: 200 m from the Civic Centre the road name changes to Strand Road and you'll see the Sanlam head office on your right. The road gradually bears right past Stikland and the surface deteriorates. Pass under the R300 Kuils River freeway about 3 km from your start. Just over 1 km from the R300 look out for the municipal offices on your left; immediately after them on the same side look for the old milestone – a national monument. Another 1 km will bring you near to the Skyvue drive-in on the left, opposite a cemetery. The road is quite bumpy and narrows here, but about 1 km further on it improves and becomes a dual carriageway.

From there you'll go across traffic lights at the Polkadraai (M12) Road, which runs between Stellenbosch (left) and Belhar/airport (right). From here on for some distance there are lovely open views across grazing lands to the peninsula mountain chain, with Muizenberg mountain easily recognizable.

The next built-up area on your right is Kleinvlei, with Penhill on the left. Between the two you follow a long S-bend to take you over the railway – Eersterivier station being just ahead. After the bridge there's a bit of a downhill to a pleasant new shopping complex, then some more nice open country while you approach and pass the bridge carrying the R310 – which runs from Stellenbosch, crosses the N2 off to your right and becomes Baden-Powell Drive running along the False Bay coast.

Cross the Eerste River 400 m ahead, noticing Faure station just before. Ahead on the right is a café (untested) next to a turn leading to Macassar and the sea. The next farms on your left are Uitkyk and Zandvliet. Now there's a wide smooth section where you can try your speed, but take care because motorists will be having the same idea. Cross the Eerste River tributary, the Moddergat, 3,4 km from the café; enjoy the view to the right covering the mountain chain from Cape Hangklip back to Strandfontein. The double dome of the Helderberg looms near on your left; did you know it is 54 m higher than Table Mountain?

Just 200 m after the Moddergat there's a right turn to Firgrove and Macassar, over the N2, and after another 400 m there's a traffic light for, left, the road to Stellenbosch and Wine Route 8, and, right, to the N2. Another set of lights lies 400 m ahead, for Firgrove traffic. Now ride another 3,8 km to pass under the R44 bridge (left to Stellenbosch, right to Strand). Over the next 1 km the road narrows, bears right, and cuts across the Somerset West Country Club golf course. At the stop street turn left onto the N2 (which has a 70 km/h speed limit on this section and a rough surface).

Pass through the next traffic lights, then cross the Lourens River. Turn left just before another bridge 1,1 km ahead, then turn left again after 200 m onto a bumpy road leading past a post office on the left followed by a short steep incline over the railway. The road levels here and acquires a pleasant border of trees. Another 300 m, bearing left, brings you to the shopping area. Notice the old Lourens River road bridge on your right (national monument), and the new Vergelegen Hospital as you ride up into the dual carriageway section with its attractive flower-planted centre island.

You're now on the main road through Somerset West. Notice Checkers on the left and then a plentiful sprinkling of cafés and bakeries right through town.

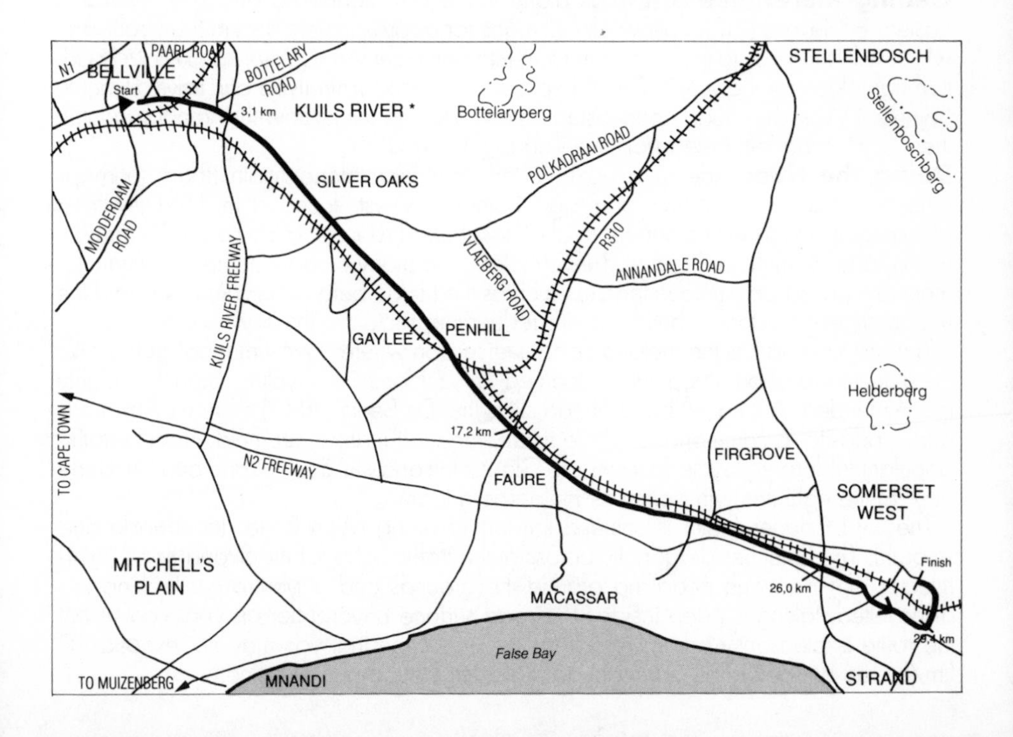

29 Somerset West to Stellenbosch

Features: This is a combined scenic/training ride in a beautiful vineyard environment, on a safe open road with high-speed descents – once you've got up the hills. Families are advised to cycle in single file. Traffic on the route is usually light but fast. Security is good.
Grade and distance: C3; 15 km each way; 90 minutes for round trip.
Best times: Autumn shades in the vineyards are lovely, but so are the fresh greens of early summer. High summer may be hot, especially if there's no wind. One of those amazing clear blue windless days after a rainy spell in winter is also suitable. Traffic is never heavy unless some big event is being held.
Special information: If a good southeaster's blowing and you have to do the round trip, then start at the Stellenbosch end so that the wind will blow you back on the return leg. The opposite applies in a winter northwester. Much of the route has a coarse road surface – not kind to worn tyres.
Sustenance: Consult a wine route brochure (from any wine route estate or co-op) for opening times; Blaauwklippen is very pleasant. There is a restaurant (untested) at Zandberg on the Lynedoch connecting road. If you prefer to eat at the end of the trip, consider the California Spur, Mike's Kitchen, Chez Michel (up-market), or Hobbits (for massive Sunday lunches) – all in Somerset West. There are also several bakeries producing very fresh goodies every day. If you end in Stellenbosch, you'll ride past the Volkskombuis where you might be tempted by their waterblommetjie bredie.
Getting there: Drive eastwards along Table Bay Boulevard and split right onto Eastern Boulevard (N2). Follow all N2 signs for approximately 49 km from your start which will bring you to the *second* left turn into Somerset West. Drive up to Main Road, turn right, look for the very visible Checkers, then park. Train users can travel direct to Somerset West and head northeast for three blocks to intersect with Main Road; start there (by turning left) instead of reversing to Checkers.
Doing the ride: Ride in a northwesterly direction along Main Road, perhaps reflecting that not so many years ago Somerset West, founded in 1820, was a picturesque village with a serene rural atmosphere. Progress, alas, has transformed it into a large commercial centre. Nevertheless, the many elegant homes, spectacular mountain backdrops, unique features such as the Helderberg Nature Reserve, and the high number of historical buildings are redeeming factors.

The first landmark is the Victoria Road intersection where a left turn leads to the N2. Next there's a short steep hill redeemed by a Home of Cycling branch – highly recommended. A long left bend ahead skirts the 'De Beers' (AECI) recreation grounds and, opposite, a commonage where interesting craft markets are held. From here the popular Helderberg Cycle Tour sets off. Glance left and you'll see Strand and Gordon's Bay; to the right the twin domes of Helderberg loom.

The Lord Charles Hotel is some 2 km further along Main Road, (now wide and smooth). The hotel lies diagonally across at the traffic lights for the Strand Road (R44) intersection; it's worth pedalling around the grounds and, if you're not looking too dishevelled, taking a peep inside. The road surface beyond here is very coarse but the route is pleasantly green; reflect on the instruction that you may not exceed 90 km/h. The bridge visible 2 km ahead indicates the top of the incline.

Stop for a breather at the crest and look back at the grand view of False Bay. Notice on the mountainside the buildings of the ingenious Steenbras pumped-storage system, where electricity is generated at peak hours by emptying the upper dam into the lower dam through turbines. At off-peak times surplus power is used to run the turbines as pumps to return the water to the upper dam.

As you pass over the top you can see Table Mountain in the distance beyond the seas of vineyards. Now you can tear down the long hill the other side, thinking with pity of those overfed under-exercised hotel patrons missing out on this exuberant sensation. Another 600 m brings you to a left turn back to the N2 and Firgrove, then 1,5 km further on there's the left turn to Wine Route 8; you'd need to go down here to reach Zandberg Restaurant and the Helderberg Co-op. Now you have a succession of hard climbs and speedy descents for 3 km, bringing you to Annandale Road which leads off left to Lynedoch along Wine Route 7; WR 9 is off to the right and would bring you to Rust en Vrede.

Proceed for 3,4 km, passing the Stellenbosch Flying Club on the left, to the popular Blaauwklippen Estate, home of Graham Boonzaier who has a collection of fine antique cars. The currently embryonic Stellenbosch Technopark is ahead on the left, followed by another dreadful hill and then the refreshing greenness of the golf course. You're now back in suburbia, as indicated by a series of traffic lights, and Strand Road runs on to eventually intersect with Adam Tas Road outside the station.

Depending on how much energy you have left, you can now wander round historic Stellenbosch and perhaps enjoy a leisurely drink.

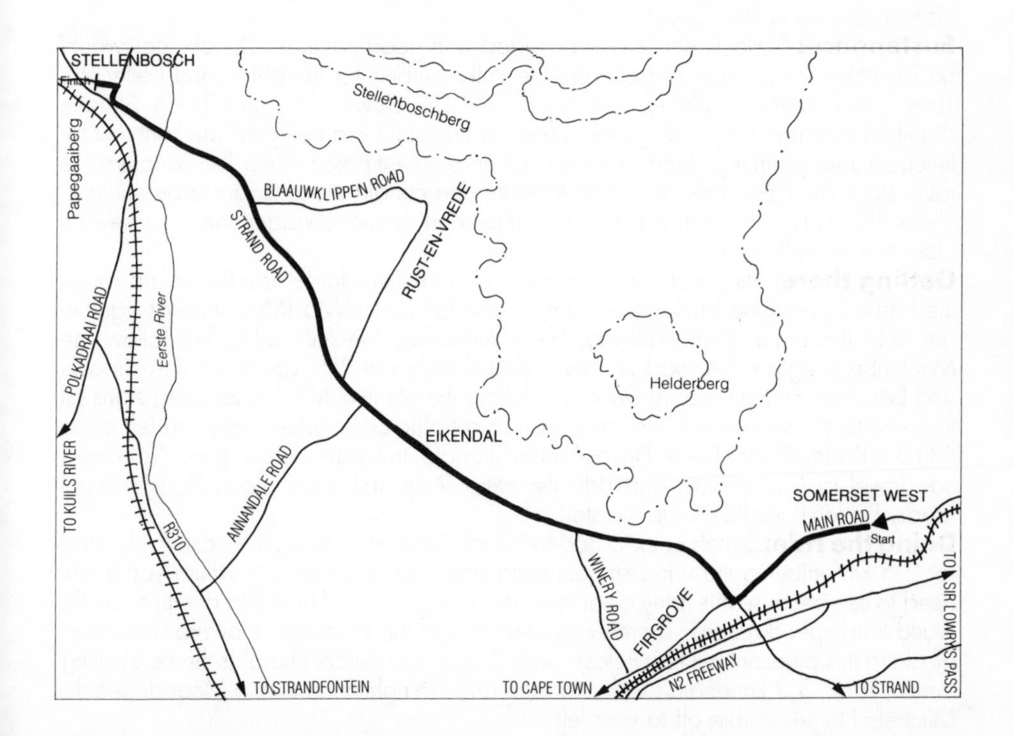

30 Strandfontein to Stellenbosch

Features: A fine longish ride from Strandfontein to Stellenbosch, combining a bracing coastal section with a very pretty rural stretch and no significant hills. Wind can make the round trip moderately tiring. The coastal stage has long, deserted sections where security is uncertain. Women and youngsters should not do the ride unaccompanied.
Grade and distance: C2; 35 km each way; 60 to 100 minutes each way, depending on wind direction.
Best times: Autumn, when the foliage is changing colour, is the best time for riding past the vineyards. Stellenbosch town is at its best when the trees are in leaf, but high summer can be uncomfortably hot for cycling. In winter there are often crystal clear, but very cold, days. The southeaster is helpful for keeping cool in summer but opposes the rider on the inland part of the return trip. Our choice would be early morning in late spring, with a stop at Spier on the way back. Weekend traffic is very heavy in summer unless you start early.
Special information: During strong southeasters a lot of loose sand blasts across the road along the coastal section; this is bad for gears and chains. Bush fires are common in this section and apart from the unpleasant smoke they produce the danger of being run down in poor visibility is increased. Consider combining the ride with a good look round the historical sights of Stellenbosch – pick up a brochure from the Visitors' Bureau in Plein Street.
Sustenance: Stellenbosch is well provided with good eateries. Our choices would be De Akker for younger people and the Volkskombuis for the older (and better-off). Those who like quiet places will appreciate De Ouwe Werf in Church Street – dignified Victorian surroundings for coffee. Spier estate is a delightful environment for lunch on your return trip. There are many other excellent possibilities. The various wine route stops are open only at certain times and in certain seasons; get a brochure to check. If you prefer to delay eating until you're nearly home, consider one of the several places at Strandfontein pavilion.
Getting there: The least confusing route is to take the Table Bay Boulevard round the harbour; pass the brick power station and follow the M5 (Muizenberg) signs to get onto the Black River Parkway. Near Mowbray the M5 splits, but follow the Muizenberg signs – the road is now called Kromboom Parkway. Later this narrows and becomes Prince George Drive, but follow the plentiful M5 Muizenberg signs all the way to the sea, which will bring you to a traffic circle where you turn left on to R310 – Baden-Powell Drive. Drive 7 km to Strandfontein pavilion and park. Train users can travel to Muizenberg and ride the extra 9 km (all level) along Beach/Royal roads/Baden-Powell Drive to the start.
Doing the ride: Set off back to Baden-Powell Drive and turn right – eastwards. Ride for 2,5 km enjoying the wide smooth road and ridable shoulder – which you might need to use because this fairly clear road attracts occasional unskilled attempts on the world land speed record. There's a grand view of the Hottentots Holland mountains all along this pleasant but featureless road. A short fast descent heralds the next rolling stretch, some 3,2 km ending with a bridge and the right-hand turn to Mnandi Beach. Mitchells Plain is visible off to your left.

What is surely, over summer weekends, the busiest pedestrian crossing in the country lies 500 m ahead. At peak times you may have to fight your way through the multitudes of beachgoers using it. That done, climb gently for 1,7 km as the road turns slightly inland to avoid the crumbling sea cliffs, much favoured by vast numbers of wheeling, screaming seagulls. From here you get wonderful views across the full width of False Bay from Hangklip to Cape Point. The road returns to beach level quite steeply then takes you past Swartklip Road on the left followed by a camping ground on the right, shortly before the Monwabisi resort area.

The road begins to take you away from the sea, passing a sewage disposal works on the left, and on the right, the turn-off to Macassar Beach. You may want to detour here to visit Sheik Yusuf's tomb; if so, chain up your bike at the beach and walk (or ride your ATB) about 2 km along it to the Eerste River mouth. Back on the route, pass through a stretch of waterlogged coastal bush with a lot of interesting bird life. Cross the N2, which may mark the point where Baden-Powell Drive loses its name and becomes known only as the R310.

Two kilometres after the N2 bridge you pass the left turn to Blue Downs, then 500 m ahead the slip road onto R102 connecting Eersterivier with Somerset West. Cross the R102 and see Faure station off to your right as you progress to a vineyard-flanked section of the route. The road cuts across a dam on the Meerlust property; the island to your left here is another good spot for bird-watchers. This section passes through beautiful farmlands and, not surprisingly, the road narrows – it's infamous for catastrophic late-night head-on collisions.

A wine route co-op, Welmoed, comes up on the right and the railway swings in from the left near the Lynedoch station where there's a modest hotel with a popular disco. The right turn opposite the station is a smooth route to Somerset West via various wine route establishments, including the Zandberg restaurant. Ahead to the right you come to the farm Spier, best known for its historic Jonkershuis restaurant (not run by the estate). In summer this is a nice place for a late breakfast outside under the trees, with the Eersterivier trickling through the grounds nearby.

Ride another 1,4 km, passing the Eersterivier Valley Co-op (which you can visit) and swing left up and over a steep little railway bridge. Just before the bridge you can make a short detour to the Van Rhyn brandy cellar, and just after the bridge to the Vlottenburg Co-op cellars. It's all too tempting for a cyclist who needs to preserve his balance. The route now hits a T-junction with Polkadraai Road from Kuils River. Turn right, although if you like you can detour left and look at Neethlingshof, with its jet fountain and rows of national flags.

Back on the route again you can enjoy a fine wide smooth road into Stellenbosch, with various distractions along the way. Over on your left, you can stop off to have a look at the interesting Oude Libertas open-air theatre (pick up a programme). Then there's the extensive SFW complex on the right, which can be visited for a conducted tour provided you telephone first – (02231) 7-3400. Papegaaiberg (parrot mountain: so called because wooden parrots were once used here as targets for shooting competitions) is up to your left. Then comes the Adam Tas bridge with its intriguing mounted plaque describing the remarkable Stone Age artefacts found there.

Swing left after the bridge then take the first turning right which dog-legs into Dorp Street past a service station. Take care riding up Dorp Street because the road width changes suddenly at some intersections and there are deep water furrows instead of roadside gutters. As you cross Strand Street look to the right and notice the old wine press on the northeast corner; this is the Stellenryck Wine Museum, next to which is the Rembrandt van Rijn Art Gallery. If you turn right into Strand Street and cross the (Eerste) river you'll find one of our recommended restaurants, Volkskombuis, and next to it the Oude Meester Brandy Museum housed in an attractive Sir Herbert Baker-designed cottage.

Further up Dorp Street (No 90) you'll find De Akker pub/restaurant, an outstanding place to eat and slake your thirst, but not if you have to ride all the way back again! Alternatively, turn left into Bird Street and end your ride a few blocks along among the lawns of Die Braak – a commonage which the town fathers have been wise enough to leave open and unspoilt.

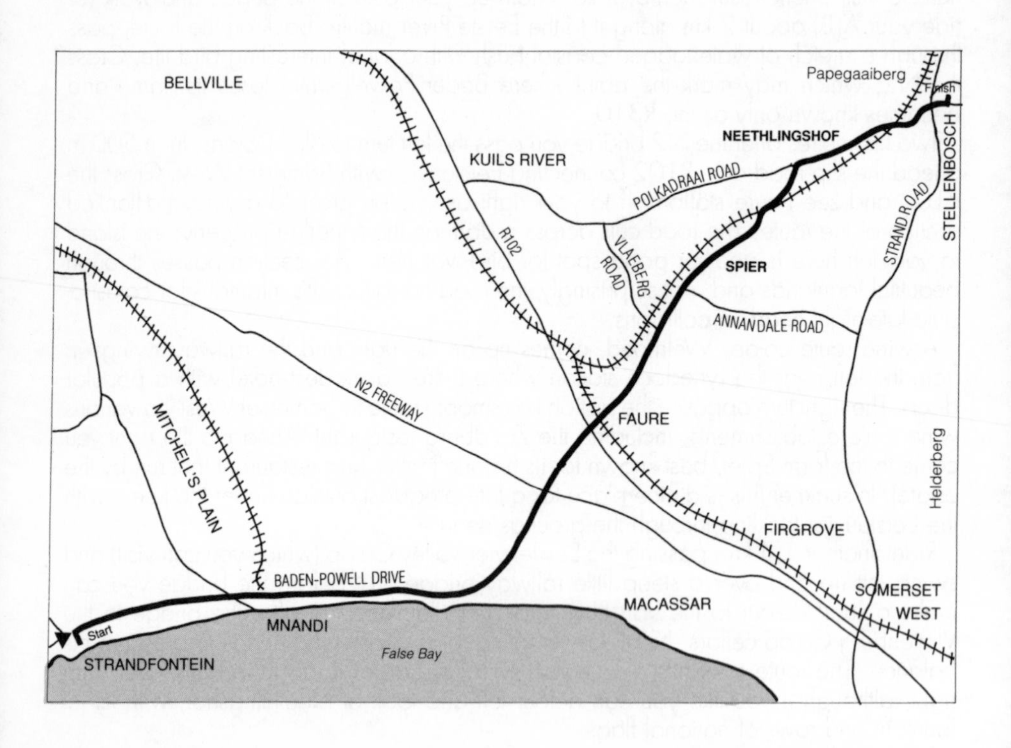

31 Stellenbosch Town Circuit

Features: A short, flat circuit of a most attractive and richly historic town with an immense variety of interesting things to look at. Make your own detours, according to what you particularly want to see. Normally this area is safe for cyclists. Suitable for family rides if the mini rush hours are avoided.
Grade and distance: A1; 10 km; 30 minutes riding time.
Best times: Stellenbosch has very little wind and a good deal of shade in summer – when it can become uncomfortably hot. In winter it can get extremely cold, with snow on the nearby mountains – but a midday ride in winter sunshine after some rain can be very enjoyable. Insignificant rush hours occur on weekdays but are easily avoided. During university terms there are large numbers of commuter cyclists in town.
Special information: Stellenbosch is the most cyclist-friendly urban area in the country, and the local population is accustomed to hordes of student (and other) cyclists. A number of central roads have deep water furrows instead of gutters and kerbs; it is easy to wobble into one while admiring the town's attractions.
Sustenance: The town is amply provided with middle- and up-market restaurants, cafés and bakeries. Some of these places are heavily dependent on student custom and extend their hours during university terms. Good low-cost meals are available at some pubs. Excellent pastas are served at Mamma Romas.
Getting there: Take the N2 freeway and follow it for about 37 km, then exit left at the Stellenbosch R310 sign. Follow the R310 for 13 km to its T-junction with Polkadraai Road. Turn right and head into Stellenbosch; note the speed limit which comes into force quite far outside the town – trapping is frequent. Bear left over the Adam Tas bridge (and if you have time, now or when you return, stop to look at the monument next to the bridge on the left marking the site at which Stone Age tools were found in 1899). Take the first turn right after the bridge, into Dorp Street, drive up 1,4 km and turn left into Bird Street. About 200 m along on the left is a large open area, Die Braak, where one can usually park. For train users, the station is conveniently situated next to Adam Tas Road barely 200 m from Dorp Street.
Doing the ride: Head off back the way you came, along Bird Street (which is called Mill Street over the short one-way section). Turn right into Dorp Street and immediately left into Piet Retief Street; note Pieter se Fiets cycle shop on the right. Cross the Eerste River and turn left into Suidwal Street alongside the river. Ride nearly 1 km along this narrow and bumpy road with Paul Roos Gimnasium on your right.

Coetzenburg sports grounds come up on your right with the Danie Craven Stadium ahead. Turn left at the traffic circle then cross a narrow bridge and immediately turn right into Noordwal Oos Street. This is also bumpy and turns to gravel further ahead, at which point turn left (bridge on the right leads to sports grounds). Turn right into Van Riebeeck Road and ride up past the beautiful lawns of university residences until you come to the fork. Take the right-hand prong to pass into the small suburb of Mostertsdrift along Van der Stel Road (poor surface) then turn half-left into Du Plessis Road at the yield sign. You're now in an even smaller suburb with the unusual name Aanhou Wen! Ride for 200 m and turn right at the T-junction. Ride for 400 m and turn right at the stop street, then 100 m and turn left into Lanzerac Hotel and vineyard where you can look around for a while before continuing.

As you leave Lanzerac down the exit road, turn left out of the gate into Martinson Road and ride down past a few side streets and extensive playing fields to the traffic circle where you turn left into newly-resurfaced Merriman Street (the R310 – main route to Jonkershoek and Helshoogte). Notice the beautiful grounds of the small but interesting Jan Marais Nature Reserve on your left. In the upper reaches of Martinson Street there are several grand university complexes with architectural styles reflecting their respective ages.

About 1,3 km after the first traffic circle turn left into Van Ryneveld Street, ride past the Carnegie Library then turn (next) left into Victoria Street. Now take the second right into Bosman Street then again the second right to put yourself in Van Riebeeck Street which becomes Plein Street lower down. Look out for Drostdy Street on the left, turn into it and ride past the magnificent Moederkerk where, weekdays, there is usually somebody happy to show you round – but perhaps not if you're togged out in sweaty cycling gear. There is a small but well stocked and very obliging cycle shop in Plein/Van Riebeeck Street, nearly opposite Drostdy Street (Cycle Circuit).

Turn right where Drostdy forms a T with Dorp Street and ride down, passing numerous national monument buildings. Stellenbosch Hotel on the corner of Andringa Street has a small roof garden where it is delightful to take a sundowner in warm weather. If you have time, ride right down Dorp Street, perhaps taking in a visit to the Brandy Museum on the corner of Strand Street. Afterwards, or instead of this, consider downing a pint and a pie at De Akker at 90 Dorp Street.

In due course return to Die Braak via Bird Street, then take a ride around it to get a look at the beautiful buildings and other objects of historical interest before riding home.

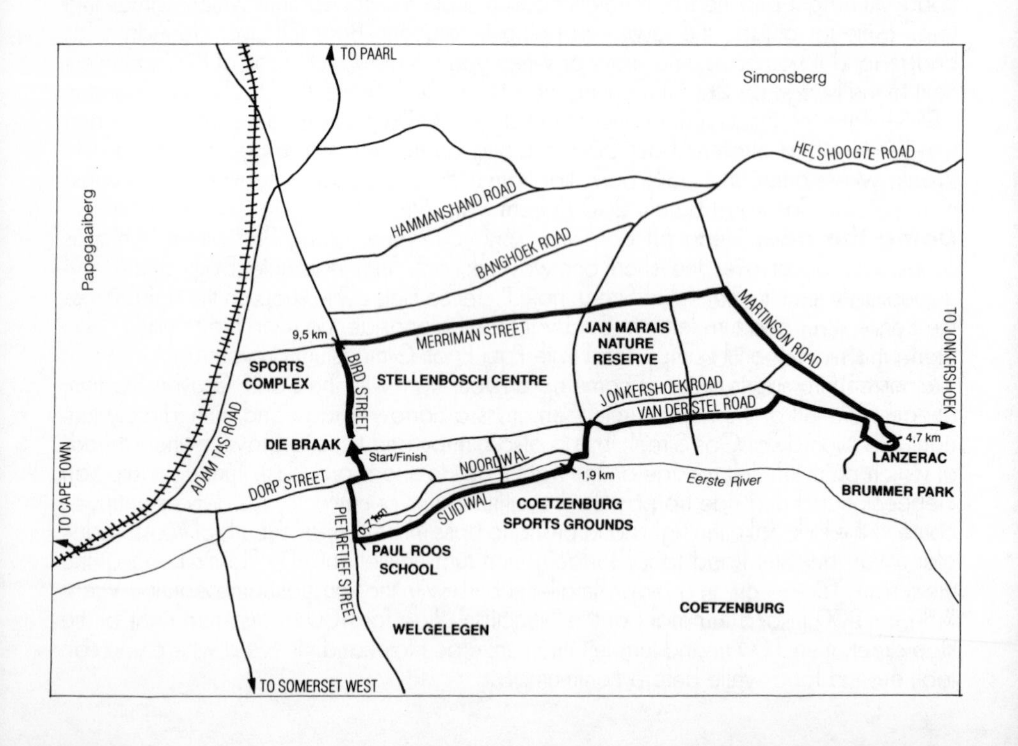

32 Jonkershoek Valley

Features: A spectacular ride that enables you to enjoy the mountains without having to climb them! Takes in lovely vineyards and an unspoilt river. If you have a mountain bike the ride can be extended to include an easy but bumpy circular trip into the forest reserve – strongly recommended. A lonely but peaceful rural area, ideal for family groups and probably safe for alert solo riders.
Grade and distance: A2; 12 km, or 18 km if you do the ATB bit. Riding time 45 minutes; add 30 minutes for the ATB section.
Best times: In summer the valley can get extremely hot and is not cooled by the southeaster – so start early. Spring and autumn are beautiful, and winter is also pleasant provided there's no northwester shrieking up the open valley. In winter go at midday otherwise you won't get much sun. Traffic is never a problem.
Special information: In late summer the reserve itself (but not the valley road) is usually closed because of the fire risk; you can check in advance by calling the forestry office on (02231) 7-2805. If you do the ATB section take a swimming costume and towel. Make time to have a look around the Lanzerac Hotel in Stellenbosch, built as a farmstead in 1830; don't overlook the Tinus de Jongh art gallery – you may bump into his flamboyant and equally successful son Gabriel.
Sustenance: No eateries along the way, but there are two obvious choices: either take *padkos* to have at one of the many delightful picnic spots, or get back to Lanzerac Hotel which serves several menus that can be enjoyed in pleasing rustic surroundings (but extremely busy over weekends). Stellenbosch itself has numerous restaurants, bakeries, and coffee shops; a favourite is Mamma Romas in Andringa Street.
Getting there: Take the N2 (airport) freeway and follow it for about 37 km to the R310 Stellenbosch exit left. Drive 13 km along the R310 (through lovely scenery) to the T-junction with Polkadraai Road. Turn right and follow this road (beware of frequent speed traps) into Stellenbosch. Pass the station and turn right (immediately after the sports grounds) into Merriman Street (still the R310). Drive about 2,2 km and cross a traffic circle, then go another 800 m and turn half-right into Martinson Street. Look out for a series of 'Hotel' signs which will direct you right and then left to the Lanzerac Hotel where you can park in the shade. Train users will find the station discharges them onto Adam Tas Road at which point they turn left and ride 650 m to the junction with Merriman Street.
Doing the ride: Ride back down the Lanzerac drive, out of the bottom gate and turn right at the stop street into Jonkershoek Road. This is quite narrow, rather bumpy and initially steep, but wind is unlikely and the view is gorgeous right from the start. After 800 m the road bends right and the gradient eases for about 1,3 km.

The road now steepens again, there are vineyards everywhere (which look particularly attractive when in their autumn colours), and the well-known wine estate Oude Nektar appears on your left. There is potential confusion here because the adjoining property is called Old Nectar, the homestead of which, built in 1780 to a Louis Thibault design, is a national monument. Old Nectar was the home of the late Major-general K.R. van der Spuy, a great South African known worldwide as an authority on roses; his wife, Una, wrote several very popular books on gardening, and the Old Nectar nursery appears still to flourish.

Now there's a short steep left-hand bend passing a handful of cottages, after which you come to the extensive and beautiful picnic sites (no fires) which reach right down to the river. This superbly clean stream (which can rage in winter) is known along these upper reaches as the Jonkershoekrivier, but somewhere near Stellenbosch acquires its better-known handle Eersterevier. Notice that the road gradually climbs to flank the northern side of the valley, the towering mountains (1 500 m) seeming to close in on you as you ride along.

A small soccer field can be spotted over on your right, followed half a kilometre on by camping sites. The road undulates gently and 1 km ahead you will reach the forest reserve entrance gates. Except at weekends, these do not seem to be manned; when they are, you can be issued a permit (currently free) to go in, and ATBs are allowed.

The reserve circuit is about 6 km long and fairly level, but very bumpy, especially after winter rains. Apart from its forestry activities, this reserve has an important trout hatchery and the office will give you full details about where and when trout may be fished. You can also arrange to be shown over the hatcheries and to have a look at the interesting aquarium.

At the far end of the loop there is a small wooden bridge, and just downstream of it the water is deep enough for a dip, even in summer. On the return side of the loop, roughly 2 km from the bridge, there are little notices pointing out walking routes to two waterfalls on the southern side of the valley. If you have the time and can lock your bike(s) these are easily reached on foot and add to the pleasure of the whole trip.

The return trip can be accomplished at high speed once you're out of the reserve, although the surroundings are so tranquil you probably won't feel like hurrying.

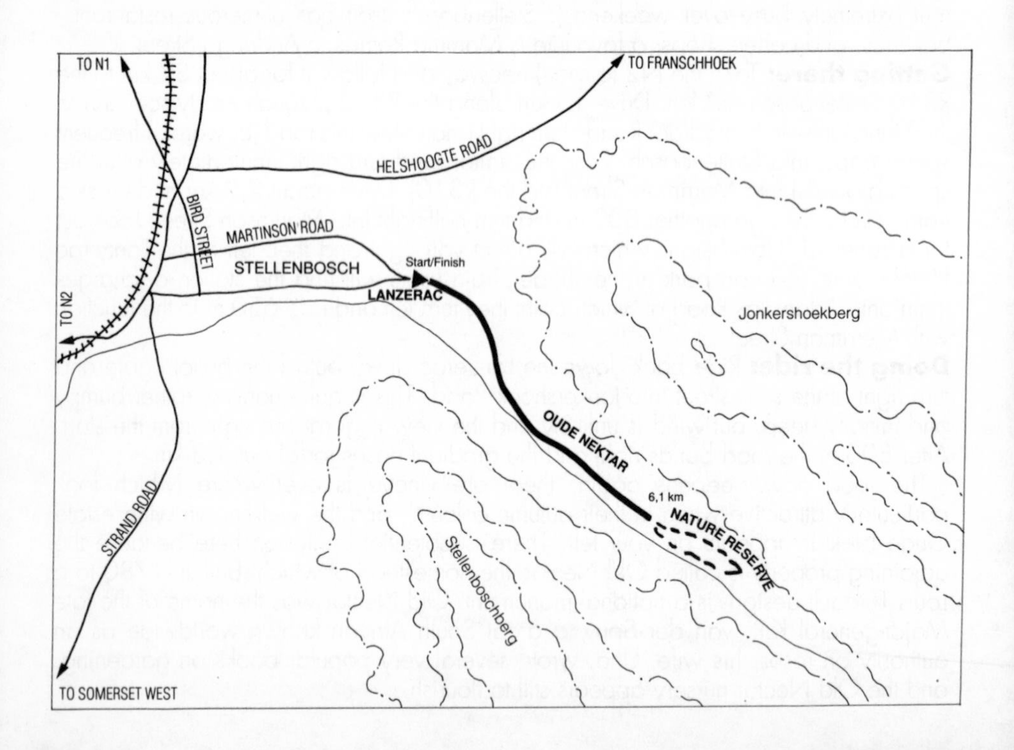

33 Circling the Simonsberg

Features: Rural cycling at its grandest, with tough hills and thrillingly rapid descents through some of the Western Cape's most spectacular scenery. Suitable for solo riders but a richer experience if shared. Family groups will manage as long as they can handle the grade and distance. Traffic is negligible except at the start and finish. Security is normally good in these country areas.
Grade and distance: C3; 42 km; minimum two hours riding time.
Best times: Choose between moderately early, before it gets too hot in summer, or mid-afternoon so as to catch the setting sun over distant Table Mountain during the later stages of the route. Winter on a sparkling day is marvellous but the air can be extremely cold, even without wind. The southeaster is not a problem. Other winds may intensify considerably up or down the Helshoogte Valley, provoking wobbles and making the ascent either even worse or quite a bit easier.
Special information: Be sure to take windcheater, water and tubes in case of punctures on lonely roads. Some of the organized cycle tour events use the Helshoogte and Klapmuts roads (but never on Sundays) so acquaint yourself with these sections in case you ever decide to compete in one of these events.
Sustenance: Buffet picnic-style lunches are served on the lawns at Boschendal during the summer. La Pommier, near the top of Helshoogte, is untested by us but looks delightful. Remember however that it's not a good idea to cycle after hefty meals – but you could start and finish your ride at La Pommier or Boschendal to get around that problem. There are several wineries offering light meals along the way – consult a Wine Route guide available from the helpful Visitors' Bureau at 30 Plein Street, Stellenbosch.
Getting there: Take the N2 freeway and follow it for about 37 km, then exit left at the Stellenbosch R310 sign. Follow the R310 for 13 km to its T-junction with Polkadraai Road. Turn right and head into Stellenbosch; note the speed limit which comes into effect quite far outside the town – trapping is frequent. Bear left over the Adam Tas bridge then take the first turn right, into Dorp Street, drive up 1,4 km and turn left into Bird Street. About 200 m along on the left is a large open area, Die Braak, where one can usually park. The station is conveniently situated next to Adam Tas Road barely 200 m from Dorp Street.
Doing the ride: Ride northwards for about 800 m along Bird Street (same direction you came) which becomes wider and easier from Merriman Street. Turn right into Muller Street, which starts off promisingly then becomes narrow and bumpy where it changes name to Hammanshand Road, approximately at the CSIR complex on your left. About half a kilometre ahead, up a short hill, turn right and come to a T-junction with a wider two-lane road – Banghoek (also spelt Banhoek) Road. Some 1,2 km ahead, after passing across traffic lights, start a stiff climb where the road name changes appropriately to Helshoogte. The suburb of Ida's Valley is on your left.

After 900 m you'll be next to a pine plantation on the right and will enjoy the recently widened road with its nice smooth shoulders although the old twisty narrow one was far more picturesque. There is a good view of the Simonsberg range to your left. Now the road steepens, believe it or not, for nearly 2 km; beware of buffeting wind as you cross the bridge. Climb steadily for another 900 m; the valley is fairly open here and the wind can be very gusty. Don't be surprised to see cyclists hurtling suicidally down – some do, and speeds over 100 km/h have been recorded (legal limit 60!). Take heart, the top is only another 700 m further on; meanwhile enjoy the smooth wide road.

Notice the hillside vineyards to your left. Because of the soil type and microclimate the grapes grown on these south-facing slopes produce very distinctive wines. La Pommier is on your left less than 1 km from the top. Also to the left, half a kilometre further on is Dangerwood, a widely-known German Shepherd kennel. The valley to your right carries the Banghoekrivier and lies between the Jonkershoek range (nearer) and Groot Drakenstein range (further). The visible peaks rise to around 1 200 m, but behind them, out of view, some reach above 1 500 m.

Another 1,5 km brings you to a narrow, mostly tree-lined section. This continues for 1,3 bumpy and twisty kilometres, bringing you to the village of Pniel, a German mission station established in 1848 on the edge of the fairy-tale Drakenstein valley with its numerous beautiful homesteads, many of which belong to the Rhodes Fruit Farms group. When you reach Boschendal (1865), a national monument some 2,6 km ahead, go in and collect a leaflet describing the remarkable events which led to the establishment of this ambitious and visionary enterprise in 1902.

Meanwhile, about 1,5 km out of Pniel is a dirt road going off to the right past the farmstead Rhône, another national monument, to the village of Languedoc – gradually and unfortunately becoming 'Langedok'. If you have time, stop off there and you will find yourself taken back in lifestyle nearly a hundred years, for this village was designed as an 'economic housing scheme' by no less an architect than Sir Herbert Baker. Cecil Rhodes retained Baker to design 110 of these enchanting and practical cottages for the farm labourers, a remarkably advanced notion in those days. The villagers have a warm old-fashioned friendliness and speak easily of the old times.

A railway crossing lies 1,5 km beyond Boschendal and then a T-junction. A right turn would take you to Franschhoek, but today turn left onto the R45 and ride past the Meerlust forest station and sawmill on the right, with Groot Drakenstein station on the left. The mountains to the left are the Simonsberg while off to the right, quite far away, are the Klein Drakenstein mountains. On the way to Simondium, 3,3 km ahead, notice the right turn to Bien Donne (1800), yet another national monument that has been very accurately and beautifully restored. As a matter of interest the Berg River flows over on your right, having risen in the mountains behind you. It winds on to reach the sea at Velddrif on the west coast.

At Simondium take the Klapmuts left turn, cross the railway, and ride past the Drakenstein Co-op on your right (wine tasting). Three kilometres after the railway notice the Backsberg turn-off on your left (tasting), and after another 1 km a right turn-off to Simonsvlei Co-op (more tasting – but don't, otherwise you'll lose your balance along the next stretch which features some tremendous ups and downs, not to speak of unexpected potholes). Notice the Wemmershoek mountains far in the distance on the right. The road now swings left, and after about 2 km brings you to the junction with the R44; turn left.

The road climbs gently, flattens somewhat, then swings right past paddocks with horses. The mountains on the left are the western end of Simonsberg, known as the Skurweberg; the knoll on your right is Klapmutskop (a *klapmuts* was the little cap once worn by Dutch sailors). Notice the left turn to Wiesenhof Wild Park. Further on you'll see the right turn-off to Simonsig (10 km from Klapmuts) and, just after, a left turn to the famous estates Muratie and Delheim. The top of the rise is 1,7 km ahead and rewards you with a very splendid view across immense vistas of winelands, with the Cape Flats in the distance, and if it's clear, Table Mountain. As you race down, spot Elsenberg Agricultural College to your right; it's become a popular starting point for triathlon events.

The next 3 km includes a short very steep hill but compensates with a stunning summit view of distant Table Mountain and the Tygerberg hills. Levelling out, notice that the steeper hillsides are planted to pine trees, with the flatter areas taken up with vineyards. The Wine Route Hotel comes up on your right, then there's a hill for nearly 1 km and the road develops into dual carriageway and acquires a 60 km/h limit.

Two kilometres ahead is a set of traffic lights at the new Helshoogte Road extension. After another 400 m turn left into Bird Street (sign 'Middedorp'). This end of Bird Street is partly oak lined and very attractive – nice and soothing if you've found this lengthy ride heavy going.

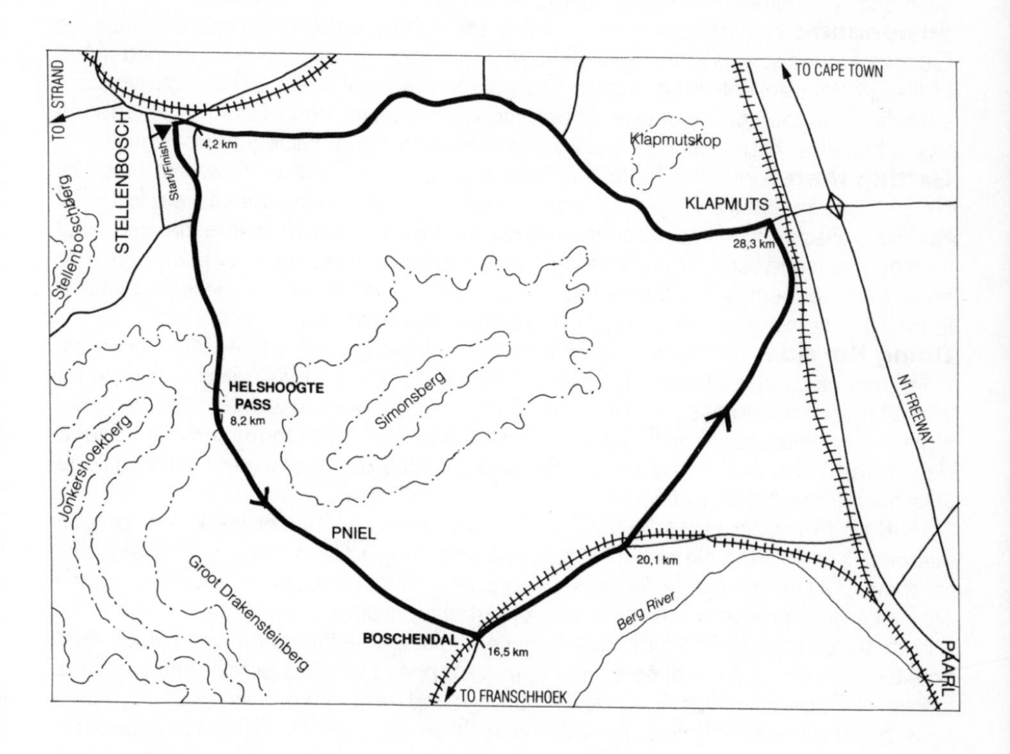

34 Huguenot Valley to Paarl

Features: A fairly long but only moderately hilly ride through stunningly beautiful scenery. Negligible traffic or other hazards. Lovely for groups or families able to manage the distance. Security should be good in that there are very few people around – but this in itself holds some threats.
Grade and distance: C2; 57 km; 2,5 to 3 hours.
Best times: In summer the Franschhoek valley can be extremely hot and windless. In winter, if it looks like rain in Cape Town it will probably be raining in Franschhoek!
Special information: Don't forget the tubes and tools – this is a lengthy ride! Put some respectable clothes and a strong deodorant in your car in case you want to sample a quality restaurant! Try to schedule time for an adequate visit to the Huguenot Memorial and museum in Franschhoek.
Sustenance: Franschhoek has several *haute cuisine* restaurants, one of which, Le Quartier Français, was formerly acclaimed as the best restaurant in South Africa. Most of these establishments have superb (but not cheap) local estate wines not available elsewhere. If you can't manage to get into one of them, have lunch at the Laborie Wine House in Paarl, but take it easy – you have to pedal back again.
Getting there: Take the Table Bay Boulevard (N1) and follow it towards Paarl for 57 km. Turn right at the Paarl/Franschhoek R45 sign and follow all R45 signs for 24 km into Franschhoek. Drive through the town and park in the lot next to the Huguenot memorial at the far end. Train travellers are not so lucky; there are very few passenger trains and the journey is unacceptably slow. The service to Paarl is better but limited to mainline trains where you may find red tape entangles your bicycle.
Doing the ride: Go back through the village, looking out for the various eateries; there's not much else of interest. Once out of town you could be riding in France for all the French farm names you will notice. First up is La Provence with its 1756 national monument homestead. You'll also pass side roads leading to farms such as La Terra de Luc, La Motte ('the lump of earth'), Beaucoup l'eau ('plenty of water'), Le Mouillage ('the anchorage'), and La Montagne ('the mountain').

Just 8 km from your start take the right turn signposted 'Wemmershoek' into Jan van Riebeeck Road. Cross the railway – you will find the road bumpy but still wide; it runs for some 600 m through shady trees. Next pass the much-frequented De Hollandsche Molen camping resort where there is a pleasant tearoom.

If you're really energetic and have the time, make a side trip to Wemmershoek dam from the right-turn 500 m ahead – but you're supposed to get a permit from the Civic Centre in Cape Town first. It's another 10 km round trip but worth the visit.

Just beyond this turn-off cross the Wemmers River, and pass through a flat floodplain section of the L'Arc d'Orleans estate. Another 2 km up some hilly bits amid rugged rocky scenery will reward you with a view ahead to Paarl mountain. The road now levels but narrows and deteriorates as it passes Victor Verster prison.

Another beautiful farm, La Paris, comes up soon, and then you have a fine run of some 9 km through delightful farmlands. Notice the left turn to Safariland, a small resort which is very pleasant during the week but overcrowded at weekends. Between there and the golf course is a camping spot, Wateruintjiesvlei. Just after the golf course on your left there's a right turn to a nut farm and then the road briefly becomes a dual carriageway as it passes under the N1, after which it narrows again and is very bumpy. Paarl is about a kilometre further on. Ride another 500 m to cross a small bridge, then turn left at the traffic circle into Market Street. Ride past sports grounds and cross the river bridge; this is where the famous four-day Berg River Canoe Marathon starts every year.

At the next circle turn left into Berg River Boulevard (you pass the police station on the left), then enjoy a wide smooth dual carriageway section. The road now veers right and climbs towards Paarl Rock (itself a national monument), meanwhile giving grand views across the river towards the imposing Du Toitsberge. Two kilometres from the police station turn left into Main Road at the traffic lights.

Follow Main Street under the N1, and 1 km later turn left onto the R45 'Franschhoek' road and pass under the railway. At the top of a slight hill pass the Berg River resort (Campers Paradise) then cruise gently down past the Paarl Nursery on the left with its lands to the right. A turn-off to a crocodile farm is 500 m ahead on the right, but we found it unwelcoming and expensive. Take care as you cross the railway 1,3 km further on, then after 600 m you will see the turn into Drakenstein Co-op.

The next right turn leads to Klapmuts and offers a 6 km round trip detour to the Backsberg Estate, which is very welcoming to all visitors. Next pass through Simondium village, then Meerlust forest and sawmills. Pass the right turn to Helshoogte/Stellenbosch, then after the little Dwarsrivier bridge notice a tiny World War I memorial to the left.

Two more right turns follow, to L'Ormarins (1694) and to Bellingham and La Garonne wine estates. Next comes a narrow road/rail bridge over the Berg River after a steep left-hand bend. A small but attractive woody picnic spot is to your left, and then you come to the Wemmershoek turn-off. From there it's an 8 km slightly uphill ride back to Franschhoek and lunch.

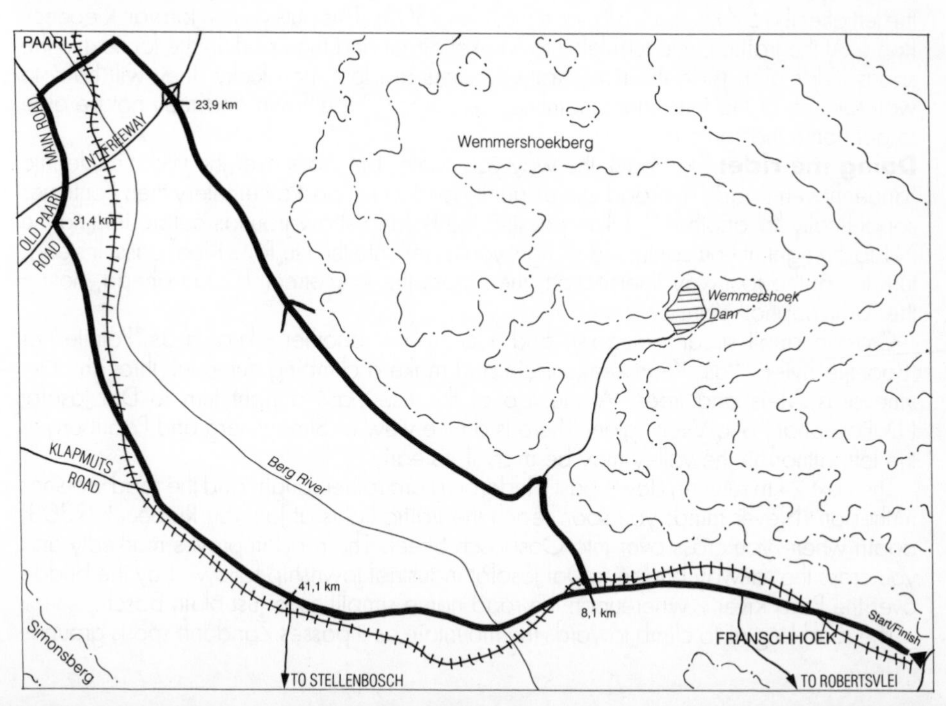

35 Le Tour de Paarl

Features: Paarl is one of the few rural centres that has become industrialized and commercialized without losing its hospitable country-town atmosphere and its historical heritage. This little ride will help you appreciate this. It is suitable for families over weekends (the industrial sections of the route are fairly busy on weekdays). Security: better than if you were a pedestrian; no lonely sections; traffic reasonable.
Grade and distance: A2; 15 km; allow an hour.
Best times: Paarl can get stiflingly hot in summer (but our route is mostly under shade) and miserably cold in winter. The surrounding mountains tend to shield the sun in the early mornings and late afternoons, making the valley comparatively cool. There is seldom much wind. Mid-mornings are the best times to do this ride in summer and mid-afternoons in winter.
Special information: Huguenot farmers settled in the district from 1687 after it was explored by Abraham Gabbema. He is credited with naming two (no one knows *which* two) of the several unique and geologically ancient granitic intrusions 'Pearl' and 'Diamond' because of their glistening appearance after rain. The town was formally established in 1720. It is richly historical and you should definitely stop at the enthusiastic Publicity Association at 266 Main Street for background literature.
Sustenance: There are plenty of acceptable eateries and takeaway places in the town, including a Spur (Pasadena). We've had good reports on Blacksmiths, Fiorinis, Troubadour and Hide-Away, but our oft-tested preference is Laborie Wine House – despite the fact that it is operated by a huge commercial organization, KWV.
Getting there: Drive along Table Bay Boulevard, N1, and take the *second* exit to the left after the 57 km mark (signpost includes R303). This puts you on Jan van Riebeeck Road. At the traffic circle turn left into Market Street and then park in the lot next to the sports fields alongside the river. Railway users are less than lucky; they will have to wait for one of the infrequent mainline trains from Cape Town and may not be able to get home the same day.
Doing the ride: Start back the way you came, but cross over the traffic circle into Langenhoven Road. The road climbs gently for 1,6 km past a cemetery then continues soporifically for another 2,1 km, passing the Boland showgrounds before joining the N1 to the right. If you continued straight you'd get onto the Du Toit's Kloof pass. Instead, turn left at the four-way intersection, then cross the stop street 100 m ahead, noting the 'Daljosophat' sign.

Cross a small stream (Hugo's), and 1,6 km on, another – known as 'Palmiet' or 'Boontjiesrivier'. Pass Klein Drakenstein and make a climbing curve left through quiet vineyards, vleis and trees. At the top of the rise pass a right turn to Dal Josafat ('Daljosophat') and Wellington. There is a nice view of Simonsberg and Paarlberg to the left, although the valley may be misty if it's early.

The next 2 km running down past Nederburg are rather rough, and the road worsens further on. Never mind; you soon reach the traffic lights at Jan van Riebeeck (R303) again where you cross over into Oosbosch Street. The road improves markedly and you cross the railway bridge in Dal Josafat industrial township followed by the bridge over the Berg River – whereupon the road name simplifies to just plain Bosch.

The road begins to climb towards the mountain as it passes Zanddrift sports grounds and brings you to Main Street (R45). Turn left here (right goes to Malmesbury). The road here is wide but bumpy, and there are lovely oaks and many attractive old houses in big gardens. After nearly 1,5 km pass into the shopping area and turn right into Lady Grey Street then immediately left to stay in Main Street. Here is your opportunity to visit the Oude Pastorie, in the next block. It was built in 1787 and bought by the town council in 1937, carefully restored and turned into an excellent museum (closed on Sundays).

The road becomes wider and smoother and brings you to the Information Office 900 m after the Lady Grey dogleg. Look out for a post office on the left and then the historical building which housed the first landdrost on the right. After the next two left turns keep a look out to your left for the old thatched roof church, opened in 1805 and still in use. About 700 m further on arrive at a major junction and turn down left into Berg River Boulevard. This is a wide smooth road which bears left and then runs alongside the river giving fine distant views of the mountains to the north.

However, if you want to visit the Laborie Wine House for lunch, do not turn left but continue down Main Street past the extensive KWV premises (of which tours are held on weekdays) and look out for the Laborie on your right.

Back on the Berg River Boulevard, you pass a police station on the right followed by the magistrates' court just before the traffic circle. Turn right here, into Market Street, then cross the river and find yourself back at the parking lot.

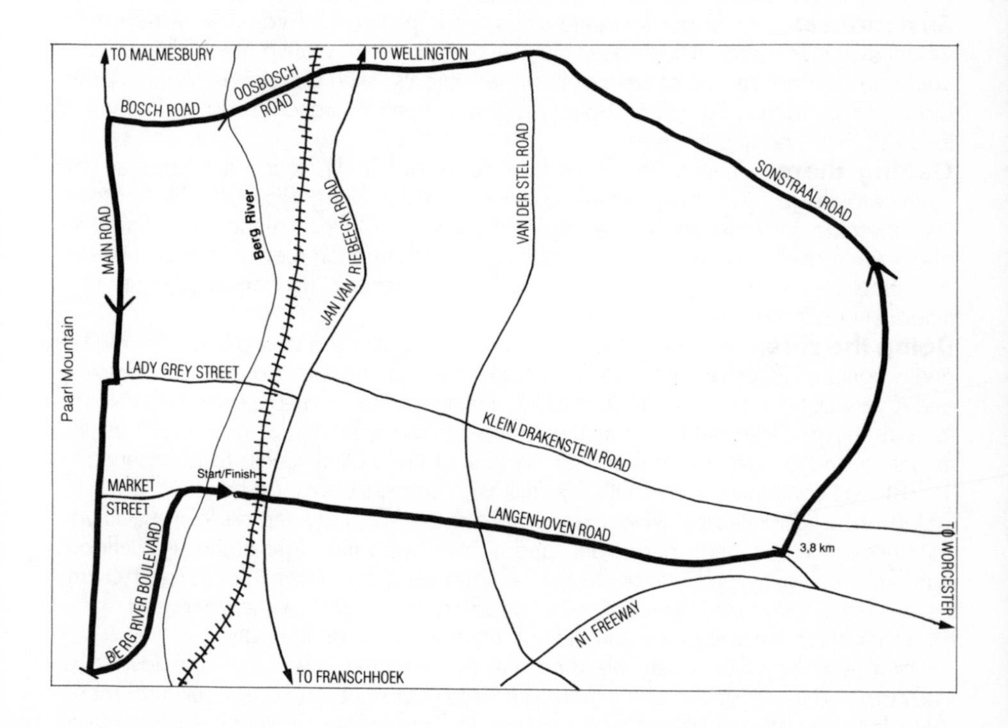

36 Riding round the Pearl

Features: This circuit of Paarlberg gives you a small taste of the town of Paarl, but mostly some splendid elevated views west and south towards Table Mountain and across great spreads of vines and cereals. There are spectacular sunsets when the conditions are right. The route is quite hilly in parts, but should not present any insurmountable challenges to the average cyclist. Security is typical of country areas, with friendly farmers but crazy drivers of farm produce trucks on some sections!
Grade and distance: C2; 30 km; 100 minutes.
Best times: Don't attempt this ride during the heat of the day in warm weather, especially as much of it is on the western side of the mountain. If a cooling southeaster is blowing it will help blow you round. Try to time it so that you can see the sunset over Table Mountain. You'll have to finish the ride quickly because Paarl town will be in shadow and getting dark. Consider a late autumn visit when the green vineyards have turned to wonderful warm reds and golden browns.
Special information: Paarl has a strong and active cycling club and there are several good events in the neighbourhood during the year – notably the Paarl Rock Cycle Race, which is a registered event on the calendar. Various fun rides are held and the mountain lends itself to ATB excursions, both organized and informal.
Sustenance: One of our favourite stops is the picturesque Fairview wine estate, where delicious goats' milk cheeses may be bought. If you want a meal, change after your ride and eat at one of several Paarl restaurants, such as Laborie Wine House, Blacksmiths, Fiorinis, Pasadena Spur, Wagon Wheels or Schoongezicht. Phone first to check their opening hours.
Getting there: Drive along Table Bay Boulevard (N1), round the harbour and northwards for 57 km, then exit left to the R45 which brings you onto Main Street. (Don't accidentally take the earlier 'Agter-Paarl' turn-off.) Drive along Main Street for about 4 km and park as near as you can to the Information Centre, corner of Main and Hout streets (left). Train travellers will need to check the convenience of very infrequent passenger services.
Doing the ride: Head back the way you came, passing a post office after 700 m and a right turn (Bosman Street) to Paarl Rock. The road becomes a dual carriageway and is very bumpy for about 600 m; along this stretch there's a café on the left. Notice the Jan Phillips Drive (which branches to the Afrikaans language monument) up the mountain on the right. More than half the cost of this 10-km scenic road (opened in 1928) was contributed personally by Phillips, a successful wagon builder.

Don't investigate Phillips Drive unless you have an ATB. Just keep pedalling until you pass under the N1, then bear right, and 1 km ahead turn right at the 'Agter-Paarl' sign. This will take you back under the N1 and up a steepish hill for some 1,6 km; the surface is rough and the road quite narrow. From the crest of the steep part of this hill another 1,8 km will place you at the Fairview turn-off on the right.

Along here the view is very pleasing; the N1 stretches away to Cape Town, the vine-carpeted lower slopes of the mountain lie to your right, and a tranquil rural scene spreads to the left and ahead. The right-turn to Landskroon, another attractive estate and winery up on the lower slopes of Paarlberg, lies 1,8 km further on; this is also well worth a visit. From there the road levels off and begins to descend slightly until,

2,3 km from Landskroon, you come to a stop street on the R44 and must turn right, towards Wellington.

This should be a very scenic section, notwithstanding the rather rough and narrow road. Alas, it is also something of a trucking route and for some reason stimulates drivers to terrifying speeds. Fortunately there are not too many trucks, and their approach can be heard – giving you ample time for escape to the shoulders.

Just 4,5 km from the stop street the R312 Durbanville turn-off appears on the left (feeding in more trucks). But meanwhile, provided it's a clear day, you can see the distant ocean and enjoy a different perspective of Table Mountain. Paarlberg's granite rocks still seem quite close by, on the right.

The various Windmeul and Perdeberg Co-op farms look like a jigsaw puzzle on your left and their wineries can be reached 4,7 km ahead on the left. But to pursue the route turn right 100 m beyond and descend a gentle incline (beware of potholes) for 1,9 km to a T-junction. Turn right again and ride for 2,5 km past Paarl's outlying residential areas to the turn-off for the Boland Co-op winery. The road is rather rough but pleasantly tree-lined. Another 300 m brings you to the junction with the R45 from Wellington and Malmesbury.

The traffic lights at Bosch Road mark your crossing into the municipal area. Go straight across these lights; the road is wide and the surface not very good but the oaks lining the pavements are lovely and a delight to cycle beneath on hot days. You are, of course, in Main Street. Take care not to be misled at the Lady Grey Street traffic lights; you must turn right and then immediately left in order to stay in Main Street. Hout Street is 900 m further on, to the right.

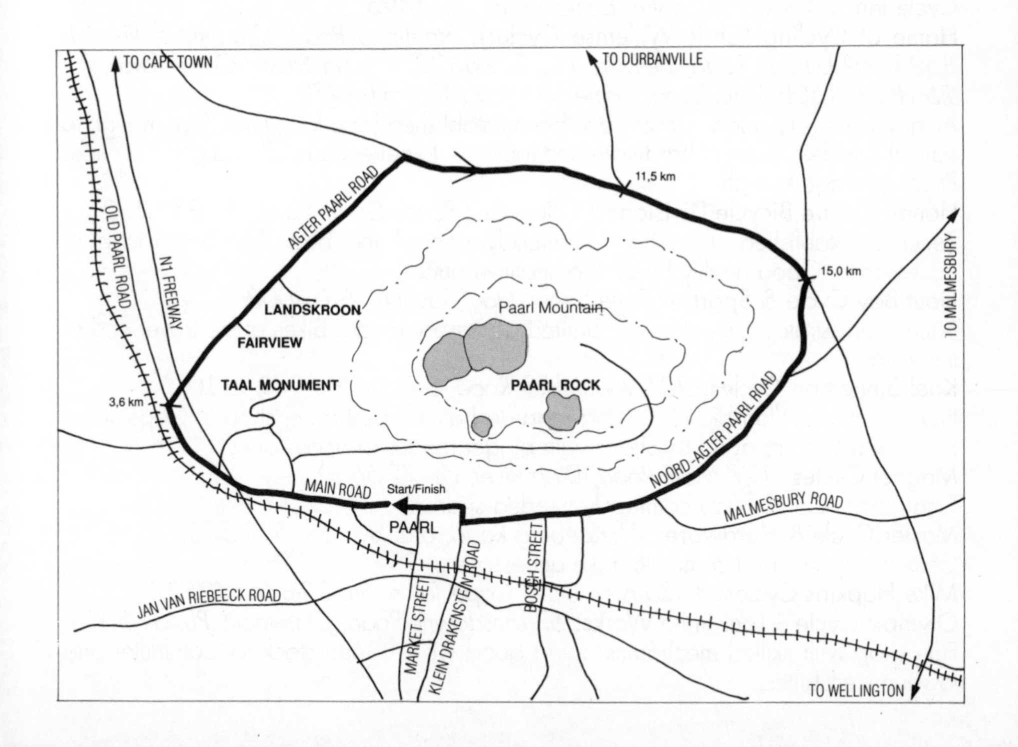

SOME PENINSULA CYCLING SHOPS

NB: This list covers only the shops we've noticed and/or dealt with fairly recently. Comments about the shops are subjective and based on our personal experience of looking for parts and advice, and comparing prices. If we found attentive service at a particular shop, that does not necessarily mean that other customers will have similar good service.

If you don't know much about cycling and bikes, but have an expensive decision to take, it's best to go to the big comprehensive shops,whose staff are likely to be the most knowledgeable. HOWEVER, don't go there when they're busy – you may not get the time and patient service you require.

Astra Cycles: *97 Voortrekker Road, Parow. Ph. 930-2630.*
Possibly the all-round best shop in the northern suburbs. Part owned and managed by friendly veteran cyclist Gerhard Genis, one of the leading Cape cyclists. Good range of accessories.
Bellville Cycles: *171 Voortrekker Road, Bellville. Ph. 94-3386.*
Good stock of spares. Limited range of bikes.
City Cycle and Hardware: *Voortrekker Road, Goodwood. Ph. 591-0013.*
Crosstique: *302 Main Road, Wynberg. Ph. 761-5362.*
Nice-looking shop. High prices. Fair facilities. Indifferent service.
Crown Cycle Works: *343 Lansdowne Road, Lansdowne. Ph. 696-1572.*
Low-priced spares. Limited stocks of bikes and accessories.
Cycle Inn: *24 Shoprite Centre, Bothasig. Ph. 58-1495.*
Home of Cycling (Chris Willemse Cycles): *Stanhope Road, Claremont; Ph. 61-8503. 49 Durban Road, Bellville; Ph. 949-8822; 2 Long Street, Cape Town; Ph. 25-1828. 150b Main Road, Somerset West (024) 51-4979.*
All branches very good – most have been established for a long time. Big enough to carry the widest range of hardware and facilities. Experienced staff and good service. Prices average to high.
Honda Centre Bicycle Division: *11 Somerset Road, Green Point. Ph. 25-1400.*
Recently established, this shop is already one of the best. Excellent range of accessories. Good quality bikes. Competitive prices.
Hout Bay Cycle & Sport: *4 Earle Street, Hout Bay. Ph. 790-4008.*
Nice shop, strategically situated. Limited accessory range. Bikes at the lower end of the range.
Kriel Binneman Cycles: *201 Voortrekker Road, Bellville. Ph. 949-9110.*
Home of Peter Allan bicycles. Long regarded as the best cycle shop in Cape Town but now being upstaged by shops with bigger ranges of accessories.
Magnet Cycles: *127 Main Road, Diep River. Ph. 72-6650.*
Small shop. Carries only commonly needed spares.
Master Cycle & Hardware: *71 Koeberg Road, Brooklyn. Ph. 511-5783.*
Common spares and commuter bike accessories.
Mike Hopkins Cycles: *133a Bree Street Cape Town. Ph. 23-8461/2527.*
Olympic Cycle & Locksmith Works: *67 Lansdowne Road, Claremont. Ph. 61-5008.*
Fine shop with skilled mechanics doing good work. Good stock for commuter and lower-priced bikes.

Parow Cycle House: *311 Voortrekker Road, Parow. Ph. 930-2836.*
Pleasant shop; helpful people. Limited stock range.
Pedalfair: *3 Baypoint, Three Anchor Bay. Ph. 434-7745.*
Pickering's Cycle Inn: *The Link, Main Road, Claremont. Ph. 61-6102.*
Very well stocked shop. Excellent technical advice from competent and knowledgeable staff. Good quality lines. Prices highish. Counter undermanned. ATBs for hire. The centre for Pickerings Cycle Tours.
Premier Cycles: *47 Voortrekker Road, Goodwood. Ph. 591-6431.*
Small-scale shop. Limited spares range.
Regal Cycles: *66 Main Road, Fish Hoek. Ph. 82-2944.*
Strategically positioned but limited range of spares, and only for commuter bikes.
Sea Point Hire: *46a Main Road, Sea Point. Ph. 434-9794.*
Has ten Bomber 12-speed bikes for hire.
Smitco Cycle & Hardware: *311 Voortrekker Road, Goodwood. PH. 591-2451.*
Limited range of spares.
Soloped: *34 Klipfontein Road (in Sportsman's Warehouse), Rondebosch. Ph. 689-2703. 94 Loop Street, Cape Town; Ph. 24-5664.*
Popular shops. The town branch is well stocked with a wide range of parts and accessories. Bicycle stock seems less comprehensive.
Speedy Cycles: *370 Main Road, Wynberg. Ph. 797-5674.*
Very good spares and service shop. Staff friendly and efficient. Limited bike range and stock.
Sports & Cycle Centre: *199 Loop Street, Cape Town. Ph. 24-5416.*
Nice shop. Good range of accessories, especially clothing.
Taj Locksmith & Cycle: *Gatesville Centre, Klipfontein Road, Gatesville (a.k.a Rylands). Ph. 637-0025.*
Union Cycles: *103 Parow Street, Parow. Ph. 930-3002.*
Van Reenen Cycle Depot: *Duke Road, Rondebosch. Ph. 686-4091.*
A father-to-son business founded in 1910! Caters mainly for school and commuter cyclists. Very knowledgeable and resourceful when it comes to technical problems or replacing rare parts. Reasonable prices. Service good except when staff 'snowed under' with repairs (often). Very limited stock range of bikes and accessories.
Znugglez: *3c SBDC Complex, Lower Scott Rd, Observatory. Ph. 47-9973.* Makes good quality low-priced cycling apparel – and other sports clothing. The shop's owner Neil Buckland is one of the Western Cape's best known riders and very attentive to cyclists' needs.

SOME CYCLING MAGAZINES

BICYCLING: An American publication that costs a fortune in the shops. Very good on training, accessory reports and latest trends in the cycling world.
LIFE CYCLE: Originally the WPPPA newsletter, currently metamorphosing into a more ambitious periodical. Attractive colour pictures. Caters mainly for recreational riders.
TRICYCLING: At the time of writing, the latest newspaper-type magazine in South Africa. Well-written monthly reports on local cycle and triathlon events. Good reading for anyone interested in racing cycling. Less so for recreational riders.

SOME CYCLING BOOKS

Duffer's Guide to cycling: Mike Gordon, Columbus Books, 1988. This is simply the best book on how to be (or how not to be) a cyclist. It covers everything from how to identify a cyclist to a translation of racing jargon.
Glenn's Complete Bicycle Manual: Clarence Coles and Harold Glenn, Crown Publishers, Inc., New York, 1973. An outstandingly clear book on adjustment and repair, with hundreds of step-by-step photographs covering almost every bike and component made. Out of date (but not incorrect) on current setting up ideas and on technical developments. A more recent edition may now be available.
Greg LeMond's Complete Book of Bicycling: Greg LeMond and Kent Gordis, Perigee Books (Putnam Publishing Group), New York, 1988. This is the best training and racing book we've seen. Its outline of co-author Greg LeMond's career and the personal anecdotes give great encouragement to aspiring stars. It goes into detail about how exactly to choose, fit, and use your bike. Training and competition tactics are well covered. Very up to date.
The Lore of Cycling: Beneke, Noakes and Reynolds, Oxford University Press, Cape Town 1989. This is quite a good book with chapters on all aspects of bicycles, cycling physiology and history. It describes the general state of cycling in South Africa.
On Your Bicycle: James McGurn, John Murray Publishers, 1987. This is a wonderful book about the history of cycling from the first 'running' bikes (no pedals) to the modern racer. Very entertaining and interesting.

INDEX